MW01534128

Preparation and Development of School Leaders in Africa

Also available from Bloomsbury

Education in East and Central Africa, edited by Charl Wolhuter
Education in Southern Africa, edited by Clive Harber
Education in West Africa, edited by Emefa Takyi-Amoako
Exploring School Leadership in England and the Caribbean, Paul Miller

Preparation and Development of School Leaders in Africa

Edited by
Pontso Moorosi and Tony Bush

BLOOMSBURY ACADEMIC
LONDON • NEW YORK • OXFORD • NEW DELHI • SYDNEY

BLOOMSBURY ACADEMIC
Bloomsbury Publishing Plc
50 Bedford Square, London, WC1B 3DP, UK
1385 Broadway, New York, NY 10018, USA
29 Earlsfort Terrace, Dublin 2, Ireland

BLOOMSBURY, BLOOMSBURY ACADEMIC and the Diana logo are trademarks
of Bloomsbury Publishing Plc

First published in Great Britain 2020
This paperback edition published in 2021

Copyright © Pontso Moorosi, Tony Bush and Contributors, 2020

Pontso Moorosi, Tony Bush and Contributors have asserted their right under the Copyright,
Designs and Patents Act, 1988, to be identified as Authors of this work.

Cover designer: Adriana Brioso
Cover image: epicurean/iStock

All rights reserved. No part of this publication may be reproduced or transmitted
in any form or by any means, electronic or mechanical, including photocopying,
recording, or any information storage or retrieval system, without prior permission
in writing from the publishers.

Bloomsbury Publishing Plc does not have any control over, or responsibility for, any
third-party websites referred to or in this book. All internet addresses given in this
book were correct at the time of going to press. The author and publisher regret any
inconvenience caused if addresses have changed or sites have ceased to exist, but
can accept no responsibility for any such changes.

A catalogue record for this book is available from the British Library.

A catalog record for this book is available from the Library of Congress.

ISBN: HB: 978-1-3500-8114-7
PB: 978-1-3502-0595-6
ePDF: 978-1-3500-8115-4
eBook: 978-1-3500-8116-1

Typeset by Deanta Global Publishing Services, Chennai, India

To find out more about our authors and books visit www.bloomsbury.com
and sign up for our newsletters.

Contents

Preface

The preparation and development of school leaders represents a significant body of research that recognizes the value of professionalizing school leadership. Concerns surrounding the preparation of school principals have been growing in recognition of the significance attached to the nature and scope of the content of the programmes used to educate those who aspire to take school leadership roles. In some contexts, as this book will show, this concern has focused on the absence or scarcity of school leadership preparation and development programmes, particularly in developing countries. To this end, this book is based on African experiences and reviews around school leadership preparation and development, taking stock of where the field is in this geographical context and what lies ahead. The exclusive focus on African countries is driven by the desire to foreground African experiences, exposing the existing body of research and highlighting gaps and critical questions for the field on the continent. This contribution is envisaged to be a timely contribution in this context, where school leadership is frail and leadership preparation and development, in particular, is in need of serious political attention. For these reasons, it is expected that the book will be attractive to students of school leadership, be it practitioners or research students interested in the subject as a field of study. It is therefore expected to serve as an important resource for educators of school leadership preparation programmes and for researchers who work in the field on the continent and the diaspora. Most importantly, it is expected to catch the attention of policy-makers who have the power to shape the agenda that guides dialogue on preparation and development programmes in different countries.

The editors of this collection have been involved in a South African project that evaluated the national pilot of a leadership development programme almost a decade ago (see Bush, Kiggundu and Moorosi, 2011). From this evaluation, a significant gap in the literature on leadership preparation and development on the African continent was identified, sparking an interest in work on the continent that addresses areas related to the preparation and development of school leaders on the continent and beyond (see for example, Moorosi and Bush, 2011; Moorosi and Grant, 2018). It is noted that South Africa pioneered a pilot of a national programme on school leadership preparation and development, what was at the time regarded as a first on the continent and a promising gesture that school leadership was finally receiving the national attention it deserves. The evaluation recommended a comprehensive framework for leadership development in the country (Bush et al., 2009). However, policy commitment from the government towards leadership preparation remains questionable.

Practice and policy on school leadership preparation on the rest of the continent has been sporadic and largely undocumented. As a body of research and knowledge, the field is beginning to emerge on the continent, but the balance is still skewed towards a few countries that include South Africa, Kenya, Nigeria and Tanzania, indicating paucity of the field in this geographical region. This book, therefore, presents an exclusive focus on Africa, with selected countries as a starting point to taking stock of work done in the field in this continent. This book is the first of its kind on leadership preparation and development in the region, and it is expected to trigger more research, contributing to this body of knowledge. It is also envisaged that it will catch the attention of policy-makers and more policy attention.

As editors, we are immensely grateful to all the authors for contributing their work to this volume. The authors include a combination of seasoned and emerging authors who have been, or are currently, researching aspects of leadership preparation and development in their respective countries and/ or elsewhere on the continent and the diaspora. It is the variety, breadth and depth of knowledge shared in this volume that makes the book special. The chapters cover research findings, reviews and conceptual analyses, and discuss implications for context, policy and practice in their respective countries. These contributions make this volume unique and an important resource that should be on the reading list of every leadership educator, researcher and student.

Pontso Moorosi and Tony Bush

References

Bush, T., Duku, N., Glover, D., Kiggundu, E., Kola, S., Msila, V. and Moorosi, P. (2009), *External Evaluation: Research Report of the Advanced Certificate in Education*, Pretoria: Department of Basic Education.

Bush, T., Kiggundu, E. and Moorosi, P. (2011), 'Preparing New Principals in South Africa: The ACE: School Leadership Programme', *South African Journal of Education*, 31 (1): 31–43.

Moorosi, P. and Bush, T. (2011), 'School Leadership Development in Commonwealth Countries: Learning across Boundaries', *International Studies in Educational Administration*, 39 (3): 59–75.

Moorosi, P. and Grant, C. (2018), 'The Socialisation and Leader Identity Development of School Leaders in Southern African Countries', *Journal of Educational Administration*, 56 (6): 643–58.

Editors

Pontso Moorosi is Associate Professor of Educational Leadership and Management at the Centre for Education Studies, University of Warwick, the United Kingdom. She is also a research associate at the University of Johannesburg, South Africa, and a rated researcher by the National Research Foundation of South Africa. Her research interests include school leadership preparation and development and leader identity development, with a specific interest in the African continent. She is also interested in gender in educational leadership. She has published extensively in these research areas, and her research covers various countries across different continents.

Tony Bush is Professor of Educational Leadership at the University of Nottingham, the United Kingdom, and he previously held similar positions at the universities of Leicester, Reading, Lincoln and Warwick. He has published many journal articles and books, including his bestselling *Theories of Educational Leadership and Management*, which is now in its fourth edition and has been translated into several languages. He is also editor of the leading international journal *Educational Management, Administration and Leadership* (EMAL). His extensive international work has included research, consultancy or invited keynote presentations in 22 countries on all six continents.

Contributors

Mohammed Abdalla (PhD) is a lecturer at the Aga Khan University – Institute for Educational Development, East Africa (AKU-IED, EA) based in Dar es Salaam, Tanzania. He has extensive experience in coordinating and facilitating educational leadership courses in East Africa. His research interest is in school leadership and in student participation in school affairs. He is a co-author of reports of head teachers' preparation and experience in their first year in Tanzania.

Michael Amakyi is a senior lecturer in Educational Statistics, Financial Administration in Education, and Management of Educational Institutions at the Institute for Educational Planning and Administration (IEPA), University of Cape Coast, Cape Coast, Ghana, and a consultant to schools in the preparation of mission statements and school improvement plans. He holds a PhD in Educational Leadership from the University of Dayton, Dayton, Ohio, the United States; an MBA from the Ghana Institute of Management and Public Administration in Accra, Ghana; and a BSc in Mathematics from the University of Cape Coast, Ghana. His major research interest is in school leadership preparation and school improvement.

Alfred Ampah-Mensah is a senior research fellow at the Institute for Educational Planning and Administration (IEPA), University of Cape Coast, Ghana, and the national coordinator of the Leadership for Learning (L*f*L) Ghana programme. He holds a PhD in Education from the University of Bristol, the United Kingdom; a Master of Arts in Educational Planning and Management from the UNESCO International Institute for Educational Planning (IIEP, Paris); and a Master of Philosophy in Educational Planning and a Bachelor of Education (Mathematics) from the University of Cape Coast. Ampah-Mensah is an independent consultant for the Ministry of Education, the Ghana Education Service and other stakeholders in education.

Frederick Ebot-Ashu is a lecturer of Educational Foundation and Administration at the University of Buea, Cameroon. Prior to this, he was a lecturer of Philosophy of Social Science and Ethics in Research and Research Methods in

Education at the University of Birmingham, the United Kingdom, and served as a senior research officer for 12 years at Community Advice and Support Services (CAASS UK), where he researched and taught courses on system reform and system leadership, community leadership, school and organizational leadership and school leaders leadership. He has pioneered projects across the United Kingdom and Cameroon in these domains. He has published over ten peer-reviewed papers and six authored books and has held fellowships with the Commonwealth Professional Fellowship and the Association of Commonwealth Universities.

Carolyn (Callie) Grant is Associate Professor of Educational Leadership and Management at Rhodes University, South Africa. Her research interests include distributed leadership, teacher leadership and learner leadership as well as school resilience. She is also interested in higher education studies, particularly as it relates to teaching and learning, doctoral education and postgraduate supervision practices.

Raphael Isibor Imoni is presently the parish priest of St Patrick's Leicester, Leicestershire, the United Kingdom, where he provides pastoral leadership to a primary and a secondary school as a school governor. He holds a Ph.D. in Educational Leadership and Management from the University of Nottingham, based on research in Nigerian secondary schools, and a master's degree in Educational Leadership and Management from the University of Warwick. The title of his thesis is 'Distributed Leadership in Government Secondary Schools in Nigeria'.

Moikabi Komiti is a doctoral student at the North-West University, South Africa. Her research explores female principals' leadership experiences in selected secondary schools in Lesotho. She holds a Diploma (cum laude) and a degree in Adult Education from the National University of Lesotho (NUL). She obtained an Honours Degree in Education Management, Law and Systems (cum laude) and a master's degree in Education Management (cum laude) at the North-West University. She currently works as a writing consultant at the North-West University's Academic Development Centre (ADC), where the primary focus is to teach academic writing skills to undergraduate and postgraduate students.

Shadreck Zola Majwabe holds a master's degree in Human Resource Management. He is currently a pursuing his PhD in Education Management at the University of Botswana. His study is on the impact of globalization in education reforms in Botswana (1976–2015). He is currently the coordinator of education reforms at the Ministry of Basic Education, Botswana. Majwabe has co-published two social-studies books.

Raj Mestry is Emeritus Professor in the Department of Education Leadership and Management at the University of Johannesburg, South Africa. His research focus is on education resource management and leadership. He has previously served as head of department and is a rated researcher. He serves on the executive of the Education Association of South Africa. He has co-authored books and written numerous chapters for books on education leadership. He has also published articles extensively in national and international peer-reviewed journals. In 2012, he was awarded the Research Medal by the Education Association of South Africa, and in 2017, he received the association's Medal of Honour.

Mweru Mwingi is an assistant professor at the Aga Khan University Institute for Educational Development, East Africa (AKU-IED, EA), based in Dar es Salaam, Tanzania. She teaches leadership in education and gender in education. Her research interests are in girls' education and teachers' professional development, and she has published *Where Are the Gaps? HIV and Gender Pre-Service Teacher Training Curriculum and Practices in East Africa*. She is currently the academic coordinator of the Centre for Education for Life Long learning (CELL), which offers professional development courses in East Africa.

Janet Mola Okoko is an assistant professor in the Department of Educational Administration at the University of Saskatchewan, Canada. Her research focuses on school leadership preparation and development. She is currently studying school leadership preparation for school and system leaders who work with minority groups. Dr Okoko has co-authored a cross-cultural analysis of school principals' preparation in Kenya, South Africa and Canada. Her recent publication reports the perceptions of school leaders in Nairobi about their leadership preparation and development.

Nkobi Owen Pansiri is an associate professor at the University of Botswana and former chairperson of the Botswana Educational Research Association. He has a Doctorate Degree in Education with specialization in Educational Management, Leadership and Policy studies from the University of Bristol, the United Kingdom. His diverse career spans working as a teacher through educational leadership to becoming a researcher, lecturer, postgraduate supervisor and international examiner in his specialization. He served as chairperson of SADC Technical Committee on Basic Education, has participated in Commonwealth Education Material Development and Training for headteachers and school inspectors and is a European Union Education Expert. He has published widely in both local and international educational refereed journals.

Nicholas Wachira is an assistant professor at Aga Khan University Institute for Educational Development, East Africa. His research interests include school leadership and technology integration in education. He has recently published a book called *Taking Making to Classrooms in Challenging Contexts*.

Charles F. Webber is a professor in the Faculty of Health, Community and Education at Mount Royal University in Calgary, Alberta, Canada. His research interests focus on higher education administration and leadership, cross-cultural leadership development, the role of the principal and student assessment policies and practices. During his career as an educator, he has served in western Canada as a classroom teacher, curriculum consultant, principal, professor, associate dean and dean.

Introduction and Setting the Scene

Pontso Moorosi

Introduction

Leadership development and specific preparation for school leadership represents a rapidly growing body of literature and has been of significant interest for scholars in the field for decades. This aspect of the field is concerned with the readiness of those who take up leadership positions and the level of professional development support while in office. Tony Bush has consistently argued over the years that the journey from teaching to leading is 'an incremental process, which generally involves the gradual substitution of leadership and management activities for classroom teaching' (Bush, Bell and Middlewood, 2010: 7). An even more compelling case is made in Bush (2018), where he posits that headship is a specific occupation requiring specific preparation in view of the increasing complexity of the demands facing school leaders in recent years. Thus, the preparation and development of school leaders has become an important issue for scholars in the wake of the now widely accepted recognition of leadership as a very significant aspect (second to classroom teaching) in influencing and shaping students' learning outcomes and for leadership succession. Accordingly, Leithwood, Harris and Hopkins (2008: 29) asserted that 'unplanned headteacher succession is one of the most common sources of schools' failure to progress, in spite of what teachers might do'.

Within many of the most advanced and developed education systems, the preparation of school leaders is typically discerned by a certificated programme of training, usually undergone by those aspiring for headship in advance of taking office. In these contexts, research primarily focuses on the nature and scope of preparation programmes, processes of recruitment and selection of participants of leadership development programmes, content and providers of training programmes and the extent to which these programmes lead to improved learning outcomes for schools. However, it has become evident over the years that this preparatory training is not a universal phenomenon and does not receive the same level of priority in other parts of the world. In some contexts, no training is provided or is provided long after incumbents have taken office, in which case the retrospective training becomes part of induction and/or ongoing professional development. In such contexts, research ought to be asking different questions that aim to unearth, understand and develop the actual practices that school leaders go through to develop skills, knowledge and dispositions that give them the confidence to lead and manage schools. This remains a gap in the literature, and this book is intended to illuminate some of those experiences.

As the chapters in this volume demonstrate, in many African countries, formal preparation training for school leadership is not a priority. However, the volume is intended to showcase other ways in which school leaders in Africa have been, and continue to be, prepared for positions of leadership, despite the absence of formal preparatory training. The book also highlights some of the experiences that shape professional development for school leaders, which are equally important in ensuring that the latter keep up with the demands of the office and provide improved learning outcomes for students. This introductory chapter sets the scene for the rest of the book, providing a conceptual background to the field and introducing key concepts central to the book. It summarizes key developments in the field and raises questions for both preparation and development research, particularly as understood, practised and experienced in the African context. The chapter ends with an overview that foreshadows the rest of the chapters in the book and highlights some good practices.

Understanding school leadership preparation and development

School leadership preparation has often been understood in the context of formal programmes that help individuals to become ready for the principalship and other leadership positions. Although school leadership entails a collective of leaders and the process of leading, both processes of preparation and development often involve individual leaders. Additionally, although school leaders and school leadership include all leaders at different levels, preparation is often understood and used to refer to preparation for school principalship or headship, while leadership development involves the advancement of those already in the headship. In earlier work, Moorosi and Bush (2011) drew a distinction between preparation and development, wherein the former was understood to be pre-principalship training normally undertaken before the assumption of duty, while the latter has more to do with post-appointment professional development that includes both induction and ongoing professional development. In addition to training, principalship preparation would also entail middle-leadership experiences through positions occupied before one is finally appointed as a school principal. However, those who are not en route to headship are often left out of the preparation programmes, and those who are not in headship do not have many opportunities to attend leadership development programmes.

In this volume, we adopt a broad understanding of leadership development as one that advances the capacity of a collective of leaders and teachers, including those teachers who are not holding managerial roles. We also define school leaders as those playing a role in leadership and management activities in schools, whether or not they are in formal managerial positions. This includes school principals, deputy principals, heads of departments and teachers. We acknowledge that school governors could, in some contexts, be broadly placed within this category, given the breadth of their responsibilities and their significance to the overall functioning of a school, particularly in the context of site-based management. However, school governance research has remained an independent sub-field, albeit complicated and under-researched. Our notion of school leaders in this chapter and in the rest of the book does not include school governors and learners.

In understanding the preparation and development of school leaders, a further distinction has often been made between the concepts of *leadership* and *management*. Here, the argument is that preparatory programmes focus more on knowledge, skills and dispositions that enhance performance for managerial roles rather than leadership roles. The latter should focus more on enabling different groups of people within an organization to work together more meaningfully towards change and the achievement of goals, regardless of whether they are holding managerial positions or not. We acknowledge these debates over leadership and management as distinct but interrelated processes by accepting the use of both terms depending on different contexts. For example, in Ebot-Ashu's chapter on Cameroon, the use of management is stronger than leadership, while Mestry uses leadership in the South African context, suggesting that leadership has now been fully embraced. Thus, for the purposes of this volume, 'leadership development' is used to refer to knowledge, skills and dispositions that enhance both management and leadership performance.

A further distinction is also made between developing a 'leader' (individual) and 'leadership' (collective). Bush (2008) argues that although the notion of 'leadership development' is often used in contrast to 'leader development', the focus usually remains on developing leaders as individuals. The argument is that, because of its collective nature, leadership development speaks more closely to school improvement and hence needs to be given more attention. Therefore, in this chapter and generally throughout the volume, leadership preparation and development is referred to in both individual and collective terms.

As many of the chapters in this volume show, most preparation for principalship is for individuals, with training (where it happens) occurring as induction. However, in a more recent analysis of school leadership socialization, Moorosi and Grant (2018) problematized the distinction between preparation and development, arguing that the lack of a clear-cut boundary renders the distinction problematic. In this understanding, a confusion arises where principals are appointed into post with no specific preparation. In this case, professional socialization, which is often defined as the acquisition of new knowledge and skills – usually prior to role acquisition and incorporating preparation training – is seen as overlapping with organizational socialization, which usually incorporates induction after role acquisition as part of leadership development. Thus, in view of these contested issues, the use of 'leadership preparation' and 'development' in this volume denotes a field of research that covers some or all the aspects referred to above and does not necessarily indicate a differentiation between the concepts.

The global context for and background to leadership preparation and development

The earliest work on school leadership preparation and development research dates back to the late nineteenth century in the United States, when school leadership as we now know it was referred to as mere supervision and the school principalship role was limited to (financial) planning, coordination and public relations, as opposed to more instruction-focused leadership (Murphy, 1998). Murphy's analysis shows that the preparation of school principals in the United States has been linked to university teaching from the 1960s, when different states required formal coursework in educational leadership for principalship positions, leading to higher numbers of school principals and superintendents embarking on university training for their administrative preparation.

According to Murphy (1998: 365), the establishment of the University Council for Educational Administration (UCEA) in 1956 fell within a period of rapid growth of the field of educational administration, marking a significant milestone that 'helped shaped the evolving conceptions' of school leadership as a field of study, leading to a high number of doctoral degrees. Brundrett (2001) argues that centring school leadership preparation in university programmes ensured an intellectually sophisticated approach to school leadership training which embedded academic critique from the get go. Consequently, research became central to school leadership preparation and open to a range of analyses, including the significant work of Greenfield (1985), which critically looked into the socialization processes of being and becoming a school principal. Greenfield scrutinized principalship role learning among teacher aspirants for the principalship and its impact on actual readiness.

In the United Kingdom, the focus on leadership preparation and development pretty much followed the US model (Bush, 1999; Brundrett, 2001). Brundrett (2001) states that programmes offering systematic preparatory training and development opportunities for senior teaching staff in schools in England were only initiated in the 1960s, followed by the establishment of researcher chairs in educational management in the 1970s. To this end, an important early work on educational management development (as it was referred to when the field started) was by Glatter (1972), following what has been famously known as the Plowden Report of 1967, which basically highlighted the inadequacy of the training programmes that were meant to prepare prospective heads and deputy heads for their roles (Brundrett, 2001). Glatter's (1972) initial work started looked into how school managers were developed and began to question the responsiveness of the then models to the needs of school management. However, Brundrett (2001) indicates that the period before 1980 was characterized by inconsistencies and lack of coherent structure at national level. Significantly, the English approach to school leadership training and development (as opposed to the US one) was characterized by bureaucratic interjections to the national programme that arrogated training to a competency-based model at the expense of academic critique that the US model enjoyed.

Although these early works focused more on processes of individual school leaders' preparation through university-led programmes as well as leaders' socialization within the school context, and less on the complexity of the interplay between the different agents involved in the socialization of school principals (as does more recent research), they kick-started a significant debate that shaped the current thinking around the preparation and development of school leaders, not only in the global north but also in the rest of the world. Significantly, they began to highlight the need for more responsive models of leadership preparation and development in view of the shifting social climate, technological advances and contextual challenges. In the same breadth, these early discourses enabled different levels of scrutiny that may not necessarily be within the context of formal preparation, such as socialization and leader identity development. The socialization and leader identity literature, as seen for example through the longitudinal research studies of Greenfield (1985) and Browne-Ferrigno (2003) and other work by Ribbins (2008) and Moorosi and Grant (2018), acknowledges that preparation can also occur outside formal training programmes.

Since the early days of the field, there has been a surge of research in school leadership preparation and development in the United Kingdom centred on the establishment and evaluation of the former National College for School Leadership and its rather comprehensive leadership development framework that became influential in many countries. In the United States, leadership development research focused around the work of the UCEA and the licensure debates around preparation of school principals (e.g. Young et al., 2009; Young and Crow, 2016). Leadership preparation research from other parts of the world also emerged. Notably, on the African continent, Kitavi and van der Westhuizen (1997), Bush and Oduro (2006), Mathibe (2007), and Otunga, Sereme and Kindiki (2008) highlighted challenges experienced at schools with implications for preparation and development. The influence of the international models on the different aspects of the field, is seen through the various chapters in this volume.

As an indication of growth in the field, many journal special issues and book volumes have been dedicated to leadership preparation and development. For example, in 2006 *School Leadership and Management* journal dedicated a special issue to leadership development (26: 2), which covered many leadership development issues in some international contexts, while the *Journal of Educational Administration* (2008, 46: 6) and *Educational Administration Quarterly* (EAQ) (2010, 47: 1) also dedicated special issues to principal preparation and leadership development, respectively, and both attempted a global focus, albeit to varying degrees. For example, while JEA attempts a more global perspective, drawing contributions from a diverse group of authors and contexts, EAQ tends to be more US-centric. *Educational Management Administration and Leadership* (2013, 41: 4) and *Management in Education* (2018, 32: 2) also followed suit, again with no focus on the African continent.

In addition to the journal special issues, several books and handbooks have also been published in different contexts. Huber (2004) provided an international analysis of leadership development models across continents. Brundrett and Crawford (2009) published a book on global perspectives on leadership development, while Young et al.'s (2009) handbook and its subsequent second edition by Young and Crow (2016), although focused mostly on US experiences, addressed important leadership preparation concerns, raising questions for research in the field. While most of these were global collections offering very useful contributions to the field, they focused mainly on the global north and particularly Europe and North America, with, notably, very limited coverage of perspectives from the global south and particularly Africa. Implications and lessons can always be learnt from these Western experiences, however, as Eacott and Asuga (2014) and Pansiri (2011) noted, relying on Western notions of leadership does not help disrupt the colonial legacies and does not serve justice in advancing contextually based African knowledge.

Individual researchers' work from the neglected context of Africa is scattered across a range of journals and book chapters, and some significant research presumably still lies buried in unpublished masters' dissertations and doctoral theses. Hallinger's (2017) review of educational leadership and management (ELM) literature on the African continent reveals a total of 48 articles on school leader preparation and development published between 1981 and 2016, while an earlier review by Eacott and Asuga (2014) revealed 20 articles (focused on Africa and inclusive of the broader field) in five of the top journals in the field of ELM. By global standards, and in view of the size of the continent that Africa is, this reflects the field in its infancy, needing much attention from researchers. Yet Hallinger (2017) seems to suggest that the field of leadership and management in general is 'ripe for systematic review' in the contexts of Kenya, Nigeria and South Africa. This suggests the skewed nature of the contribution that is dominated by a handful of countries out of the total of more than 50 countries in the continent.

Specific attention to the developing world, and to Africa in particular, is seen in Bush's (2008) book on leadership development, which provides a comprehensive coverage of international practices covering both developing and developed contexts. Lumby, Crow and Pashiardis (2008) provide a global coverage of leadership preparation and development with some attention to Africa and extensive focus on the developing world in general. Although both Bush (2008) and Lumby et al. (2008) highlight the limited research attention to the developing world and particularly Africa, this remains a gap in the literature which this volume attempts to address. While we observe the need for a more comprehensive country-by-country analysis and comparative analyses that would inform cross-cultural learning, this book only focuses on some of the identified African states where research on leadership preparation and/ or development has been conducted. It is significant, however, that the book presents a unified voice focused on Africa where the field is at the emerging status. This is a useful starting point for a dialogue that is geared towards theorization based on local experiences.

Overview of leadership preparation and development research in Africa

This section provides an overview of existing literature on the subject of school leadership preparation and development on the African continent, while foreshadowing the rest of chapters in this volume. It highlights different aspects which have influenced research in this field thus far, putting the spotlight on the uniqueness of issues affecting the field in the African context that may differ from other parts of the world. These aspects are categorized into broad areas, including the historical legacy of colonialism, lack of resources and political will and other contextual problems that are compounded by the lack of sufficient preparation of school principals. Often, these are challenges that uniquely face school leaders in the African context. Earlier, Kitavi and van der Westhuizen (1997) argued that principals may not always be in a position to solve all the contextual problems they experience, but that their awareness of them means that they are alert.

Historical legacy of colonialism and apartheid

Context and history are important in shaping current policy and practice, not only in school leadership but also in education in general. Undoubtedly, education systems in Africa are hugely shaped by the legacy of colonialism, and the field of leadership preparation and development has not escaped. Inevitably, this has meant that even in times when post-colonial countries claim their independence, their education systems are still tied to colonial ideals in their curricula, approaches to teaching and approaches to leadership and management.

Pansiri (2011) criticized the adoption of Western models that are unsuitable for the African context. He argued that despite the claim of independence by post-colonial countries in sub-Saharan Africa, education systems, and particularly leadership and management, are still blindfolded by colonial ideals including 'school calendars' and 'homeworks' that make school leaders completely ignorant of contextual realities that make these ideals challenging. As a consequence, models adopted from the West do not quite explain the situation in Africa due to the nature of its complexity. Eacott and Asuga (2014) augmented this critique by also problematizing the dependency on Western intervention and models, arguing that the colonial chains may never be shuffled off the ankles of African education systems. Indeed, in Chapter 2 of this volume, Pansiri and Majwabe use a post-colonial lens to analyse the history of Botswana's school leadership and management and its attempt to develop its leaders. The significance and relevance of this historical background lies in the poignant point they make about the chances that school leadership and management development have of turning themselves around to be more responsive to the context. Their analysis shows that despite efforts made by the Botswanan government since independence, the country has failed to decolonize its policies. The authors call for an indigenous and endogenous policy that is in line with the historical, cultural and socio-political contexts of the community that would make leadership preparation and development relevant.

The failure to decolonize policies is perhaps attributable to many, if not all, of the post-colonial countries, and it is arguably the reason why the success of leadership preparation and development is still measured by the amount of training or lack of it. In Chapter 3, Moorosi and Komiti present an analysis of another post-colonial country, Lesotho, which attained independence around the same time as Botswana. Although Moorosi and Komiti choose to highlight the different ways in which school leaders become prepared outside of the context of formal leadership training, which include reliance on their initial teacher training, experiential preparation and networking, all happening outside of any formal leadership training programme, the fact that the majority of schools in which these preparation and development processes occur are owned by churches speaks volumes about the challenges government has and the prospect it could ever have a handle on training and development for school leaders. From their different research studies, the authors highlight alternative ways in which school leaders are being prepared outside the context of formal training. Although their analysis shows that the lack of training is attributed to reduced levels of funding, it is arguable that formal training is made unattainable by its conceptualization, influenced by Western models of leadership preparation. Indeed, Pansiri (2011) argued that in the context of donor funding, school leaders have become passive recipients of prescribed international policies.

Unlike two of its sub-Saharan neighbours that had British protectorate status, Namibia was under the rule of its most immediate neighbour, the Republic of South Africa, until 1990, which puts it in the unique position of being under both colonial and apartheid rule. In Chapter 4, Grant shows how since independence, Namibia has attempted to reform its education policy, prioritizing 'access', among other ideals. However, these priorities have not yet translated to access to opportunities for universal formal leadership preparation. Grant uses career socialization theory to identify the different phases through which school leaders learn the role of leadership within the context of a haphazard and inconsistent training. Indeed, Lopez and Rugano (2018: 2) argue that against the backdrop of colonialism, 'education continues to produce a system in which student disengagement, inequity, and social injustice continues to exist'. In referring to social justice, Grant makes an important distinction between (leadership) role-taking and role-making, which, she argues, are equally important in shaping experiences of school leadership socialization. She argues that school leaders need to develop competencies that would enable stronger role-making, as this would ensure that they are more responsive to the context in ways that are sustainable and socially just.

Social justice as a constitutional ideal in South Africa underpins Mestry's Chapter 5, wherein he problematizes the lack of meaningful policy shift on the preparation of school principals since the end of apartheid rule, despite a series of evaluations of the pilot programme that provided evidence that the programme significantly benefitted school principals to lead schools effectively. The analysis helpfully demonstrates the effect of school leadership preparation on learning outcomes, showing that the latter has been consistently poor in South Africa as a result of poor leadership in most schools. Although the focus is on poor outcomes in schools that are suffering poor leadership in general, it is worth noting that the majority of these schools are in Black communities that were segregated under apartheid rule. This issue is quite on point, as the literature shows that the lack of leadership preparation comes under the spotlight when students' performance is poor (Mathibe, 2007) and how the majority of students who suffer are Black students who were disadvantaged under the previous apartheid regime.

Resources, context and political will

Most of the literature on school leadership preparation and development highlights the lack of resources and other socio-economic challenges facing the newly appointed school principals in most African schools (Bush and Oduro, 2006; Kitavi and van der Westhuizen, 1997). Bush (2018) argues that problems experienced in the African context by school leaders are highly complex, making it even more important for school principals to be prepared for their role so that they have the skills to address the problems in context. Onguko, Abdalla and Webber (2012) stated that school leaders in Africa must be prepared to deal with broader socio-economic issues over and above lack of learning resources and planning for leadership succession. Lack of political will emerges in contexts where there is a failure to make the expected resources available.

Chapters 6 and 7 focus on the East African region, which (in addition to South Africa) is also active in the development of school leadership research (see e.g. Asuga, Eacott and Scevak, 2015; Onguko, Abdalla and Webber, 2008, 2012; Okoko, Scott and Scott, 2014). School leadership preparation and development in this region is sufficiently well-documented due to the specific effort of some of the governments and the help of private funders and private–national providers, professional associations and consultants (Asuga et al., 2015; Lopez and Raguna, 2018). However, Lopez and Raguna (2018: 7) argue that school leadership preparation and development programmes in Kenya have not been responsive to the needs of both current and aspiring school leaders. Accordingly, in Chapter 6, Okoko's secondary analysis of data to examine context-specific school leadership preparation and development needs in Kenya is quite pertinent. She uses this rich body of literature to argue that framing school leadership preparation and development within context-specific considerations could assure quality and consistency in the modes of delivery, engagement and partnerships, which would arguably make school leadership preparation and development more responsive.

In Chapter 7, Abdalla and colleagues provide a critical analysis of the efficiency model in Tanzania that gives school leaders a more supervisory role, which, as they show, fails to address the complexity of education in the Tanzanian context. In earlier work, Onguko et al. (2012) had suggested that Tanzania uses an apprenticeship model for school leadership preparation whereby incoming school leaders learn from their predecessors. As the socialization literature has shown, the problem with this model is that it leads to conformity and lack of innovation (Moorosi and Grant, 2018). However, as the authors show in this chapter, serious questions are to be addressed about the effectiveness of the efficiency model of school management. The chapter raises important questions for leadership development that is context specific, so that school leaders can be trained to deal with deeply entrenched problems.

In Chapter 8, Ebot-Ashu explores factors that influence school leadership preparation and development in Cameroon, using both primary and secondary data from his previous work. He establishes that central educational agencies, schools and communities all recognized the importance played by policy in the preparation of aspiring head teachers. As other literature from the continent suggests, the role of on-the-job training (and seminars) also appears important in this context as opportunities for leadership development, and this is actually found to align with some international best practices, particularly when it is coupled with a well-structured programme of leadership training.

The last two chapters are based on the West African analyses of Ghana and Nigeria respectively, where a great deal of research is also found. In Chapter 9, Amakyi and Ampah-Mensah provide a conceptual analysis, arguing the importance of craft knowledge in the development of school leaders. They show that Ghana has no shortage of programmes of school leadership development as these are provided by local universities. Yet, the practical realities suggest a reliance on craft knowledge that is not based on theoretical learning. In this chapter, they therefore explore the opportunities and challenges in relying on craft knowledge for practising school leaders and suggest ways in which effective instructional leaders could be developed in order to meet contemporary Ghanaian expectations.

In Chapter 10, Imoni reviews the literature on school leadership and leadership preparation and development in Nigeria. Indeed, Nigeria is identified by Hallinger (2017) as one of the contexts ready for reviews given the amount of literature available on school leadership and management as a field. Imoni's review shows that despite this broad coverage of leadership and management literature, very little attention appears to have been given to specific aspects of leadership preparation and development.

The chapters in this volume confirm what has been established previously about the lack of formal leadership preparation programmes in the African continent. However, they also reveal other ways in which school leaders are being developed, and significantly, ways that work outside formal preparation. Perhaps more significantly, the chapters reveal, in different ways, the effect of international influence on local practices, raising further questions about models of leadership preparation and development that are contextually relevant.

There are, however, some positive experiences showcased in these chapters, signalling good practices that need underscoring. For example, the focus on the richness of context, and the benefits to be gained from practices outside schools, suggest that a great deal can be drawn from community and highlight the need to view the development of leadership skills more broadly than just within the school context. Some in-house and/or district or regional initiatives such as mentoring, networking and collaborative learning are good practices that can be built on and learnt from.

Conclusion

It is an important development that in the past decade or two, literature on school leadership preparation and development in the African context has expanded. The interest in this aspect of the field is growing, suggesting a healthy starting point from which to build scholarship that addresses key questions and to develop a strong, contextually driven body of knowledge. What this development suggests is the possibility for more 'home-grown' models and approaches to preparation and development, models that are more responsive to the context and the realities faced by African children. As indicated, other researchers have called for more relevant models in post-colonial Africa. Perhaps even more important is the need to develop more extensive and longer-term projects that provide more convincing evidence to enhance cross-cultural learning and influence policy to shape school leadership preparation and development.

References

Asuga, G., S. Eacott, and J. Scevak (2015), 'School Leadership Preparation and Development in Kenya: Evaluating Performance Impact and Return on Leadership Development Investment', *International Journal of Educational Management*, 29 (3): 355–67.

Browne-Ferrigno, T. (2003), 'Becoming a Principal: Role Conception, Initial Socialization, Role-Identity Transformation, Purposeful Engagement', *Educational Administration Quarterly*, 39 (4): 468–503.

Brundrett, M. (2001), 'The Development of School Leadership Preparation Programmes in England and the USA: A Comparative Analysis', *Educational Management & Administration*, 29 (2): 229–45.

Brundrett, M. and M. Crawford, eds (2009), *Developing School Leaders: An International Perspective*, London: Routledge.

Bush, T. (1999), 'Crisis or Crossroads? The Discipline of Educational Management in the 1990s', *Educational Management & Administration*, 27 (3): 239–52.

Bush, T. (2008) 'From Management to Leadership: Semantic or Meaningful Change?' *Educational Management Administration & Leadership*, 36 (2): 271–88.

Bush, T. (2018), 'Preparation and Induction for School Principals: Global Perspectives', *Management in Education*, 32 (2): 66–71.

Bush, T. and G. Oduro (2006), 'New Principals in Africa: Preparation, Induction and Practice', *Journal of Educational Administration*, 44 (4): 359–75.

Bush, T., L. Bell, and D. Middlewood (2010), 'Introduction: New Directions in Educational Leadership', in T. Bush, L. Bell and D. Middlewood (eds), *The Principles of Educational Leadership & Management*, 2nd edn, Sage: London.

Croft, J. C. (1968), 'The Principal as Supervisor: Some Descriptive Findings and Important Questions', *Journal of Educational Administration*, 6 (2): 162–72.

Eacott, S. and G. N. Asuga (2014), 'School Leadership Preparation and Development in Africa: A Critical Insight', *Educational Management Administration & Leadership*, 42 (6): 919–34.

Glatter, R. (1972), *Management Development for the Education Profession*, London: Harrap.

Greenfield, W. D. (1985), 'The Moral Socialization of School Administrators: Informal Role Learning Outcomes', *Education Administration Quarterly*, 21 (4): 99–119.

Hallinger, P. (2017), 'Surfacing a Hidden Literature: A Systematic Review of Research on Educational Leadership and Management in Africa', *Educational Management Administration & Leadership*, 46 (3): 362–84.

Huber, S. (2004), *Preparing School Leaders for the 21st Century: An International Comparison of Development Programs in 15 Countries*, London: Routledge Falmer.

Kitavi, M. and P. van der Westhuizen (1997), 'Problems Facing Beginning Principals in Developing Countries: A Study of Beginning Principals in Kenya', *International Journal of Educational Development*, 17 (3): 251–63.

Leithwood, K., A. Harris, and D. Hopkins (2008), 'Seven Strong Claims about Successful School Leadership', *School Leadership & Management*, 28 (1): 27–42.

Lopez, A. E. and P. Rugano (2018), 'Educational Leadership in Post-Colonial Contexts: What Can We Learn from the Experiences of Three Female Principals in Kenyan Secondary Schools?' *Education Sciences*, 8 (3): 99.

Lumby, J., G. M. Crow, and P. Pashiardis (2008), *International Handbook on the Preparation and Development of School Leaders*, New York: Routledge.

Mathibe, I. (2007), 'The Professional Development of School Principals', *South African Journal of Education*, 27 (3): 523–40.

Moorosi, P. and C. Grant (2018), 'The Socialisation and Leader Identity Development of School Leaders in Southern African Countries', *Journal of Educational Administration*, 56 (6): 643–58.

Moorosi, P. and T. Bush (2011), 'School Leadership Development in Commonwealth Countries: Learning across the Boundaries', *International Studies in Educational Administration*, 39 (3): 59–76.

Murphy, J. (1998), 'Preparation for the School Principalship: The United States Experience', *School Leadership and Management*, 18 (3): 359–72.

Okoko, J. M., S. Scott, and D. Scott (2014), 'Perceptions of School Leaders in Nairobi about Their Leadership Preparation and Development', *International Journal of Leadership in Education*, 17 (1): 1–26.

Onguko, B., M. Abdalla, and C. F. Webber (2008), 'Mapping Principal Preparation in Kenya and Tanzania', *Journal of Educational Administration*, 46 (6): 715–26.

Onguko, B., M. Abdalla, and C. F. Webber (2012), 'Walking in Unfamiliar Territory: Headteachers' Preparation and First-Year Experiences in Tanzania', *Education Administration Quarterly*, 48 (1): 86–115.

Otunga R., K. Sereme, and J. N. Kindiki (2008), 'School Leadership Development in Africa', in J. Lumby, G. Crow, and P. Pashiardis (eds), *International Handbook on the Preparation and Development of School Leaders*, 367–82, New York: Routledge.

Pansiri, N. O. (2011), 'Performativity in School Management and Leadership in Botswana', *Educational Management Administration & Leadership*, 39 (6): 751–66.

Ribbins, P. (2008), 'A Life and Career Based Framework for the Study of Leaders in Education', in J. Lumby, G. Crow, and P. Pashiardis (eds), *International Handbook on the Preparation and Development of School Leaders*, 61–80, London: Routledge.

Young, M. D., G. Crow, J. Murphy, and R. T. Ogawa, eds (2009), *Handbook of Research on the Education of School Leaders*, New York: Routledge.

Young, M. D., G. Crow, eds (2016), *Handbook of Research on the Education of School Leaders*, New York: Routledge.

2

A Historical Analysis of Educational Leadership Preparation and Development in Botswana

Nkobi Owen Pansiri and Shadreck Zola Majwabe

Introduction

This chapter discusses educational leadership training, development and preparation in Botswana for public schools. The discussion applies the socio-political and historical analysis as a methodological approach to examine the development of school leadership preparation from 1966 to 2018. School leadership is presented here as a combination of special traits or characteristics that heads of schools possess and that enable them to motivate their staff and learners to accomplish tasks. In this view, leadership is more than a position or job. It is a well-calculated, visionary and driving spirit that ignites organizational change and improves performance and success. Leadership practice in schools, as in any organization, derives power and impetus from positional legitimacy, expert power and coercive power (Northouse, 2004; Armstrong, 2007). In its varied forms and practices, leadership cannot be left to chance, hence the need for leadership training in the Botswana education system. To put the discussion into logical perspective, a brief historical background of Botswana and its educational evolution will be provided. This background is important in that it has implications for the performance of school heads and for human capital development in general.

Socio-political and historical analysis of Botswana's educational evolution

Botswana was a British colony for 81 years (1885–1966) under an arrangement that has been defined as a protectorate (Coles, 1985). This arrangement was motivated by the three *dikgosi* (chiefs) (Khama III of the Bangwato, Sebele I of the Bakwena and Bathoen I of the Bangwaketse ethnic groups) of the then Bechuanaland, who went to Great Britain in 1895 to seek Britain's protection against C. J. Rhodes, who had threatened to attack and annex Tswana-speaking people from the south to the then Rhodesia. The protectorate administration ran the country from Mafeking in South Africa until 1966. At independence, Botswana had 250 primary schools (Chiepe, 1984), eight secondary schools (Kann et al., 1988) and two teacher training colleges for a population of 550, 000 (Coles, 1985).

After 1966, Botswana developed through three periods of education development with the support of different international funding agencies. The first period (1977–1993) was the era of Education for Kagisano (the first education policy). This period saw educational leadership preparation that was supported by British funding agencies and focused more on school administration and management. The second period (1994–2014) saw the introduction of the Revised National Policy on Education (RNPE) (the second education policy). Some projects were funded by the American Development Agency. This period introduced the concepts of staff development and instructional leadership. The third period covers 2015 to date, the period of the Education and Training Sector Strategic Plan (ETSSP – an education transformation strategy). The period emphasized continuous professional development (CPD), improved school planning and decentralized leadership, management and governance. Some projects of the ETSSP were financially and technically supported by the European Union (EU). As indicated earlier, reference to the pre-history of the country is imperative because the success and/or failures of school leadership preparation depended heavily on the socio-cultural determinants of colonialism.

Africa is a known terrain of diverse geographic and socio-political heritage. Sub-Saharan African governments borrowed their development strategies from their colonizers. Adopting the best models and mobilizing adequate resources within the legacy of colonialism was a challenge (Zadja, 2014). The socio-cultural and political spelling of Botswana are drawn from its pre-history, that is, the protectorate governance system anchored on the Batswana kingdoms of the perceived eight major ethnic groups: Rolong, Kwena, Ngwaketse, Ngwato, Tawana, Lete, Kgatla and Tlokwa (Parsons, 1984). These ethnic groups created the geographical boundary of Bechuanaland and they are concentrated along the eastern coast of the country (Mgadla, 2003). The 1965 Constitution of Botswana adopted a new country and uncritically legitimized the social construction of ethno-linguistic and cultural majoritization and minoritization of Botswana society (Pansiri, 2012). Even in the absence of any statistical and cultural hegemonic pointers, the country was imagined as having major and minor ethnic groups (Gardiner, 1950; Youngman, 2003). The perceived minor ethnic groups, which Coles (1985) calls 'other associated tribes' (p. 1) were BaSarwa (also known as Bushmen), BaKgalagadi, BaBirwa, BaTswapong, BaKalanga, BaYei, BaHerero, BaSubiya and BaMbukushu (Republic of Botswana, 1965). These ethnic groups are found in the vast land of the country stretching from the central part to the western land of Botswana (Mgadla, 2003). These groups are non-Setswana speaking. They have different ethnic or indigenous languages, cultures and traditions. During the Protectorate's creation of geographical boundaries, these communities and their land areas were made subservient to the major ethnic groups. For example, some BaKgalagadi found themselves under BaNgwaketse and Bakwena cultural and historical hegemonies. In the same type of historical development, the BaSarwa found themselves enclaved within the BaNgwato (Parsons, 1984). This colonial social construction and legitimization of imagining Botswana as an ethno-linguistic and culturally majoritized and minoritized society has impacted on the development of education in Botswana and has affected the performance of schools and school leaderships. Viewed through the lenses of post-colonial theory, Botswana's education system has, therefore, been managed out of context by applying a one-size-fits-all approach despite the country being an ethno-culturally heterogeneous society with diverse geo-climatic regions. Since the colonial regime, the education system has been mechanically and uniformly run, without any flexibility to adapt to varying conditions and contexts. In the final analysis, Botswana's education system has failed to decolonize, and the school head remains a victim of performativity.

History of the education system

Western education was introduced by Robert Moffat, a member of the London Missionary Society (LMS) as far back as 1821 (Coles, 1985). Twenty-six years later (in 1847), it was spread by David Livingstone – another LMS guru – in some parts of the land of Setswana-speaking communities. In particular, the Christianity of the Bible school, focusing more on the New Testament, was introduced to the Bakwena under Kgosi Sebele (Parsons, 1984). By 1860, a mission school was introduced among the Bangwato community of Shoshong with a curriculum that included reading, writing, arithmetic (the 3Rs) and scripture in Setswana. With the arrival of the Lutheran and Dutch Reformed missionaries, missionary work carried the Western education agenda further to other Batswana Kingdoms. Parsons (1984) argues that by 1880, the eight Batswana kingdoms had Christianity as their religion. Christianity therefore became the nation-state religion. Missionaries masterminded the introduction of the Western education curriculum and schooling systems and took control of institutional leadership. For example, Miss Mary Livingstone ran the LMS infant school (Parsons, 1984). At the time, school leadership and education management did not feature as a critical issue. The Batswana had little idea about the school system that had been introduced. Questions about school leadership emerged gradually during the Protectorate's introduction of a new colonial government system with new district administration (Coles, 1985).

Sephuma (1991: 129) however, observes that

> the administrative control of education ... was the general adoption of a committee system of management which was first introduced at the joint request of LMS and chief of the Bangwaketse tribe in 1910.

The appointment of an inspector of education, Mr H. J. E. Dumbrell, in 1928 legitimized supervision of teachers in the Protectorate (Coles, 1985). Dumbrell's education leadership provided improved coordination and management of schools and teachers' work. Responding to the Bangwaketse Kgosi and in the interest of neutralizing the influence of religious movements, Dumbrell introduced a Board of Advice on Native Education to allow joint participation between *dikgosi* and missions in educational committees. The approach marked the adoption of the decentralization of education management in the eight Batswana kingdoms. It was formally ratified by the Bechuanaland Protectorate administration in 1938. This then meant that in each of the kingdoms' committees, made up of selected members of the ethnic groups, the Mission and District Administration were responsible for the management of schools. The adoption of the Native School legislation in 1938 (Parson, 1983) separated mission schools from ethnic group schools. The District Administration gained firm control over Native Schools.

During the Protectorate period (1885–1964), Batswana kingdoms, with the help of the colonial government administration, built schools. Following Bathoen's plea, the concept of teacher training also emerged, and it was agreed that a teacher training school should be built (Coles, 1985). In the late 1800s and early 1900s, the colonial government administration assisted the Protectorate kingdoms to raise funds to build schools. School fees were introduced. For example, Coles (1985) argues that in around 1894, schools in Palapye community (the Bangwato kingdom) charged 5 shillings (50 thebe) a year. This mushrooming of schools and the need for financial accountability in schools marked the beginning of a demand for the training of school leaders. In the mid-1900s, teacher training institutions were constructed by the colonial government under pressure first from Bathoen and then from other tribal leaders. That is how the first teacher training centre was started in Kanye (headquarters of Bangwaketse) in 1940, which later transferred to Lobatse and was renamed Lobatse Teacher Training College. The second such centre to be opened was the Serowe Teacher Training College in 1963. At the time, both the Missions and *dikgosi* played a significant role in appointing school heads, depending on who owned the school. Moreover, no one thought of leadership training for those who would lead schools. Only teachers were trained for classroom work (Mgadla, 2003).

The Protectorate's education development introduced through missionaries took place predominantly around the major ethnic groups' boundaries (Parsons, 1984; Coles, 1985). Schools were created under the control of missionaries and were gradually introduced to the ethnic groups' leaderships or *dikgosi*, and in many cases schools were named after the *dikgosi* or the ethnic groups themselves. School leaders were appointed and paid by their missions, and later, or during the Protectorate period, by the ethnic groups through the *dikgosi*, depending on the school ownership. This remained so until 1966. The Protectorate leadership handed to Batswana a country and/or society characterized by socio-political inequalities, uncoordinated education sub-sectors, weak school community relationships, and people without useful and productive skills (Mgadla, 2003). Failure to decolonize meant that Botswana's education development approach was, in one way or another, a response to this heritage.

School leadership preparation period 1966–1976

The 1965 Education Act, introduced before independence, borrowed heavily from the British system: Her Majesty's system of educational governance, known as the Inspectorate. The first inspector of education, Mr H. J. E. Dumbrell, drafted a managerial approach to the management of schools. The Act pronounced public schools as being of two types, namely government schools, owned by either local or central government; and government-aided schools – those shared by government and the church or mission. It also pronounced the position of a school inspector as the gazetted supervisor of schools and of the school head in particular. Right at the beginning of the new country, inspectors as supervisory officers were recruited and appointed to preside over education development in districts. Sub-section 2 of section 26 of the Act states that

> an Inspector may at any time, with or without notice, enter and inspect any school or any place at which it is reasonably suspected that a school is being conducted, and may inspect and take copies and extracts from any records kept. (Republic of Botswana, 1967)

With this legislation, the colonial imperative inevitably transferred its education supervisory legacy to the new country. In this regard, the School Inspectorate became a legitimately and administratively empowered law-enforcement cadre. School inspectors emerged as the most feared people in educational development. Their role was perceived to be more focused on a punitive than a guiding approach. This approach signals the centrality of how managerialism and performativity has been embraced in the running of schools in Botswana. It emphasized mechanical compliance to rules and regulations with little attention given to leadership development. It amplified the roles of the supervisor and supervisee as separate entities.

Upon obtaining self-rule in 1966, Botswana immediately adopted the Transitional Plan for Social and Economic Development Strategy. The strategy recognized the fact that

> primary schools were inadequate, overcrowded, and poorly staffed, without teaching aids and other educational facilities and there were only a handful of secondary schools. (Chiepe, 1984: 54)

The plan embraced a more inclusive dispensation of building a pluri-ethno-linguistic and diverse, tribal, divided country into a united nation. For example, one major goal of education was to increase educational opportunities for all age groups and reduce inequalities of educational opportunity (Republic of Botswana, 1985). To accelerate development, Botswana's education development projects depended on grant-in-aid from the United Kingdom with a focus on acquiring basic skills (SIDA, 1972). It would appear that the concept of leadership, although critical, was at that time neither conceptualized nor understood.

In 1975, Botswana adopted the Unified Teaching Service Act, which established the Unified Teaching Service Department in the Ministry of Education (MoE). This Department was mandated to recruit, select, deploy and manage all teachers employed by the (MoE). This consequentially withdrew the powers of the local authorities from teacher employment and management issues. Since then, Botswana has never had a succession and talent management plan for leadership development. Teachers are recruited mainly on the basis of their teaching qualification. Their career progression is determined by experience and assessment by the supervisors as and when vacancies arise. This process is devoid of capacity building because the system does not have institutionalized leadership development programmes. This defeats the essence of effective leadership development in the education system.

In 1976, the government appointed a national commission on education to review the education system, which resulted in a document known as the Education for Kagisano (Education for Social Harmony) and the 1977 Education Blue Print (1st Education Policy). The policy aimed at re-building a nation characterized by principles of unity, development, self-reliance and democracy. Between 1985 and 1991, with the support of the United States Agency for International Development (USAID), Botswana launched the Junior Secondary Education Improvement Project (JSEIP). This project resulted in the mushrooming of Community Junior Secondary Schools (CJSS), demanding better school leadership and community participation in school governance. This exerted pressure on the government to intensify school inspection. However, the need for training school heads for leadership became more pronounced.

Formalization of School Leadership Training: 1977–1993

By 1977, it had been found that 'Botswana students at both primary and secondary level score far below their peers in industrialized countries' (Republic of Botswana, 1977: 30). The same report shows that the number of untrained teachers was as high as 34 per cent for primary and 22 per cent for secondary schools, respectively. The rapid and accelerated education development approach enabled Botswana to increase the number of primary schools from 250 in 1966 to 500 in 1986 and the number of teachers from 1,673 in 1966 to 6,000 in 1986; universal primary education in 1986 was estimated at 85 per cent (Sephuma, 1988). This implies that the Plan for Social and Economic Development strategy focused more on the quantitative challenges and mainly on more schools and classrooms and on training teachers.

The first major effort to focus on formal school leadership development and training was the introduction of the Primary Education Improvement Programme (PEIP) at the University of Botswana in 1980. The main goal of the project was to improve the performance of school heads and learner achievement in primary schools. The project was technically and financially supported by USAID. The University of Ohio academic staff in the United States of America came and worked with both the MoE and the University of Botswana on the PEIP project. According to Sephuma (1988), the project had two components. The first component offered a bachelor's degree in primary education, the graduates of which were sent to colleges of education as lecturers. The target here was to improve the quality of teacher education. The second component produced diploma holders, who were sent to primary schools to occupy positions of responsibility in school leadership. The intakes into this programme were not necessarily school heads. Entrants were screened by what the University of Botswana called the 'Mature Age Entry Examination'. Only those who passed this examination were admissible. The first ten diplomates graduated in 1983 and were all sent to primary schools, but not necessarily as school heads. They returned to the positions they held prior to going on study leave.

It is not clear whether PEIP achieved its goal or not. However, the project's immediate result was to localize staffing at colleges of education. Attention then shifted to supplying bachelor's degree holders to primary education. This was seen as a 'comprehensive in-service project for leadership training for all head teachers in Botswana including deputy heads and senior teachers' (Sephuma, 1988: 92). Many of the earlier B.Ed. graduates were appointed education officers – many in inspectorate (education law enforcement) roles and a few in in-service sectors of the MoE. During the same period, USAID technically helped the ministry to develop 14 education centres to serve as in-service centres. The in-service education officers served as the professional staff to manage and run the centres. In-service activities also spread to include developing in-service packages to be used to assist teachers in schools. However, most of the education centre–based activities were focused on training school heads. Activities focused on helping to improve classroom teaching. In-service packages included specific teaching methods projects, namely Breakthrough to Setswana, Project Method, Botswana Teaching Competency Instruments, Special Education, Differentiation Method and Environmental Education.

In 1990, Botswana joined the international community at the Jomtien Conference on Education for All. While many issues of concern on access, equity, relevance and quality in education were raised, very minimal attention was paid to school leadership training. At the time, and to a certain extent, Botswana was already ahead in terms of focusing attention on the training of school heads. In 1992, Botswana joined Ghana, Kenya, Namibia, Nigeria, Uganda, Zimbabwe, Zambia, Sierra Leone, Tanzania and Zambia under the coordination of the Commonwealth of Africa to develop a set of seven training modules on school management known as Better Schools (Commonwealth Secretariat, 1993).

Combining these modules and PEIP activities, Botswana focused on a national school heads' training programme at the beginning of 1993. All public schools heads (primary and secondary) were supplied with a set of seven modules. These were used as self-study materials as well as school management guides. Botswana therefore used both the PEIP and Better Schools training modules to provide nationwide in-service activities for school heads on educational management. The training was a school inspector-led activity. However, there is no evidence that these projects (PEIP and Better Schools) were evaluated. Also, there does seem not to be any correlation between the leadership training and school performance. For example, there is a trend of poor learner performance, as depicted in Tables 2.1 and 2.2, in which the majority of learners achieve a pass grade of C and below in national examinations.

Coinciding with the PEIP and the Better Schools project in 1993, Botswana and the British Overseas Development Agency (ODA), later known as the Department for International Development (DfID), entered into a partnership project called the Secondary Schools Management Development Project (SSMDP) (Monyatsi, 2005). The project package included six technical advisers from the ODA (from the United Kingdom) who provided the design and guidance on the project's implementation. Like the PEIP, the SSMDP involved upgrading the qualifications of school heads to a master's degree in Educational Management, as well as in-service training, through cluster and school-based professional development activities. The project engaged the University of Bath in the United Kingdom to provide a master's degree in education. A cohort of 24 school heads were first to enrol in the project, which established a coordinating structure that ran from the MoE Headquarters to the then five regions of the country. New positions of the education officer cadre, called Secondary School Management Development Officers, were created to co-ordinate CPD for secondary school management teams (SMT). These officers were made advisers rather than inspectors (education law enforcers). The project purchased books on school management which were used by both trainers and the school heads who enrolled for the master's degree. In this period, from the late 1980s to the early 1990s, Botswana education focused heavily on the training of school heads at all levels (primary and secondary schools) in school management. However, the implementation of this project coincided with the 1993 Botswana National Commission on Education. The commission resulted in the adoption of the RNPE of 1994.

Table 2.1 National Performance for Years 2010–2017 by Grades A to E, Grouped Quality Grades A–C and Grouped Grades D–E (%)

Grade	2010	2011	2012	2013	2014	2015	2016	2017	Difference (2016 to 2017)
A	15.1	12.9	13.20	12.74	14.18	14.65	16.05	17.11	+1.06
B	18.9	15.9	15.20	17.57	17.35	17.84	17.88	18.78	+0.9
C	35.4	35.2	36.60	37.28	37.61	37.25	36.58	35.73	−0.85
A–C	**69.4**	**64.0**	**65.0**	**67.49**	**69.14**	**69.74**	**70.51**	**71.62**	**+1.11**
D	29.3	32.7	34.40	26.08	25.35	23.27	22.09	21.62	−0.47
E	1.3	3.2	0.70	5.81	5.22	6.81	7.30	6.55	−0.75
D–E	**15.3**	**17.95**	**17.60**	**15.95**	**15.28**	**15.04**	**14.70**	**14.09**	**−0.61**

Source: Department of Education Planning and Research services (2018). *National Performance for Years 2010 to 2017 by grades.* Gaborone.

Table 2.2 National Summary of Overall JCE Results 2012–2015

Grade	2015			2014			2013			2012		
	Count	%	Cum%	Count	%	Cum%	Count	%	Cum%	Count	%	Cum%
Merit	1	0.0	0.0	2	0.0	0.0	0	0.0	0.0	5	0.0	0.0
A	197	0.47	0.47	367	0.9	0.9	325	0.8	0.8	590	1.5	1.6
B	3662	8.73	9.2	4007	9.9	10.8	3788	9.7	10.7	4745	12.4	13.9
C	10154	24.21	33.41	9669	23.8	34.6	9626	24.7	35.3	10386	27.1	41.0
D	14030	33.41	66.86	12914	31.8	66.5	13662	35.1	70.4	13641	35.6	76.6
E	5987	14.28	81.14	6201	15.3	81.8	5540	14.2	84.6	4889	12.7	89.3
U	6932	16.52	97.67	6395	15.8	97.5	5592	14.4	98.9	4093	10.7	100.0
X	975	2.33	99.99	1004	2.5	100.0	412	1.1	100.0	0	0.0	100.0
Total	41938			40559			38945			38349		

Source: Botswana Examinations Council (2016). Botswana Examination Council (2015). *2015 Provisional Summary of results, Junior Certificate examinations.* Botswana Examination Council:Gaborone.

Institutionalization of instructional leadership: 1994–2015

The RNPE became the blueprint for education in Botswana. It states:

> The heads as the instructional leaders, together with the deputy and senior teachers, should take major responsibility for in-service training of teachers within their schools, through regular observations of teachers and organizational workshops, to foster communication between teachers on professional matters and to address weaknesses. (Republic of Botswana, 1994: 47)

This policy confirmed the validity and the mandates of the PEIP, Better School Module and SSMDP projects. However, the policy introduced an education expert–led training rather than the inspector-led approach taken across the basic education institutions. The system adopted a concept of 'instructional leadership' and therefore continued with numerous school head training projects. In addition, and responding specifically to the RNPE, the Botswana Primary School Management Development Project (PSMDP) was launched in 1999 to train and develop primary school heads. This was funded by the DfID. The project was an innovation for school improvement and quality of primary school leadership (in relation to all members of the SMT). The first achievement of this project was to identify 30 primary school head teachers (assumed to be the best) and to send them to three different UK universities to pursue a two-year tailor-made bachelor's degree in educational management. Upon completion of this overseas training, new positions of the education officer cadre were created, and these overseas-trained primary school heads were redeployed as Primary School Management Advisors (PSMAs) to serve as site-based school leadership facilitators to support and improve primary school leadership. In both the SSMDP and PSMDP, the newly created education officer cadre were appreciated as advisers or a team of personnel with expertise in leadership, and more supportive to CPD than the inspector cadre, whose main duty was to ensure school heads' compliance with the law. However, the irony of the structure was that the inspectors were appointed from the school headship cadre to serve as school heads' supervisors were more in number than the in-service officers, had control over budgetary allocations that supported schools and were always part of the in-service training teams. Inspectors controlled the day-to-day conduct of the school. The in-service officers worked mainly with classroom teachers (save for the PSMDP advisers). This led to role conflict and operational contradictions between the cadres as the two competed for schools.

To understand the contradictions in leadership training in Botswana, one has to apply the theory of managerialism. The Botswana education system has remained predominantly an inspector-controlled structure, leading to little flexibility and teamwork in the running of schools. This contradiction, which is predominantly inspector-driven, points to the degree to which managerialism remains influential in leadership practices. This is a system which neither motivates nor inspires employees to transform. In a managerialistic approach, the inspectorate submerges the in-service system. The inspectorate emphasizes performativity at the expense of empowerment and inclusivity, which are critical to organizational performance.

Monyatsi (2005) argues that, at secondary school level, school heads did not respect in-service officers because they felt they were too inexperienced and too junior to train them on leadership. The conflict in responsibility regarding the two cadres continues to date. Kuiper (2014) argues that, instead of Botswana concentrating on the mass production of school inspectors, the country should develop an institutionalized self-quality assurance system in which the schools quality assure themselves against stipulated standards. In any case, there is no official evidence or formal evaluation of these projects to show the impact of the SSMDP and PSMDP projects on school leadership and learner performance.

The second technical achievement of the PSMDP was the launch of a full-time B. Ed. Educational Management programme at the University of Botswana in 2002. The programme was developed to service the Republic of Botswana, particularly staff in school management positions, from both primary and secondary schools, with lower qualifications so that they could upgrade to a degree qualification. Each year, the ministry sends a cohort to this full-time degree programme in educational management.

Despite the absence of a national evaluation of the school head training initiative, some studies motivated new thoughts. For example, Monyatsi (2005) suggests that the SSMDP improved the secondary school climate. This success is only mentioned as mechanical because it does not point to improving learner achievement. Pansiri (2011) argues that the education policy lacked grounding in the socio-cultural heterogeneity of Botswana, and that it contributed to the decline in school performance, not to mention serious socio-economic inequalities and disparities in society. Jotia and Pansiri (2013) argue that, between 2002 and 2004, 88 per cent of the children from Remote Area Dwellers (RADs) progressed to secondary education with pass grades of C and D. They also reveal that, between 2004 and 2010, 27,552 children withdrew before they completed their primary education. This record translates into an average of 1.2

per cent loss per annum in school retention. Literature identifies weaknesses in primary school management (Pansiri, 2008, 2011, 2014) and links them to high levels of low learner achievement (Pansiri, 2011; Jotia and Pansiri, 2013). The problem is also associated with the homogenized education policy of mono-culturalization in the spirit of Kagisano (harmony) (Pansiri, 2011). In summary, the impact of leadership preparation and the institutionalization of instructional leadership remains unclear.

Recent developments: 2015–2018

In 2015, the Government of Botswana launched the ETSSP as a strategy to guide the transformation and implementation of education, focusing on transiting Botswana from a resource-based to a knowledge-based economy. The strategy aims, among other things, to improve school planning, leadership and management. The overarching goal of the ETSSP is 'to equip head teachers and other managers with knowledge, skills and attitudes needed to improve performance management and positively impact quality of education' (Republic of Botswana, 2015: 75). In the same year, the University of Botswana engaged an external examiner, Professor Tony Bush, to review its B. Ed. Educational Management programme. The examiner's report (Bush, 2015) noted that since its introduction, the B.Ed. Educational management programme has not been evaluated. It observed that the programme had too many management components at the expense of 'leadership'. It also faulted the programme for being too academic and examination-oriented and noted that it lacked experiential learning opportunities. The External Review Report calls for an emphasis on leadership and experiential learning in the programme (Bush, 2015). In response to both the ETSSP and the external examination report, the university reviewed the programme in 2016 and launched a revised programme, renamed the Bachelor of Educational Leadership and Management, in August 2017. This new programme has a clear emphasis on leadership, and the training component includes four weeks of experiential learning. Recently, the Ministry of Basic Education, with the technical support of the European Union is developing in-service modules on school leadership. These developments coincide with a new phenomenon in education development in Botswana, whereby all training must be accredited by the Botswana Qualification Authority (BQA). It is hoped that this accreditation approach will ensure sustainability and quality in school leadership training. This signals a clear consciousness of the value of school leadership training in Botswana.

Challenges of school leadership preparation

Since Botswana's independence, there has been a tremendous growth in the number of schools in the country. As of 2018, there are 754 primary schools, 207 CJSS, 32 senior secondary schools, 37 vocational brigades, eight technical colleges and five colleges of education (Republic of Botswana, 2015). The management of these institutions warranted leadership training. Despite its commitment to training and preparation for school leadership, Botswana has not been successful in improving school leadership and management. This problem could be attributable to four factors: a failure to decolonize polices of development in the post-colonial period, the homogenization of education strategy, role conflict and operational contradictions in education management and a lack of monitoring and evaluation for sustainability. These four factors are explored briefly here.

Firstly, from the perspective of post-colonial theory, the cultural legacy of colonialism influenced the subsequent exploitation of the colonized people to adopt an exported or transplanted policy to further entrench the colonial master's interests (Oliveira, 2011). Botswana adopted a society constructed under the majority–minority imagination. This contributed to unequal linguistic and ethno-cultural social relations among Batswana (Nyati-Ramahobo, 2004; Jotia, 2008). School leadership that serves minority communities has little chance of success. It has been found that many such schools continuously under-perform (Pansiri, 2011). They experience high rates of early withdrawal and poor learner performance in national examinations.

Secondly, the 1st and 2nd Education Policies homogenized curriculum, language and the school calendar despite the vastness of a country with diverse heterogeneous ethno-linguistic, cultural, socio-cultural, geographic and climatic conditions (Nyati-Ramahobo, 2004; Pansiri, 2011). The policies provided a menu of an assimilationist education approach. Since 1966, evidence of resistance to this approach by ethnic-minority children has been seen in their higher rates of school withdrawal and continued decline in learner performance in national examinations in almost all affected regions. This has made the job of school head difficult, as the training of school heads in the affected areas is not focused on their needs (Pansiri, 2011). It is safe, therefore, to conclude that the evolution and transformation of Botswana's education leadership preparation was eclipsed by the policy of homogeneity, resulting in a failure to achieve the intended results.

Thirdly, there have been role conflicts between inspectors and in-service education officers regarding management and school heads' training. Monyatsi (2005) argues that school heads resisted the training provided by management advisers. Due to this conflict, the education officers who were designated to be SSMDP and PSMDP advisers were absorbed by the inspectorate. As of 2018, there are 120 inspectors compared with 60 in-service officers. The inspectors are predominantly officers who have been school heads, while in-service officers are predominantly subject specialists and are perceived to be junior to the school heads. Arguably, pedagogically, there should be more in-service officers, who guide instructional delivery, than inspectors, who police compliance. The school inspectors are inspecting schools for control or for 'witch hunting' instead of developmental goals (Moswela, 2010). Continuous training of educational leaders is not followed by support on the ground (Republic of Botswana, 2015) because the in-service system under the SSMDP and PSMDP has collapsed.

Fourthly, the success of any development project depends on the quality of monitoring and evaluation. The Republic of Botswana (2015) observes that subsequent leadership training on education in Botswana has not been monitored and evaluated. It is thus difficult to establish if the training programme ever achieved its intended objectives. As the external reviewer has observed, Botswana school leadership training has been incremental than transformational in that there has been more emphasis on management than leadership. Lundy (1986) argues that many institutions find themselves in a tradition where they can hardly distinguish leadership, management and supervision. Botswana's school leadership training seems to be trapped in this tradition.

Conclusion

Substantial progress has been made regarding school leadership development in Botswana, particularly post-independence. However, there are some deficiencies which need mitigation in line with the contemporary demands of school leadership. Botswana's education leadership approach manifests a policy of homogeneity, which is a colonial legacy. There is a need to decolonize the leadership policies inherited from the British government by customizing them within the context of the varied ethnic groups in Botswana's heterogeneous society. School leadership should be applied flexibly to cater for each socio-geo-political context in recognition of the ethno-pluralistic nature of the nation-state. This calls for a reformation of the current assimilationist education approach to adopt an indigenous and endogenous policy in line with the historical, cultural and socio-political contexts of each community. Colonialism and its remnants in the inspectorate approach have subjected school leadership and training to a managerial perspective anchored on compliance. Notwithstanding the substantial commitment to school leadership training in the country, there is little correlation between such training and school-level performance. School leadership in Botswana is largely managerialistic because it is neither empowering nor inspiring. Against this view, Botswana must adopt a leadership development programme which embraces talent management and succession planning.

Botswana leadership preparation approaches have not embraced monitoring and evaluation; therefore, their strengths and weaknesses are not precisely documented. There is a need for institutionalized and systematic monitoring and evaluation of all school leadership programmes embarked upon.

References

Andre de Oliveira, V. (2011), *Actionable Postcolonial Theory in Education*, New York and London: Palgrave Macmillan.

Armstrong, M. (2007), *Human Resource Management Practice*, London: Kogan Page.

Bush, T. (2015), *External Review of the B.Ed (Educational Management)*, Gaborone: University of Botswana.

Chiepe, G. K. T. (1984), 'Botswana Development Strategy', in M. Crowder (ed), *Education for Development: Proceedings of the Symposium Held by the Botswana Society at the National Museum and Art Gallery*, 53–8, Gaborone: Botswanan Society & Macmillan Botswana.

Coles, T. E. K. (1985), *The Story of Education in Botswana*, Gaborone: Pula Publishers.

Commonwealth Secretariat (1993), *Better Schools - Resource Materials for School Heads*, London: Commonwealth Secretariat.

Gardiner, J. (1950), *Bechuanaland Protectorate Annual Report of the Education Department for the Year Ended 31st December, 1950*. Bechuanaland Protectorate.

Jotia, A. L. (2008), *Educating for Deep Democratic Participation in the Post-Colonial Botswana*, Saarbrucken: VDM Verlag Dr Muller.

Jotia, A. L. and O. N. Pansiri (2013), 'Multicultural Education: The Missing Link in Botswana Education Policy', *European Journal of Educational Studies*, 5 (1): 101–10.

Kann, U., G. Ahmed, B. Chilisa, W. Dikole, J. King, D. Malikongwa, M. P. T. Marope, and G. N. Shastri (1988), *Education and Employment: A Study on Behalf of the Ministry of Education*, Gaborone: Ministry of Education.

Kuiper, J. (2014), *Study on Declining Learning Results: Investigating Senior Secondary Education*, Gaborone: Government printer.

Lundy, J. (1986), *How to Lead so Others Follow Willingly*, London: Kogan Page.

Mgadla, P. T. (2003), *A History of Education in the Bechuanaland Protectorate to 1965*, Latham: University Press of America.

Monyatsi, P. P. (2005), 'Transforming Schools into Democratic Organizations: The Case of Secondary School Management Development in Botswana', *International Education Journal*, 6 (3): 354–66.

Moswela, B. (2010), 'Instructional Supervision in Botswana Secondary Schools: An Investigation', *Educational Management Administration & Leadership*, 38 (1): 71–87.

Northouse, P. (2004), *Leadership; Theories and Practice*, London: SAGE Publications.

Nyati-Ramahobo, L. (2004), 'The Language Situation in Botswana', in R. B. Baldauf, Jr. and R. B. Kaplan (eds), *Language Planning and Policy in Africa*, Vol. 1: 21–78, Clevedon: Multilingual Matters LTD.

Pansiri, O. N. (2008), 'Improving Commitment to Basic Education for the Minorities in Botswana: A Challenge for Policy and Practice', *International Journal of Educational Development*, 28 (4): 446–59.

Pansiri, O. N. (2011), 'Performativity in School Management and Leadership in Botswana', *Educational Management Administration and Leadership*, 39 (6): 751–66.

Pansiri, O. N. (2012), 'Improving Retention of Rural Ethnic Minority Children: A Theoretical Analysis of Botswana Education Policy', *Mosenodi*, 17 (1): 3–15.

Pansiri, O. N. (2014), 'Managing Educational Change: A Critique of the Top-Down Primary School Management Development Project in Botswana', *European Journal of Business Social Sciences*, 2 (12): 26–37.

Parsons, Q. N. (1984), 'Education Development in Pre-Colonial and Colonial Botswana to 1965', in M. Crowder (ed), *Education for Development: Proceedings of the Symposium Held by the Botswana Society at the National Museum and Art Gallery*, 21–45, Gaborone: Botswanan Society & Macmillan Botswana.

Republic of Botswana (1965), *Botswana Constitution,* Gaborone: Government Printer.

Republic of Botswana (1967), *The Education Act: CAP 58:1 Education*, Gaborone: Government of Botswana Gaborone, Government Printer.

Republic of Botswana (1977), *Education for Kagisano: Report of the National Commission on Education*, Gaborone: Government Printer.

Republic of Botswana (1985), *National Development Plan 6 1985–91*, Gaborone: Ministry of Finance and Development Planning Gaborone, Government Printer.

Republic of Botswana (1985), *National Development Plan 8 1998–2003*, Gaborone: Ministry of Finance and Development Planning Gaborone, Government Printer.

Republic of Botswana (1994), *The Revised National Policy on Education of 1994*, Gaborone: Ministry of Education, Government Printer.

Republic of Botswana (2015), *Education and Training Sector Strategic Plan (ETSSP 2015–2020)*, Gaborone: Government Printer.

Sephuma, P. V. (1988), *Department of Primary and Teacher Training Papers on Primary Education, Special Education and Teacher Training*. In a report on departmental papers and discussion, 81–96, Gaborone: Ministry of Education.

Sephuma, P. V. (1991), 'Decentralisation of Education System in Botswana', in S. Siesa and F. Youngman (eds), *Education for All in Botswana*, 129–37, Gaborone: Macmillan.

SIDA (1972), *Education and Training in Botswana: A Survey by a Mission from Swedish International Development Authority*, Gaborone: Ministry of Education.

Youngman, F. (2003), 'The State, Adult Literacy Policy and Inequality in Botswana', in E. R. Beauchamp (ed), *Comparative Education Reader*, 139–61, New York: Routledge Falmer.

Zajda, J. (2014), 'Globalization and Neo-Liberalism as Educational Policy in Australia', in H. Yolcu and D. Turner (eds), *Neoliberal Education Reforms: A Global Analysis*, 164–83, New York: Taylor & Francis/Routledge.

3

Experiences of School Leadership Preparation and Development in Lesotho

Pontso Moorosi and Moikabi Komiti

Introduction

Issues of school leadership and management in Lesotho are guided by the Education Act 2010, which clearly spells out the role of school principals as managers of schools in collaboration with school governing boards. In terms of the Act, the only requirement for the appointment of school principals is qualified teaching status, with no provision for any specific form of preparatory training for the principalship. There is a dearth of literature available on school leadership and management in Lesotho and, more particularly, in leadership preparation and development. A recent publication on school leadership preparation and development (Moorosi, 2017) acknowledges the absence of formal leadership preparation in the country yet points to the unique ways in which school principals in Lesotho may consider themselves prepared. This is one of the main points pursued in this chapter, which attempts to highlight different forms of preparing and developing leadership within Lesotho schools.

The growing body of research in the field of school preparation and development on the African continent consistently makes points about the absence of formal training for aspiring principals (Bush and Oduro, 2006; Mathibe, 2007; Pheko, 2008; Moorosi and Bush, 2011). Yet millions of children continue to be taught on a daily basis in schools that are led by these supposedly untrained school principals. It is often argued that the lack of preparation means that the responsibility of school management is placed in the hands of technically unqualified people (Mathibe, 2007), who are likely to lack motivation to innovate and support new practices (Mulkeen et al., 2007). Eacott and Asuga (2014: 920) contend that leaders 'matter in relation to the quality and improvement of schools and schooling', and that untrained school principals do not often grasp fully the need for them to be competent instructional leaders.

In this chapter, we acknowledge that in the absence of formal preparation and development, there exist ways in which school principals develop the skills, knowledge and confidence to lead schools. Bush and Oduro (2006) note that where there is no formal preparation available, newly appointed principals often rely on a pragmatic approach. It is these largely undocumented practices that we are interested in bringing to the fore with regard to Lesotho. This chapter is therefore based on the lived experiences of what constitutes preparation and development for some practising school leaders in Lesotho, drawing from two studies conducted between 2013 and 2016. This introduction is followed by a discussion of the background to educational leadership and management (ELM) in Lesotho, which is followed by a methodology section. The main body of the chapter is divided into broad thematic areas as sub-sections that summarize experiences of leadership preparation and development by school leaders. This is followed by a discussion and a conclusion highlighting implications for school leadership preparation and development in the country.

Background to school leadership and management in Lesotho

Lesotho's governance system is highly centralized but divided into ten geographically demarcated administrative districts that bring educational (and other) services closer to the public. Although Lesotho has traditionally invested in education, some recent reports show a declining investment in education by the Lesotho government. In 2009, the World Bank Fast Track Lesotho Report (2009) reflected a high budget allocation of 20 per cent of the national budget towards education, regarded as high by international standards (Khaahloe, 2011). However, a more recent UNICEF (2017) report points towards a decline in educational spending, with the country's education budget among the lowest in Southern Africa, falling below both domestic and international targets. According to this report, Lesotho is failing to meet its Education for All target by 6 per cent, the same targets exceeded by other Southern African countries such as Botswana and Namibia, which, among other things, share similar population numbers with Lesotho. The falling budget in education spending is attributed to an economic slowdown and declining donor funding (UNICEF, 2017).

Lesotho's formal education system is still largely characterized by the legacy of colonialism, which has resulted in contentious ownership of schools between government, communities and churches, with the latter having the majority ownership of 80 per cent. Khama (2017) provides a detailed historical analysis of the partnership between government and churches, which will not be rehearsed in this chapter. However, it suffices to state that, in an attempt to maintain some form of control over the education system, the Lesotho government, through its Ministry of Education and Training (MoET), assumes the role of educational policy development and implementation and has centralized the curriculum and employment of teachers. This means that, although the government does not own most of the country's schools, it pays all teaching and non-teaching staff salaries and subsidizes basic primary education across the board. It has also centralized all major decisions, including those on curriculum, inspectorate and financing, all of which are made at the headquarters in the capital Maseru (Moorosi, 2017). The ten administrative districts serve as educational administration hubs, meant to provide closer administrative support to schools. Magau (2005) argues, however, that the district offices have minimal impact as important decisions are made at the central offices, and the day-to-day running of the schools is overseen by the schools and their governing boards.

The Education Act of 2010 (hereafter, the Act) considers school principals responsible for the management of schools. However, there is no mention of school leadership and management in the *Education Sector Plan 2016–2026*, nor in its predecessor, the *Education Sector Strategic Plan (2005–2015)*, the two most recent documents carving out the vision for Lesotho's education. The Act stipulates that the role for school management is a shared one between school principals and school governing boards. While school principals have the responsibility for the overall professional management of the school, the role of school boards is three pronged: 1) determination of school policies; 2) recommendation of staff appointments and 3) financial management. Yet, Mncube and Makhasane's (2013) study shows that in some areas, particularly where the governing boards are not very educated, the latter role falls to the principal, who may not always be equipped with financial management skills. Although school governing boards oversee, inter alia, the selection of teachers and school principals, these posts are centrally ratified, suggesting that school governors only make recommendations, lacking the power to make the final decision. Notwithstanding these questionable powers, it is perhaps a progressive indicator that the country has made significant steps towards the democratic governance of schools. Parents and communities are regarded as critical components in the running of schools in Lesotho; 'hence the metaphor that is often used to describe the "three-legged-pot" symbolizing the partnership between the government, community and the parents, which is intended to increase accountability and a sense of ownership in school governance' (Lekhetho, 2017: 2). Clearly, there is a strong community involvement within school boards; however, Nthontho (2017) makes a salient point about the diminished role of parents since the implementation of Free Primary Education in 2000, which made them feel redundant. It is unclear, however, the extent to which parents feel valued in education outside of the primary phase. Poor school governance, moreover, remains an overall challenge to the education sector in Lesotho (UNICEF, 2017).

Although the Act and other policies make provision for teacher professional development, there is silence around the preparation and/or development of school managers or leaders (principals). The Act stipulates only the teaching qualification status for the appointment of a school principal, yet Mulkeen (2010) appears to suggest that there is an expectation that the principal would hold a university degree and have several years of experience. The Lesotho College of Education (LCE) and the National University of Lesotho (NUL) are the main providers of teacher education and, as will be seen, they are also by default providers of training for school leadership. The NUL provides some postgraduate programmes in educational leadership and management intended for current and prospective principals of schools. Evidence of the effect of such programmes remains sparse.

Methodological considerations

This chapter is based on findings that speak to aspects of leadership preparation and development of school leaders in Lesotho. It draws from two different data sets located in the two studies that were conducted with school leaders by two separate projects between 2013 and 2016. Although conceptualized at different times and by different researchers, the studies both used in-depth semi-structured interviews, which suited the investigations by probing deeper into the experiences of the school leaders involved. Both studies were conducted with practising school leaders in the capital district (Maseru); one study explored the leadership socialization of both male and female school leaders of both primary and secondary schools, while the other study examined the career development of female principals of high schools.

The first study, initially reported in Moorosi (2017), was based on school leaders' socialization into leadership and involved principals and deputy principals of both primary and secondary schools in the capital district of the country. The sample was drawn from the greater Maseru area that included both rural and urban schools. The original study involved four countries (Lesotho, Botswana, Namibia and South Africa), where each country was treated as a case study in its own right. The study was completed in 2016, and an overview of findings from the four case studies was published in Moorosi and Grant (2018). Moorosi (2017) reported on the Lesotho case study, and it is from these sources that the material pertaining to Lesotho for this chapter are drawn. Semi-structured interviews were conducted with a total of 29 participants that included both male and female principals (16) and deputy principals (13) of primary and secondary schools. In this study, a deliberate attempt was made to select the principal and deputy principal from the same school so as to counter self-reports from participants already in the top leadership positions. However, some schools (particularly small primary schools) did not have deputies. In addition to the school leaders, three officials were also interviewed. One was from the national office, while the other two were from districts.

The second study was also conducted in Lesotho with female principals of high schools in the inner Maseru area (Komiti, 2017). It comprised eight female principal participants who were aged between 37 and 60. This study was conceptualized as a career development study using career development theory. It examined female principals' career transitions from teaching to principalship and also explored questions on how the women were prepared for and supported in leadership as school principals. Data were collected by means of in-depth semi-structured interviews that followed a narrative account of the women's life stories.

Both studies were characterized by the presence of older and younger generations of school leaders. The older generations were in their 50s and 60s and nearing retirement and had worked mostly in the dispensation when there were no promotion posts in middle-school management. This was the generation of principals across primary and secondary schools. These leaders had become teachers and leaders when appointment was determined largely by the school proprietors and had not necessarily followed an open process of recruitment. Hence, there were a significant number who had just been instructed to assume the school headship role out of emergency, and they had no say in the matter. The younger generations, in their 30s and 40s and, constituted the majority of participants that tended to have benefitted from the new system whereby middle-management positions were officially recognized in 1996. Both studies observed the relevant ethical protocol and were conducted with integrity.

Findings: Experiences of school leadership preparation and development

Several aspects characterized the experiences of school leadership preparation and development in the two studies. These aspects include the role played by initial teacher training in preparing leadership aspirants for leadership roles, learning leadership and management on the job, as well as self-development and networking.

i) Teacher preparation for leader preparation

The findings from both studies confirmed the absence of dedicated leadership and management preparation programmes in Lesotho. This finding was not surprising, given the vast amount of literature showing the lack of specific training in school leadership preparation in Africa in particular (Bush and Oduro, 2006; Mathibe, 2007). As per the legal requirement, the studies also confirmed the need for each principal to have a professional teaching qualification, as almost all participants (except one acting principal of a small rural primary school) were qualified teachers. This finding was also not surprising, given other practices across the continent, such as in Ghana (see Bush and Oduro, 2006). However, it was found surprising that participants in both studies regarded initial teacher training as leadership preparation. This was attributed to the fact that there was no other specific leadership training available and that their initial teacher training did include some basic introduction modules to school administration or management. The extent to which this was actual preparation for leadership is questionable, but these studies do establish the potential for pre-service teacher training to provide a platform for universal leadership training (Moorosi and Grant, 2018).

Participants in the study by Moorosi (2017) were found to have been introduced to some basic leadership and management modules and concepts during their teacher preparation programme. It appeared that these modules were a deliberate attempt to introduce teacher trainees to management concepts, as it was normal for newly qualified teachers to become principals very early on in their teaching career. Indeed, in both studies, there were participants who had been asked to take over the headship of the school unexpectedly quite soon after they took their first teaching post. A participant in Moorosi (2017) was made to take over the principalship hardly six months after starting her teaching career, due to the unexpected departure of the principal.

Komiti (2017) established that such unexpected promotions to the principalship were usually triggered by sudden departures of existing principals, and the most highly qualified (usually a degree holder) would be instructed to act in the post. One of Komiti's participants reported that she 'was just starting to enjoy teaching and wanted to enjoy the classroom and her students and did not think of anything else, let alone taking such a huge position with tough responsibilities' (p. 64). Several other participants, both men and women, confirmed 'that this type of unexpected appointment was a common occurrence where they were instructed by the school proprietors to take up a principalship position of the school when they had not even applied for it' (Moorosi, 2017: 186). In both studies, participants had been introduced to basic management concepts during their initial teacher training, and these had unwittingly prepared them for the principalship.

Perhaps these findings should not be surprising given the stipulations of the law with regard to the appointment of principals. While the teaching qualification requirement may be in line with international standards, which Bush and Oduro (2006) identified more than a decade ago as the trend in most African countries, it remains the only requirement that is statutorily binding for the position of principalship.

Indeed, the presence of leadership and management modules was reflected in the web pages of the initial teacher training programmes at both the NUL and LCE programmes, the only two institutions of teacher training in the country. A government official at the national office, interviewed in Moorosi (2017), confirmed the absence of specific preparatory training for school principals and acknowledged the government's reliance on the leadership and management modules offered by the two national providers, in the absence of enough resources to provide training for school leaders. It is on this basis that Moorosi and Grant (2018) concluded that, despite their obvious limitations, initial teacher training programmes were a source of principalship role conception through which student teachers implicitly learnt about the role of a principal. We align with the authors' suggestion that initial teacher training could be used more purposefully as a useful platform of leadership preparation, but should be coupled with other forms of training.

ii) Self-development improves promotion into the principalship

Although the official requirement for the school principalship in Lesotho is the teaching qualification status, the reality of the situation of current school principals suggests there might be an unwritten expectation for secondary school principals to hold at least a university undergraduate degree. Almost all principals and deputy principals of secondary/high schools in both studies held a university degree. The only deputy principal of a secondary school who did not have a degree was registered for one at the time of the study. Some of these degrees were upgraded from the teaching diploma obtained as the teaching qualification. Of the participants in Komiti's study, 37 per cent held postgraduate honours or master's degree qualifications, while the figure in Moorosi's study was 24 per cent. While the undergraduate degrees were mostly subject based, postgraduate degrees were in leadership and management, suggesting intent to develop a deeper theoretical knowledge of the field.

A significant point linked to these qualifications is that they were pursued by those participants who had aspired to the principalship and actively sought means of facilitating the promotion. Findings showed that such participants did not just sit and wait for promotion to happen, but they chose to self-develop by improving their qualifications and actively seeking promotion into middle-leadership positions, leading to the principalship. Komiti (2017) described these go-getters' journeys to the principalship as 'intentional' as opposed to the 'unintentional' ones that just happened without much effort from the participants. In the intentional journeys, the leadership aspirants actively sought promotion and upgraded their qualifications. Thus, their determination to become school leaders informed their decisions to upgrade their qualifications in the quest to prepare themselves for the top positions. Although a firm link remains to be established as to the necessity of the master's degree for promotion, there is evidence from these studies to suggest that postgraduate study improved participants' chances of promotion.

The studies did not explore the details of leadership and management degrees to establish the content of what was studied and how relevant it was for practice. Mncube and Makhasane's (2013) study, conducted with high-school principals in one of the districts in Lesotho, illustrates the difficulties that principals experienced in managing school finances. An interview with the government official confirmed that financial management is one of the most significant challenges facing school principals as chief accounting officers. It would therefore be prudent to establish the extent to which such studies are relevant to practice. We observe the level of agency, drive and initiative shown by aspirants of school leadership who elected to self-develop. It is in this sense that we align with Moorosi and Grant (2018) to argue for better coordination and oversight of leadership development, which might actually help aspirants make choices that are relevant to their practice.

iii) Experiential preparation

In the absence of formal preparation for the top leadership positions, three types of experiential preparation were observed from these two studies: (1) *observation during teaching experience*, (2) *the promotion route* and (3) *on-the-job training*. Although not overtly acknowledged as preparation by participants, mention was made of instances where former principals were role models and their practice was emulated. Equally, participants also noted bad practices that they would not copy. Thus, the *teaching experience* itself became an important 'socialization period' (Moorosi and Grant, 2018) that inadvertently prepared the would-be leaders for the principalship as they indirectly observed their predecessors. Crow and Glascock (1995) found principal observation, as well as teachers' own experiences, as important sources of principalship role learning whereby principals were witnessed in their role and where teachers' own experiences indirectly socialized them into the organization.

The *promotion route* was where many of the principals in both studies gained hands-on managerial experience through middle-leadership positions such as head of department and deputy principal. The promotion posts were not formalized in Lesotho until 2006. However, some of the older generation participants from both studies acknowledged going through and occupying these promotion positions informally, although they were not paid for these roles. This is recognized as *teacher leadership* (Moorosi and Grant, 2018) as it is arguable that participants exhibited qualities that helped them to stand out as good leaders. Grant (2006) argues for the significance of developing teachers by exposing them to leadership roles at different levels in order to ensure a pool of capable leaders. In both studies, the opportunity to act in these promotion posts was acknowledged to have improved the participants' skills and equipped them with new knowledge on how to do their jobs as principals effectively. One of the female principals in Komiti's (2017: 89) study reported:

> The HOD position that I held developed me and prepared me for the principalship because of the leadership skills I learned in the position … Moreover, being a deputy principal stretched my horizons and my skills in preparing me for the

principalship position. Whenever I came across a certain challenge in this position I incorporated the skills I acquired from these positions and what I have learned from school and come up with a solution which will work best for the situation.

Such utterances were evidence of how the promotion route afforded participants the opportunity to learn through practice. This had been vital for the participants' preparation and ability to cope while new in the principalship role. The positions provided them with leadership skills and self-confidence – arguably what a training programme alone would not achieve. One could deduce from participants' narratives that those who got the chance to act in these middle-leadership roles prior to becoming principals did not struggle to adjust to their new principalship roles to the same degree as did those who moved directly from being teachers to becoming principals. The latter is seen as *on-the-job preparation*, as there was no opportunity for them to learn administrative roles before they became principals. In a previous study outside the Lesotho context, on-the-job preparation was found to be the most common experience for female principals who had also unexpectedly found themselves in the principalship post (Moorosi, 2010).

It is noted, however, that the promotion-route positions were not always effectively and intentionally used for principalship preparation. In Moorosi's (2017) study, wherein some of the participants were deputy principals who were aspiring to become principals in the future, interviewing them revealed some tensions about 'lack of role clarity', where the deputy principals were not always clear about their roles and principals were not always confident who their successors were going to be. The lack of role clarity for the deputy principal would perhaps find its explanation in the Education Act of 2010. This important piece of legislation does not provide for the role of the deputy principal or any other professional manager but only enshrines the role of the school principal. To this effect, Moorosi (2017) suggested that the deputy principal role should be utilized more concertedly as a pre-socialization experience for the principalship and for succession planning.

iv) In-service training and networking

In both studies, there was a mixture of participants who remembered attending induction workshops after being appointed as principals and those who did not. Those who had to self-teach and socialized themselves into the principalship role regretted not joining induction programmes. This group of participants generally felt as if they had been just 'dumped' in the principal's office and left to their own devices; hence they drew from their previous observations, common knowledge and their 'own gut feelings'. Indeed, previous research has established feelings of anxiety and loneliness where no proper induction into the principalship exists (Kitavi and van der Westhuizen, 1997; Mathibe, 2007).

Although there was no evidence of consistency with regard to the availability of induction training for new incumbents, there was evidence of existing leadership development workshops for practising principals organized by the MoET. The interviews with the two district officials reported that some training for school principals (and governors) exists, not only in the Maseru district but in other districts as well. None of the deputy principals had attended any workshop by the department as yet, and the officials confirmed that plans were only underway for the training of deputy principals in the capital district. However, no interviews were conducted with school leaders in other districts to confirm the extent or availability of workshop training.

Linked to in-service leadership training was what was described as networking of clusters in which most principals actively took part. In Komiti's (2017) study, female principals appreciated the support they received from the association of high-school principals, facilitated by the MoET, in making sure that they developed their skills to become better managers in their schools. Talking about the opportunities of being part of the association, one of the female principals stated:

> I think one of the things that is good about being a principal is that one gets to know a lot of important people, networking is very important in this job. ... you find opportunities like that once you are in the position, you get to know what is out there, they also hold or organize workshops for us, seminars and conferences so we improve a lot in our work.

In Moorosi's (2017) study, participants also spoke about network clusters that they found helpful in updating them with information. This was found to be a regular form of professional development for the principals that was district co-ordinated and involved principals of both primary and secondary schools. School principals who were part of the study were all part of the regional network clusters. Through these cluster networks, principals met regularly to discuss common issues of concern and shared experiences that developed and empowered them. Stating the benefit of the clusters and how they used them to empower themselves and develop each other, one of them, who also happened to be a cluster leader, stated that we have clusters and we empower each other within the cluster. … I always say, I will find things for you and I find that it empowers me even more.

It was clear in this study that, although these networks were initiated at district level, it was the cluster leaders, who happened to be other principals, who co-ordinated and ensured that regular interaction with other principals and continuing peer support took place. In one of the schools, it was the cluster meeting day when the researcher visited and the amount of support the principals provided for each other could be discerned. It is through these networks that most principals attested to feeling empowered and learning more from their peers. Indeed, networking has been found to be an important element of leadership development for school principals in South Africa (Bush, Kiggundu and Moorosi, 2011; Kiggundu and Moorosi, 2012). However, the extent to which this networking extended to the whole school management team was not established, as the latter did not appear to be part of the network, and this was found not to bode well for succession planning.

Discussion and implications

School leadership and management are generally under-researched in the Lesotho context, particularly the preparation and development of school leaders. In addition, it is an area that appears to be neglected by the MoET as there is no policy for the development of school leaders. In this context it is perhaps not unusual for initial teacher training programmes to introduce school leadership theory. What is unusual, however, is the reliance on initial teacher training as the only form of universal training available for the preparation of both teachers and school leaders. While it is sensible to introduce leadership learning early in the preparation for a teaching career, to raise awareness for teachers about school leadership and to build capacity for leadership among teachers (Hamilton, Forde and McMahon, 2018), Bush (2018: 67) reiterates that 'being a [school] principal is a different role from classroom teaching and requires specific preparation'. It has been advocated elsewhere (see Moorosi and Grant, 2018) that contexts that are poor and have limited resources may need to use initial teacher training much more concertedly, but evidently, the latter would need to be supplemented with ongoing leadership development training and support. Bush (2018) makes a compelling case for why specific leadership training is not negotiable, particularly in low-economy countries, where school leaders often have to work in far more challenging circumstances with a barrage of socio-economic problems. He gives several reasons, one of which involves the larger accountability pressures facing school principals in all contexts across the world as well as the devolution of power to local levels, which is an international policy trend (Bush, 2018). Mulkeen et al. (2007) confirms that decentralization of educational administration in sub-Saharan Africa has increased the responsibilities of school principals but that this is not often accompanied by appropriate training.

The government of Lesotho realizes this international trend by making parents and the community partners in the running of the school. Nthontho (2017) acknowledges this as a sign of democratic governance for the country, wherein parents and the community constitute the main composition of the school governing boards, even though, in practice, school principals still bear the largest responsibility. Of most significance and relevance is that the most important piece of legislation, the Education Act of 2010, does not recognize other school managers in this democratic management of schools. Without the recognition of school leadership teams, and in light of the different roles played by the different managers and staff, the Act basically assumes school principals to be sole managers, and this is not in line with current trends in school leadership that encourage leadership to be shared. Significantly, it illegitimates what is already in practice. In one of the local newspapers in 2015, the association of school principals was reported to be drafting an amendment to this law as it has significant omissions (Lesotho Times, 2015). For this to be realized in practice, it has to be driven by the relevant guidelines and this oversight leads to tension and lack of role clarity.

When there is no preparatory training, and when induction training is not consistently available, leadership and management knowledge and skills are acquired on the job through the promotion posts or on the actual principalship. On-the-job learning, or experiential learning (as it is often called), is known to be more reflective, encouraging problem-solving and learning from each other. In its classical application, experiential learning works entailed four elements: 'concrete experience, observation and reflection, the formation of abstract concepts, and testing in new situations' (Kolb, 1984) and works well when it is integrated with theory learning. We believe that learning leadership and management on the job holds prospects for transmission of ideas and skills from those who know to those who are novices, creating social capital for broader leadership capacity. However, for this to work effectively, there has to be collaboration between teachers and leaders at different levels, such as experienced principals who can offer mentoring and support to the deputy principals and (HoDs) under the overall guidance of district and/or national leadership. It should be noted, however, that learning on-the-job that is not accompanied by theory, is no guarantee that the right skills will be acquired as leaders may be socialized into existing systems in which they could just conform to ineffective practices and become less innovative and agentic. The extent to which current practices lead to improved learning outcomes was not established in either of these studies. This may be the next focus of research.

There is also the networking of clusters, and through associations, that are driven by the principals, albeit with MoET support. This is good practice which needs to be commended, improved, supported and extended to other districts. Moorosi and Grant (2018) advocate good examples of in-house leadership development where, within one school, the principal works together with staff to build capacity for leadership and plan for succession. These would form part of the larger context that would create the 'social capital' for leadership development, where 'networked relationships' among individuals can be built to 'enhance cooperation and resource exchange' within the school (Day, 2000: 586). We believe that this could work better in collaborative partnerships and shared resources within and across different schools, as also observed by Cliffe, Fuller and Moorosi (2018). The model of collaborative school management driven by the legislation, symbolized by a three-legged pot, recognizes the collaborative African way of raising a child, wherein a child is raised by a village and not an individual nuclear family. This is fundamentally informed by the Ubuntu concept that recognizes the existence and interdependence of collaboration in the effective running of schools (Msila, 2008). Likewise, bringing community leaders and parents into partnering and working together with school principals is something that should be studied and understood so that it can be built on, improved and learnt from. We believe that this collaborative Ubuntu-driven approach to school management may have significant implications for leadership development, wherein the culture of inclusiveness is ensured and nurtured within schools as workplaces and within the system of education. Significantly, this could offer some sound theoretical grounding that informs practice for generations to come. After all, experiential learning is known for giving leaders an opportunity to put theory into practice.

Finally, networking or learning from each other emerges strongly as one aspect of experiential learning that is ongoing and contributes significantly to the development of current school principals, as seen in both studies.

Moorosi (2017) linked the lack of role clarity for deputy principals directly to the Education Act of 2010, section 20–21, which clearly stipulates the duties of a school principal but makes no mention of the roles of deputy principal and/ or (HoDs). It was this lack of role clarity, and the lack of involvement of deputy principals, that denied them the visibility they needed to pro-actively use and be used for principalship succession planning. Although one district official mentioned the effort to treat and develop deputy principals as 'principals in the making', the experiences of deputy principals suggested otherwise. Principals were not always confident about who their successors would be within the school and, equally, deputy principals were not always confident that they were ready for the principalship. Thus, the recognition of current deputy principals would augur well with the rhetoric of leadership development and in tandem with the good intentions of the district to treat deputy principals as 'principals-in-the-making'.

Conclusion

This chapter demonstrates some good practices around school leadership development that can be used as a basis for a model of school leadership preparation and development in Lesotho. We suggest that a link is made between teacher preparation and leadership development. Moorosi and Grant (2018) acknowledged that the introduction of basic leadership and management concepts during initial teacher training provides a real chance of universal leadership learning, which is an important step towards preparation for principalship, leadership development and leadership capacity building. However, we appreciate that, in and of itself, initial teaching training cannot be sufficient to build capacity for leadership and to prepare aspirants for school leadership. Hence, a clear strategy, starting with initial teacher training and progressing to elements of teacher leadership and dedicated leadership preparation, would work more effectively. This could be followed by induction guidelines after appointment and ongoing leadership development programmes that build on existing practice. We believe that linking initial teacher training to teacher leadership would ensure the involvement of teachers in building broader capacity for leadership which would ensure collective capacity of knowledge, skills and resources within and across schools. This holds better prospects for leadership preparation and development, and succession planning, for principalship in Lesotho.

References

Bush, T. (2018), 'Preparation and Induction for School Principals: Global Perspectives', *Management in Education*, 32 (2): 66–71.

Bush, T., E. Kiggundu, and P. Moorosi (2011), 'Preparing New Principals in South Africa: The ACE School Leadership Programme', *South African Journal of Education*, 31: 31–43.

Bush, T. and G. Oduro (2006), 'New Principals in Africa: Preparation, Induction and Practice', *Journal of Educational Administration*, 44 (4): 359–75.

Cliffe, J., K. Fuller, and P. Moorosi (2018), 'Secondary School Leadership Preparation and Development: Experiences and Aspirations of Members of Senior Leadership Teams (SLTs)', *Management in Education*, 32 (2): 85–91.

Crow, G. M. and C. Glascock (1995), 'Socialization to a New Conception of the Principalship', *Journal of Educational Administration*, 33 (1): 22–43.

Day, D. V. (2000), 'Leadership Development: A Review in Context', *The Leadership Quarterly*, 11 (4): 581–613.

Eacott, S. and G. N. Asuga (2014), 'School Leadership Preparation and Development in Africa: A Critical Insight', *Educational Management Administration & Leadership*, 42 (6): 919–34.

Grant, C. (2006), 'Teacher Leadership: Some South African Voices', *Educational Management, Administration and Leadership,* 34 (4): 511–32.

Hamilton, G., C. Forde, and M. McMahon (2018), 'Developing a Coherent Strategy to Build Leadership Capacity in Scottish Education', *Management in Education*, 32 (2): 72–8.

Khaahloe, M. B. (2011), 'Lesotho', in F. M. Kelleher, F. O. Severin, M. Khaahloe, M. Samson, De Anuradha, T. Afamasaga-Wright and U. Sedere, *Women and the Teaching Profession: Exploring the Feminisation Debate*, 116–42, Paris, France: UNESCO.

Kiggundu, E. and P. Moorosi (2012), 'Networking for School Leadership in South Africa: Perceptions and Realities', *School Leadership & Management*, 32 (3): 215–32.

Kitavi, M. and P. van der Westhuizen (1997), 'Problems Facing Beginning Principals in Developing Countries: A Study of Beginning Principals in Kenya', *International Journal of Educational Development*, 17 (3): 251–63.

Khama, D. (2017), 'Church and State Relations in the Development of Education System in Lesotho: A Historical Perspective', in M. Lekhetho (ed), *Education in Lesotho: Prospects and Challenges*, New York: Nova Science Publishers.

Kolb, D. A. (1984), *Experiential Learning: Experience as the Source of Learning and Development*, Englewood Cliffs: Prentice-Hall.

Komiti, M. (2017), 'Exploring the Career Paths of Female Principals in Lesotho High Schools', Unpublished MA thesis, North-West University, South Africa.

Lekhetho, M. (2017), 'Education in Lesotho: An Overview', in M. Lekhetho (ed), *Education in Lesotho: Prospects and Challenges*, New York: Nova Science Publishers.

Lesotho Times (2015), 'Teachers Are Being Appointed Illegally', *Lesotho Times*, 27 November. Available online: www.lestimes.com (accessed October 2018).

Magau, T. (2005), 'Lesotho: the Uphill Journey to Development', in S. Akoojee, A. Gewer and S. McGrath (eds), *Vocational Education and Training in Southern Africa: A Comparative Study*, 32–45, Pretoria, South Africa: HSRC.

Mathibe, I. (2007), 'The Professional Development of School Principals', *South African Journal of Education*, 27 (3): 523–40.

Moorosi, P. (2010), 'South African Female Principals' Career Paths: Understanding the Gender Gap in School Management', *Educational Management Administration Leadership*, 38 (5): 547–62.

Moorosi, P. (2017), 'School Leadership Development in Lesotho', in M. Lekhetho (ed), *Education in Lesotho: Prospects and Challenges*, New York: Nova Science Publishers.

Moorosi, P. and C. Grant (2018), 'The Socialisation and Leader Identity Development of School Leaders in Southern African countries', *Journal of Educational Administration*, 56 (6): 643–58.

Moorosi, P. and T. Bush (2011), 'School Leadership Development in Commonwealth Countries: Learning across the Boundaries', *International Studies in Educational Administration*, 39 (3): 59–75.

Mncube, V. S. and S. Makhasane (2013), 'The Dynamics and Intricacy of Budgeting in Secondary Schools in Lesotho: Case Studies of Three High Schools', *Africa Education Review*, 10 (2): 347–63.

Msila, V. (2008), 'Ubuntu and School Leadership', *Journal of Education*, 44: 67–84.

Mulkeen, A. (2010), *Teachers in Anglophone Africa: Issues in Teacher Supply, Training, and Management*, Washington DC: The World Bank.

Mulkeen, A., D. W. Chapman, J. G. DeJaeghere and E. Leu (2007), *Recruiting, Retaining and Retraining Secondary School Teachers and Principals in Sub-Saharan Africa*, Washington DC: The World Bank.

Nthontho, M. A. (2017), 'The Voices of Parents as Partners in Education in Lesotho', in M. Lekhetho (ed), *Education in Lesotho: Prospects and Challenges*, New York: Nova Science Publishers.

Pheko, B. (2008), 'Secondary School Leadership Practice in Botswana', *Educational Management Administration & Leadership*, 36 (1): 71–84.

UNICEF (2017), Lesotho Education Budget Brief. Available online: https://www.unicef.org/esaro/UNICEF-Lesotho-2017-Education-Budget-Brief.pdf (accessed October 2018).

4

An Analysis of School Leadership Preparation and Development in Namibia

Carolyn (Callie) Grant

Background and context

Namibia, a country in south-western Africa, gained independence from South Africa on 21 March 1990. A secular and democratic state, Namibia is headed by a president together with a Cabinet. The capital of Namibia is Windhoek, situated in the Khomas region, one of 13 regions in the country. Namibia remains largely a rural society with 57 per cent of its citizens living in rural areas (Namibia. Government of Namibia – www.gov.na, 2018). Despite it being a large country, for its size it has a notably small population, being the least densely populated country in the world (Kraft, 2014). While English is the official language, more than 11 languages are indigenous to Namibia and spoken by the people (Namibia. Government of Namibia – www.gov.na, 2018).

Post-independence Namibia is serious about education and takes pride in its four major goals of access, equity, quality and democracy, outlined in the policy document *Toward Education For All* (Namibia. Ministry of Education and Culture, 1993). Though the goal of access to education has largely been achieved, the education system is not yet generating outcomes that are even close to the expectations and needs of the nation (Kraft, 2014). While Namibian learners have improved dramatically in functional literacy and functional numeracy in the Southern and Eastern African Consortium for Monitoring Educational Quality surveys (Taylor and Spaull, 2013), the education system is still perceived to be underperforming, and it remains a key strategic area under the country's 4th National Development Plan (Kraft, 2014).

With respect to leadership within the education system, the policy *Toward Education For All* (Namibia. Ministry of Education and Culture, 1993), as well as the Education Act No. 16 of 2001, are relatively silent on issues of school leadership, and while Namibia's Education and Training Sector Improvement Programme (Namibia, 2007) does refer to leadership, this is largely in relation to capacity development of Ministry of Education (MoE) officials. *Leadership*, for the purposes of this chapter, is defined as the process through which change is brought about in an organization and exercised by leaders, regardless of whether or not they occupy formal management roles. Leadership is often contrasted with *management* as a related concept. Management is an organizational construct which has to do with systems and processes and which is undertaken by those holding formal administrative roles in an organization such as a school (Christie, 2010). It has often been argued that leadership and management are two sides of the same coin and that both are needed for an organization (such as a school) to prosper.

A review of published literature on educational leadership and management (ELM) across the globe reveals that this literature is dominated by studies from developed countries, particularly those located in the West (Bush, 1999; van der Mescht, 2008). Hallinger's (2018) systematic review of research on ELM across English-speaking African countries is a direct response to this gap in the literature. His findings reveal that, while South Africa, Nigeria and Kenya lead ELM knowledge production across the continent, ELM research in Namibia is limited (Hallinger, 2018). And while there is an emerging body of research on school leadership development in some African countries such as Botswana, Kenya and South Africa (Bush and Oduro, 2006; Pheko, 2008; Onguko, Abdalla and Webber, 2008; Moorosi and Bush, 2011; Eacott and Asuga, 2014), this is not the case in Namibia. For the purposes of this chapter, *leadership development* is defined as a complex and continuous process, shaped by context and spanning the lifetime of an individual as she interacts with the social and organizational environments and develops a leadership identity (Moorosi, 2014).

This chapter is therefore dedicated to an exploration of the socialization of school leaders in Namibia and is guided by the following questions:

i) How do Namibian school leaders get socialized into the principalship role?
ii) What factors shape school principals' leadership development and how?
iii) How do socialization processes inform leadership development initiatives?

In light of Hallinger's urgent call to make 'locally derived knowledge [in this case Namibian] ... more broadly accessible' (2018: 363), it is envisaged that this chapter will provide a small contribution towards ELM knowledge production in Namibia. The chapter begins with a discussion of school leadership socialization as the theoretical framework of the study. Thereafter, the methodology and methods of the study are described. The findings of the study are then discussed, and four lessons learnt from this case study research are presented.

School leadership socialization: A theoretical framework

A central feature of leadership development is the socialization of future school leaders into 'the cognitive and affective dimensions of social roles related to the practice of this occupation' (Brody, Vissa and Weathers, 2010: 615). Through this socialization process, aspiring school leaders 'acquire the values and attitudes, the interests, skills, and knowledge, in short the culture, current in the groups of which they are, or seek to become a member' (Merton, Reader and Kendall, 1957, in Brody et al., 2010: 615). This being the case, career socialization theory was an obvious choice as the theoretical framing for this exploratory study. Despite its Western roots and the concomitant criticisms levelled against it (see Eacott and Asuga, 2014; Pansiri, 2011), this framework was adopted because of its premise that 'leadership practice and leadership socialization processes are informed not only by what occurs formally within the school, but also by what happens in the school leader's broader local and social contexts' (Moorosi and Grant, 2018: 2).

Within the field of ELM, career socialization theory with a specific focus on school leadership has been used and developed by several authors over the years (for an account of this evolution over time, see Moorosi and Grant, 2018). School leadership socialization, therefore, has become connected to the complex shift in role from teacher to that of principal. This complexity, particularly in the African context (and Namibia is no exception), requires a framework that looks inwards to the professional and organizational school setting and also outwards to the pre-organizational life of the school principal (Crow, 2006). Therefore, in line with the broader study (Moorosi and Grant, 2018), this chapter is informed by the classic work of Van Maanen and Schein (1979) and draws particularly on three of the four stages of socialization (anticipatory, professional and organizational) for its analysis.

Anticipatory socialization is a category of socialization of beginning principals which goes beyond what happens in a school leadership preparatory programme at a university (*professional socialization*) and entry into a school as a principal (*organizational socialization*) (Crow, 2006). It incorporates the more conventional socialization that occurs during the early teaching career when one engages as a teacher in a school (Crow, 2006). It is during this period that teachers have the opportunity to develop as leaders in their classrooms and beyond (Grant, 2017). Additionally, anticipatory socialization incorporates childhood responsibilities and family values as pre-socializing experiences which are not directly linked to the teaching profession but which, nevertheless, are subconsciously influential in developing early characteristics of leadership (Ribbins, 2008; Moorosi and Grant, 2018).

Professional socialization, particularly in developed countries, has been traditionally understood as the process of acquiring new knowledge and skills in preparation for the leadership work of the aspirant principal, either through dedicated preparation programmes or by accident through job experiences, thus implying the ongoing and incremental nature of the process (Duke, 1987; Bush, 2016). However, it has been argued that many of these programmes do not succeed in developing school leaders 'who can engage their schools in reforms that will enable students to meet the demands of a global economy, rapidly changing technology, and increasingly diverse societies' (Brody et al., 2010: 612). Therefore, as Lumby and English contend, such programmes should be treated as 'initiation into identity construction and subsequent performance' (2009: 97), given that leadership development is a career-long process, with expertise being built over time (Moorosi, 2014). Crow (2006) makes a related but significant point that, as societies become more complex, what is crucial is that university-based leadership preparation programmes should be offered in collaboration with districts and schools so that learning is immediately transferable to authentic contexts. Here the role of internships and mentoring becomes important, although, as Brody et al. (2010) warn, the type of situated learning that normally occurs in traditional mentorship opportunities is a limited form of organizational socialization.

Organizational socialization involves the new school leader learning how things are done in a particular institution – in other words, learning 'the ropes' of the role in the particular organization in which she finds herself (Moorosi and Grant, 2018). However, this stage typically involves an assault on the new principal, who is immediately faced with the suite of responsibilities the role demands and, as Crow explains, 'this lack of mediated entry creates burnout, stress, and ineffective performance as beginning principals develop quick fixes and unreflective practices' (2006: 318). Organizational socialization extends throughout the career of the school leader and includes all aspects of in-school socialization, coupled with the socialization that occurs as the school leader networks with other schools as well as with community agencies and entities (Crow, 2006).

Having presented these stages of socialization as discrete entities, it is important to note that the distinctions among them often become blurred and the categories have a tendency to overlap with each other. Notwithstanding, they provided a useful language of description and analytical framework for the study on which this chapter is based.

Methodology and methods

The study on which this chapter draws forms part of a larger study which explored the socialization of school leaders in Southern African countries. I was lead researcher for the South African and Namibian cases, while my colleague was responsible for the Lesotho and Botswana studies (Moorosi and Grant, 2018). This chapter is dedicated to the Namibian case.

The selection of the educational region for this Namibian case was conveniently facilitated through my contact with the regional director who took responsibility for inviting a sample of his principals and heads of departments (HoDs) to participate in the study (the post of deputy principal does not exist in the Namibian schooling system). Given that the face-to-face component of data collection took place during a school holiday in 2014, participant involvement was solely dependent on their availability. A total of 16 people (eight principals, seven HoDs and the regional director) participated in the study, with an equal representation of women and men. Participants were drawn from ordinary public schools regulated by the Namibian MoE. Primary schools dominated the sample. Given the constraints of the sampling process, the findings of this case study cannot be generalized, neither within nor across the region. However, the self-reporting nature of the participants' accounts of their own lived experiences provided a series of narratives that can be used to better understand leadership preparation and development experiences.

Data were generated from all 16 participants in the form of closed questionnaires and in-depth, face-to-face, semi-structured interviews. Data were analysed using an open method of coding in order to identify common themes and patterns of difference (Braun and Clarke, 2012). Thereafter, the three stages of career socialization theory were brought to bear on the data. Ethical principles were observed throughout the study, and participants were involved in member checking of the interview transcripts. Copies of the research report were also emailed to the regional director for distribution to all participants. In the next section of this chapter, a simple coding system is used in the presentation of data.

Participants are anonymized using the numbers 1–16, but their designation as either principal (P) or head of department (HoD) is acknowledged. Interview transcripts (I), where they are used, are numbered from I1 to I16.

Findings and discussion

Four key findings emerge from this Namibian case study:

1) that anticipatory socialization, conceptualized as socialization to leadership during childhood and early schooling, is an unconscious, yet significant form of leadership development;
2) that anticipatory socialization, conceptualized as socialization to leadership during the preparatory and early stage of the participants' teaching careers, is also a potential form of leadership development;
3) that while professional socialization in the form of formal leadership training is offered, more can be done in this regard; and
4) that in-school mentoring as part of organizational socialization is a productive strategy, particularly as it relates to succession planning. Each of these findings will now be discussed.

Anticipatory socialization, conceptualized as socialization to leadership during childhood and schooling, is a significant form of leadership development

Socialization to leadership during childhood and schooling emerged as an unconscious yet significant form of leadership development. These subconsciously influential, early forms of socialization can be loosely categorized into four types of influences; the influence of 1) parents, 2) the church, 3) significant teachers during schooling and 4) learner leadership opportunities afforded participants while learners at school.

First, and for the most part, participants were members of large families in poor communities, struggling against the pernicious injustices of colonialism and apartheid. Three participants (5, 13 and 14) described their early years as exiles in one of the neighbouring countries as a consequence of apartheid. Despite these contextual hardships as a consequence of growing up in an unequal and discriminatory society, biological parents – and also foster parents (I10, HoD; I14, P) – emerged as a powerful influencing factor in the leadership development of the participants.

Participant 9 speaks of his father as 'a very strong and a vivid character; a person who did not conceal any emotion, anything that he thought has come to run through his mouth' (I9, P). This father had a close relationship with the Chief Council of the Herero leadership during that time, which resulted in Participant 9 attending many council meetings with his father. In this context, he learnt much about leadership as it pertained to the Herero people: 'So listening to them and you know, taking note of how they are, you know, sensitising the people, how they were putting emphasis on very important things' (I9, P).

Participant 5 reminisced about how his mother played such an inspirational role during his childhood. Although he and his siblings went 'without shoes and sometimes with no proper shoes' in lower primary school, his mother would encourage them by saying 'I want you to go to school, one day you buy a cow or something for us' (I5, P). For Participant 4, it was his father who had a huge influence on his life, chiefly because of the hardships he had withstood:

> Actually it was not the easy way, it was very tough, because my father was a man that was working on the farm of white farmer, so he was struggling actually to get bread on the table; it was not that easy. But he managed to take me to the schools, different schools … so he was struggling. He was a very brave man and I am very thankful for him. (I4, HoD)

Second, Christianity, with its espoused set of values, was deeply significant in the childhood narratives of all the participants in the study. A participant reminisced how, at her Catholic school, she attended church almost every day, under the trees (I6, HoD). Participant 7 recalled teaching the pre-primary children in the Sunday school at her church, which was 'where I started helping and I really was getting that interest in children, loving them, caring for them' (I7, HoD). For Participants 4 and 14, the priest or pastor was an influential leadership figure who played a big role in their lives. In the case of Participant 4, the pastor began to call him a teacher and let him read the Bible in front of the church members;

> When he was giving me a task of reading in front of the community, it was like I'm becoming a leader. It was like I'm joining leadership … because I was reading in the Church and I was given some other tasks, also to let people sing and so on. So actually it started there. (I4, HoD)

These early church experiences did not wane but continued into the adult lives of the participants. One participant became a deacon in the church (I7, HoD) while another became a pastor (I9, P). Participant 12 draws strength from her faith in school leadership matters, while Participant 15 describes himself as a religious person with a feeling that 'I am placed on earth by God to make a difference in other peoples' lives. And I'm not talking it, I'm doing it, or I am trying to doing it' (I15, P).

Third, school teachers also contributed significantly to the anticipatory socialization experiences of the participants. Whether a mathematics teacher (I1, HoD; I11, P), a Grade 1 teacher (I4, HoD), an accounting teacher (I10, HoD), a science teacher (I5, P) or a school principal (I3, HoD; I14, P; I7, HoD), teachers emerged as positive socializing influences in the early lives of the participants. This was likely because teachers, at that point in Namibian history, were members of the local community and had standing in the community; 'We looked up to teachers, we really did. And the teachers knew that they had to stand out in the community because the parents believed in them and the learners believed in them' (I3, HoD). Because these communities were small and homogenous,

> everybody [including teachers] was involved in bringing up the children, even if it was not your family. But then many of those Aunties, later on you started feeling like they are a part of me, they are family. Because the community was so small we used to love each other, and help each other. I think nowadays you don't find that anymore. (I3, HoD)

Teachers impacted on the early lives of the participants in this study, either because of the way they taught in class or because they noticed talent and engendered self-confidence in learners. These teachers were often hardworking and strict, and yet they went the extra mile on behalf of their learners. To illustrate, Participant 1 described a situation where she recently saw her school mathematics teacher and acknowledged that 'it's because of that man that is standing there, that I'm here where I am. Because the way he taught me in the class. It was serious business and I took it very serious' (I1, HoD). The experiences of Participant 11 were similar: 'My maths teacher was teaching at the High School. A very strict woman, but we learnt maths and the effects, the results were there. These were a set of rules put into my education, into my life long ago, and now they have value and are to fall back on' (I11, P). Participant 12 reflects on a hardworking primary school teacher who had an impact on her early life:

> I mean he saw something in me and he would tell me, you are such a bright kid, you must never go stop, and you must never drop out of school, always study hard. He encouraged me a lot, so that is the one person that I always remember when it comes to my upbringing. He played a very influential role. Encouraged me to read and to know what to want to become in life, and so on. (I12, HoD)

Fourth, leadership responsibilities, both in the schooling and post-schooling context, emerged as yet another pre-socializing experience for the participants. In the schooling context, these included election to prestigious leadership positions, including head boy (I10, HoD), head girl (discipline and life skills) (I7, HoD), hostel prefect (I2, P), library prefect (I3, HoD), class captain (I6, HoD; I12, HoD; I9, P) and prefect (I6, HoD; I9, P). At college/university level, these elected leadership positions included student representative council member (I4, HoD; I8, P; I15, P) and learner representative for the university hostel (I2, P).

Anticipatory socialization, conceptualized as socialization to leadership during the preparatory and early stage of the participants' teaching careers, is also a potential form of leadership development

Aside from childhood and schooling experiences, anticipatory socialization was also evidenced during the preparatory and early stage of the participants' teaching careers. For a select few, initial teacher training appeared to be regarded as a form of leadership preparation, as illustrated in the following excerpt:

> Yes, Educational Management, we have done it at the College, a portion of it, to run the subjects. That was actually more in the terms of teaching methodology, but also then managing a class, classroom management, that's what we have done in our Diploma year … It is included there, and I think it is properly and sufficiently covered – the areas that should need attention for them. (I9, P)

While introductory and undoubtedly not dedicated to leadership preparation, this initial teacher training did lead some participants to think about issues of leadership and management as they began their teaching careers. However, had the training 'been treated more intentionally as leadership preparation, with school leaders [as teacher trainees] being more conscious of the principalship role at the time of teacher training' (Moorosi and Grant, 2018: 7), more could have benefitted from it.

The majority of participants in this study had been exposed to leadership opportunities as teachers, as a precursor to the position of either HoD or principalship. Teacher leadership roles were enacted firstly in relation to the zone of the classroom: 'As a teacher, you are a leader because you are leading the learners that are in your classroom' (I3, HoD). Secondly, they were enacted in relation to the core curriculum, the co-curriculum and the extra-curriculum taking place outside the classroom in the form of the supervision of afternoon classes (I6, HoD), subject head (I10, HoD; I7, HoD), Grade Head followed by

Head of Phase (I8, P), Sports Organizer (I1, HoD; I4, HoD) as well as facilitator of the extra-mural activity 'Window of Hope' (I1, HoD). Finally, and to a much lesser degree, teacher leadership was enacted as a school board member (I4, HoD) and taken up as a whole school activity (Grant, 2012).

While professional socialization in the form of formal leadership training is offered, more can be done in this regard

Professional socialization, as discussed earlier, focuses on what happens in the university through qualifications and internships (Crow, 2006). However, a more expansive version of this category engages 'districts and schools, as well as universities, working together as agents in the process of learning the role' (Ibid, p. 317).

At the time of this study, Namibia did not have a dedicated and systematic national preparatory training for principals and aspiring principals. Instead, preparatory leadership short courses and workshops, organized at regional level, were offered to newly appointed principals *and* HoDs. This is in contrast to countries such as South Africa, Botswana and Lesotho, where it was principals alone who received post-appointment training (Moorosi and Grant, 2018).

The regional workshops for newly appointed HoDs were appreciated by many participants in this study, primarily because they explored and unpacked the job description of the HoD and offered guidance on how to run a department (I14, P). Furthermore, experts in leadership and management were invited to deliver some sessions and motivate participating HoDs (I16, RD). Generally, there was consensus among the HoD participants that the HoD induction workshops were useful and equipped them well for their job (I4, HoD). These sentiments are illustrated in the following quotation:

> While I was still acting [as HoD], we were taken through a workshop kind of, where we were told what a leader is, what a leader should be; the roles of a Head of Department, everything about HoDs. It was very, it was good because I learnt a lot from there. The material that we were given, everything is basically there. So that is the training that I had. And then of course from my own side, reading a lot on leadership. (I12, HoD)

It appears from the data that leadership training workshops for newly appointed principals were offered by the region (I8, P). In addition, and when funding was available, additional courses for a select group of principals in the region were presented. For example, Participant 11 referred to a good leadership course offered in response to the introduction and implementation of the Education and Training Sector Improvement Programme (ETSIP) (2007) in schools. However, the concern was that the training did not reach all principals in the region (I11, P).

Additional courses, some certificated, were offered by private companies at a national level and, more often than not, were sponsored by external funders. These additional courses varied in terms of their duration.

Reference was made by Participants 2, 5 and 9 to courses offered by the Rossing Foundation (https://www.rossingfoundation.com/). Participant 9 reminisced about his HoD years and the leadership courses he attended, organized by the MoE and delivered by consultants. These courses dated back to 1994 when the ministry decided that it was 'important that all HoDs and Principals should be subjected to a kind of a training for them to be properly equipped with management skills, administration skills and leadership skills' (I9, P). The courses were offered through the Rossing Foundation over an eight-week period and included modules such as 'Project Management, Finance Management, that is now School Project Management, that is now School Finance Management, and General Administration Management; those are the courses that were given' (I9, P).

More recently, a leadership training course was organized by the MoE and offered by the African Leadership Institute, an independent private institute, in Okahandja (https://www.ali.com.na/). This certificated course was delivered on a part-time basis over a two-year period. Participants were either nominated by their region to attend the course (I5, P; I13, P) or they could volunteer (I9, P). Sponsorship varied, but Old Mutual was particularly mentioned as a sponsor by one participant (I13, P). The course was highly regarded (I9, P; I13, P; I16, RD) and run by a retired principal who was perceived to be knowledgeable, having been part of the Namibian education system for many years. In the words of the regional director, 'He [the retired principal] has been one of the most, most successful Principals that Namibia has ever had, not even in this Region alone; in Namibia' (I16). This view was reinforced by Participant 13, who spoke about this retired principal as a well-resourced person who 'mainly used his experiences to tell us how to become successful, because when he was a Principal, he was quite successful during his days' (I13). This approach to leadership development is similar to that in the United States, where veterans are used as mentors to socialize beginning principals (Crow, 2006).

A short leadership training course, delivered in the form of a series of workshops and offered by the British Council, was also mentioned. This certificated course was designed as a part-time programme and presented during one week of each school term for three terms (I8, P). Content covered included leadership and mentoring (I10, HoD) and monitoring and developing of teachers (I7, HoD). While some participants found the course helpful (I7, HoD), others found it frustrating. For example, Participant 11 was of the view that 'they had another agenda and that was publishing, working together with British Schools'. This principal argued that while in theory this was a good idea, in practice 'we are two worlds apart; they've got the money to do that, we don't. We try to survive on the basics' (I11).

Because of the lack of mediated entry (Crow, 2006), the world of the newly appointed Namibian principal was one of chaos and accompanying hardship, specifically during the first year or two of the principalship, 'Because, if you become a principal, the first year you, you don't know actually where you are … You don't even know how that year passes by, because you, you are busy learning and touching here and touching there, and busy learning how things have to be done' (I14, P). Participant 3 described how she found it very difficult, despite having seen how her principal did things; 'when you get into it, that's when you really know what it is. There you are just an outsider still, you don't know. You are a Financial Manager, you are a Human Resource Manager, you are an Administrator, you are heading so many Departments. Ja, so during that time really, I had difficulty' (I13, P).

Given the increasing complexity of the principal role, the data suggests that while the induction workshops offered at a regional level were necessary and beneficial, they were insufficient on their own. However, the ad hoc and uneven delivery of the privately funded supplementary leadership training courses across the region posed challenges, as not all principals had an equal chance of attending. It stands to reason then that participants (principals and HoDs) articulated a need for additional systematic leadership development and training opportunities and suggested ways in which leadership training in their region might be improved.

In essence, participants argued for a holistic approach to leadership development, beginning with the induction workshops at the onset of principalship but then continuing in-service as updates and revisions became necessary (I3, HoD; I4, HoD; I7, HoD and I13, P). There was also a call for improved links between the theoretical knowledge of courses and the practical application thereof in schools (I9, P). To illustrate, Participant 5 called for an on-site follow-up to the induction workshop where the principal was observed and monitored and offered further support: 'So it should be before. But then, thereafter, there should be someone who helps us to find out whether you are still on track or not. Then that you are not just to be left there alone, and then you see that you still need to be monitored thereafter' (I5, P). In essence, this is in line with Crow's (2006) contention that there should be collaboration between the coordinators of preparatory leadership programmes and the districts (regions, in this Namibian case) and schools from which the participants come.

Within this holistic approach to leadership development, it was also recommended that principals routinely get together to discuss and be instructed on different matters (I11, P). The data did reveal that a principals' association existed in the region. It met once a term for the purposes of getting principals together to share information and best practices, discuss common problems and take common decisions before taking up issues with the regional office (I11, P; I16; RD). It was noted, though that, unfortunately, the meeting seldom had a 100 per cent attendance (I11, P; I13, P). Despite this, the association offered a platform to support committed principals in their development as leaders.

In-school mentoring as part of organizational socialization is a productive strategy, particularly as it relates to succession planning

Organizational socialization involves learning the culture of a particular organization and the ways things are done with regard to school leadership and management. In this Namibian case study, there was substantial evidence of coaching and mentoring in schools by senior staff, most notably, the principal. This coaching and mentoring was regarded by the majority as a positive influence in their development as school leaders. Consequently, it strengthened organizational socialization and enhanced succession planning.

Some participants had the role of acting HoD or principal foisted on them when the previous incumbent vacated the school. This was particularly the case with HoDs 4, 7 and 12. One HoD explained his situation: '[There] was no HoD at the school, so I was actually doing the HoD duties, all the time. So actually that Principal equipped me a lot, and I was given all different tasks and the way forward' (I4, HoD). Another HoD explained how, as HoD, she would be asked by her principal to stand in for her whenever she was away (I12, HoD).

In-house coaching and mentoring was considered effective when school principals invoked the leadership of their colleagues and involved them in the daily routines of leadership and management: 'I was prepared by him by being part of certain principal decisions; he dragged me in and asked my advice, and, over the years, we came to work quite well together' (I11, P). Principals who 'walked the talk' and role modelled good practice were particularly appreciated. One HoD narrated how her principal would discuss something with her and then immediately get up and put the idea into practice. She gave the example of the problem of litter in the school, and how her principal would role model good practice by gathering litter off the school ground and placing it in the bins provided. What she learnt was that as school leaders, 'we don't only need to talk, we have to act also. You have to be the one doing the task for others to follow you' (I7, HoD). Another participant learnt not to be too hasty in leadership decision-making but instead to first pause and reflect: 'He [my principal] was the one that said, let us wait until tomorrow, sleep on something … Well I was the one wanting to do it now' (I11, P)!

In schools with one HoD, it seems that the leadership work was divided in half and shared between the principal and the HoD (I9, P). In schools with more than one HoD, mentoring of HoDs was organized per trimester and accordingly rotated (I14, P). Succession planning was taken a step further in some schools, with teachers being mentored into leadership roles: 'I have told the teachers so that they even one day when I am not in or the HoD is not in, even at my school an ordinary teacher can run my school' (I5, P).

However, despite good preparation, a sound mentor and practical engagement in school leadership and management activities, the actual move into principalship was still experienced by some as a lonely and difficult period: 'It can become a very lonesome office ja, so the first year really, it, it passes and you don't know how it passes' (I14, P). With reference to mentorship, Participant 14 went on to say, 'That first year was still very hard for me. So what about the one that did not even have a principal like that?' (I14, P)

Indeed, a few participants in this study did not receive strong mentorship and, instead, were left to fend for themselves: 'Because my previous principal didn't guide me that much; it was like she was saying they threw me in the deep side of the water and I must swim' (I2, P). This participant explained how she was able to swim, rather than sink, because of her innate interest in wanting to know how things worked and her agency in finding out through engaging in research (I2, P).

Conclusion

This Namibian case study of school leadership preparation and development has revealed firstly that anticipatory socialization, in its different forms, is an often unconscious, albeit significant, form of leadership development. In particular, stories of the constructive influences of parents, the church and significant teachers as well as learner leadership opportunities during the schooling years emerged. Teacher leadership opportunities during the early career years also contributed to anticipatory leadership socializing experiences. Further narrative or story-based research, which is able to probe the pre-socializing experiences of school leaders, would add value to our understanding of this crucial, yet under-researched, stage of leadership development, both in Namibia and on the African continent as a whole.

Secondly, examples of professional socialization were plentiful in this Namibian case study, including regional induction workshops and a range of certified leadership preparation programmes of varying duration. Nevertheless, there was an urgent call for a more holistic, ongoing and systematic approach to professional socialization, rather than reliance on outsourced, ad hoc certificated programmes that were not available to all school leaders. This has policy implications for Namibia and requires the involvement of the MoE in a debate about the most appropriate, sustainable and just way to support the development of *all* the country's school leaders.

Important also to mention is that, while the merits of a certificated preparatory programme offered by a successful retired principal were recognized, there is a need to tread cautiously in this regard. When relying on veterans to socialize beginning principals, Crow (2006) warns, it is important to acknowledge that the learning passed on to the newcomer may serve to reproduce the status quo and stifle innovative practices. This has implications for both policy and practice in the Namibian context. If the MoE decides that a mandatory national leadership preparation qualification ought to be developed for school leaders, then it is imperative that sound principles inform the programme, principles that acknowledge complexity, embrace diversity and encourage critique.

Thirdly, in-school coaching and mentoring, for the most part, were experienced positively in this Namibian case, with participants being of the view that they strengthened organizational socialization. Principals who 'walked the talk' and modelled good practice were appreciated and their role in effective succession planning acknowledged. Here we see a degree of conformity in the socialization process and a 'role-taking' rather than a 'role-making' outcome (Hart, 1993 in Crow, 2006: 321). Indeed, there was little evidence in the case to indicate that the participants had the confidence to challenge regional norms and practices and initiate new ways of being and doing. What this chapter argues is that role-taking is a necessary but not sufficient outcome of socialization. While role-taking is appropriate in the early stages of leadership socialization, there comes a point where role-making competences are vital if schools are to stay relevant to a complex and dynamic society. Although beyond the scope of this study, a question for future research is to explore how these role-making competences are developed in school leaders, both in Namibia and beyond its borders.

References

Braun, V. and V. Clarke (2012), 'Thematic Analysis', in Cooper, H. (ed), *APA Handbook of Research Methods in Psychology*, 57–71, Washington DC: APA.

Brody, J. L., J. Vissa, and J. M. Weathers (2010), 'School Leader Professional Socialization: The Contribution of Focused Observations', *Journal of Research on Leadership Education*, 5 (14): 611–51.

Bush, T. (1999), 'Crisis or Crossroads? The Discipline of Education Management in the late 1990s', *Education Management and Administration*, 27(3): 239–52.

Bush, T. (2016), 'Preparing New Principals: Professional and Organizational Socialization', *Educational Management Administration & Leadership*, 44 (1): 3–5.

Bush, T. and G. Oduro (2006), 'New Principals in Africa: Preparation, Induction and Practice', *Journal of Educational Administration*, 44 (4): 359–75.

Christie, P. (2010), 'Landscapes of Leadership in South African Schools: Mapping the Changes', *Educational Management Administration & Leadership*, 38 (6): 697–711.

Crow, G. M. (2006), 'Complexity and the Beginning Principal in the United States: Perspectives on Socialisation', *Journal of Educational Administration*, 44 (4): 310–24.

Duke, D. (1987), *School Leadership and Instructional Improvement*, New York: Random House.

Eacott, S. and G. N. Asuga (2014), 'School Leadership Preparation and Development in Africa: A Critical Insight', *Educational Management Administration & Leadership*, 42 (6): 919–34.

Grant, C. (2012), 'Daring to Lead: The Possibility of Teacher Leadership in KwaZulu-Natal Schools', in V. Chikoko and K. M. Jorgensen (eds), *Education Leadership, Management and Governance in South Africa,* 51–68, New York: Nova Science Publishers.

Grant, C. (2017), 'Excavating the South African Teacher Leadership Archive: Surfacing the Absences and Re-Imagining the Future', *Educational Management, Administration and Leadership*. Available online: http://journals.sagepub.com/do i/10.1177/1741143217717274

Hallinger, P. (2018), 'Surfacing a Hidden Literature: A Systematic Review of Research on Educational Leadership and Management in Africa', *Educational Management Administration & Leadership*, 46 (3): 362–84.

Kraft, R. (2014), 'The Namibian Socio-Economic Landscape', in M. Schäfer, D. Samson and B. Brown (eds), *Namibia Counts: Stories of Mathematics Education Research in Namibia*, Grahamstown: Education Department, Rhodes University.

Lumby, J. and F. English (2009), 'From Simplicism to Complexity in Leadership Identity and Preparation: Exploring the Lineage and Dark Secrets', *International Journal of Leadership in Education*, 12 (2): 95–114.

Moorosi, P. (2014), 'Constructing a Leader's Identity Development through a Leadership Development Programme: An Intersectional Analysis', *Educational Management Administration Leadership*, 42 (6): 792–807.

Moorosi, P. and C. Grant (2018), 'The Socialisation and Leader Identity Development of School Leaders in Southern African Countries', *Journal of Educational Administration*, 56 (6): 643–58.

Moorosi, P. and T. Bush (2011), 'School Leadership Development in Commonwealth Countries: Learning across the Boundaries', *International Studies in Educational Administration*, 39 (3): 59–76.

Namibia (2007), *Education and Training Sector Improvement Programme: Planning for a Learning Nation. Programme Document: Phase I. (2006-2011)*, Windhoek: Ministry of Education.

Namibia. Government of Namibia (2018), Namibia Population. Available online: http://www.gov.na/population (accessed August 2018).

Namibia. Ministry of Basic Education and Culture (1993), *Toward Education for All: A Development Brief of Education, Culture, and Training*, Windhoek: Gamsberg Macmillan.

Onguko, B., M. Abdalla, and C. F. Webber (2008), 'Mapping Principal Preparation in Kenya and Tanzania', *Journal of Educational Administration*, 46 (6): 715–26.

Pansiri, N. O. (2011), 'Performativity in School Management and Leadership in Botswana', *Educational Management Administration & Leadership*, 39 (6): 751–66.

Pheko, B. (2008), 'Secondary School Leadership Practice in Botswana', *Educational Management Administration & Leadership*, 36 (1): 71–84.

Ribbins, P. (2008), 'A Life and Career Based Framework for the Study of Leaders in Education', in J. Lumby, G. Crow and P. Pashiardis (eds), *International Handbook on the Preparation and Development of School Leaders*, 61–80, London: Routledge.

Taylor, S. and N. Spaull (2013), *The Effects of Rapidly Expanding Primary School Access on Effective Learning: The Case of Southern and Eastern Africa since 2000*, Stellenbosch Economic Working Papers: 1/13 January 2013, Stellenbosch: University of Stellenbosch.

van der Mescht, H. (2008), 'Educational Leadership and Management – Some Thoughts from the Field', *Journal of Education* 44: 7–24.

Van Maanen, J. and E. H. Schein (1979), 'Toward a Theory of Organizational Socialization', in B. M. Staw and L. L. Cummings (eds), *Research in Organizational Behavior*, Vol. 1: 209–64, Greenwich: JAI Press.

5

Leadership Preparation and Development for Principals in South African Public Schools

Raj Mestry

Introduction

South Africa's education system is improving at a very slow pace, and this is demonstrated by poor student performance in national and international tests and examinations. Although the 2014 Annual National Assessment (ANA) results showed slight increases across all provinces in the overall scores of languages and mathematics compared to the 2011 ANA results (Department of Basic Education [DBE], 2014), the literacy and numeracy levels of primary school students are pitched at two grades lower than normal (Spaull, 2017a). In the National Senior Certificate (NSC) (Grade 12) examinations, the results for the past three years were 75.6 per cent (2017), 72.5 per cent (2016) and 70.7 per cent (DBE, n.d). Spaull's (2015) analysis of the NSC results indicate that only about 50 per cent of students that enrol in Grade 1 in public schools annually were able to complete the Grade 12 examinations successfully. For example, in 2014, only 532,860 students wrote matric, even though there were 1,085,570 students in the cohort that started Grade 1 twelve years earlier.

The performance of South African students in international tests is also bleak. Spaull (2015) explains that the Southern and Eastern African Consortium for Monitoring Educational Quality (SACMEQ) test of 2007 highlighted huge geographic inequalities in the country: 41 per cent of rural Grade 6 students were functionally illiterate, compared to only 13 per cent of urban students in the same grade. Also, the local Grade 6 students performed worse than students in many poorer African countries like Kenya and Tanzania, even after accounting for non-enrolment and higher drop-out in those countries. The pre-Progress in International Reading and Literacy Study (PIRLS), now referred to as PIRLS Literacy, of 2016 showed that the figure for children that cannot read for meaning in South Africa is 78 per cent (Mullis et al., 2017; Spaull, 2017b). The 2015 Trends in Mathematics and Science Study (TIMSS) results also showed very little improvement in Grade 8 mathematics or science achievement (Mullis et al., 2015).

Globally, these poor academic standards at school level could be symptomatic of a lack of effective leadership and management in schools (Spaull, 2013), among other reasons. Two pertinent aspects come to the fore. Firstly, there are no stringent criteria for the appointment of principals (Townsend and MacBeath, 2011). According to the Employment of Educators Act (South Africa, 1998), applicants for principalship positions should hold at least a three-year teacher's diploma and have had seven years' teaching experience. This implies that a post level one teacher may be appointed as a principal on the recommendation of the school governing body (SGB) without having any leadership and management qualifications or experience. This means that a teacher can bypass the ranks of head of department or deputy principal to take up a principalship position. Secondly, there are no formal leadership development programmes to prepare aspiring or practising principals (Bush, Kiggundu and Moorosi, 2011). It is for these reasons that changes in the new system of governance in schools may have resulted in principals being unprepared for their new roles as leaders (Mestry, 2017). Principals may also experience difficulty in adapting to their new roles and to new channels of communication, resulting in role ambiguity (Dimmock, 2012). Perhaps one of the major changes in principalship has been the range of expectations placed on principals, and these expectations have moved from the demands for management and control to demands for an educational leader who can adapt to educational changes (Steyn, 2002; Tucker and Codding, 2002). Many practising principals lack basic leadership and management training prior to and after their entry into principalship and are thus not prepared for their new role (Van der Westhuizen, 2007).

This chapter accentuates the role principals play in changing the education landscape of South Africa. Research has established that leadership of principals is a key factor in raising academic achievement (Leithwood, Harris and Hopkins, 2008; Bryman and Lilley, 2009). Leithwood, Day, Sammons, Harris and Hopkins (2006) assert that school leadership is second only to classroom teaching as an influence on student achievement. Principals as instructional leaders can foster high academic achievement on the part of all students by instilling a shared vision of teaching and learning (Stronge, Xu and Leeper, 2013). Other studies reiterate that leadership development of principals is critical for raising standards in education (Bush et al., 2011; Leithwood et al., 2010; Shelton, 2011; Simkins, 2005).

Researchers in South Africa concur with the belief that many principals lack the relevant knowledge and skills to lead schools effectively, and this has serious implications for student performance (Mestry and Singh, 2007). The appointment of principals with poor leadership and management skills has created an array of problematic issues, criticisms and expectations, thus making schools more difficult to lead. Recurring budget shortfalls, the complex needs of students and the cry for higher standards and achievement are only a few daily realities faced by principals. Thus, there is a need for education authorities to continually develop and support principals so that they can lead effective schools. Goslin (2009) argues that principals tend to overlook their responsibilities of curriculum or instructional leadership because they are not fully aware of their primary task, or they are too busy attending to their administrative duties and either resolving conflicts among role players or maintaining student discipline. There is a need for principals to be empowered and professionally prepared for their roles as heads of schools and to continually enhance their skills, attributes and competencies through structured leadership development programmes. The general aims of this chapter are to

- advance a clear understanding of leadership development and its importance for principals;
- use secondary data of research to examine leadership preparation and development programmes for principals in a South African context;
- explore findings regarding principals' experiences to become effective leaders through strengthening the delivery of leadership development programmes.

Methodology

A literature review was undertaken on leadership preparation and development of principals to establish what research has already been done in this field. Essentially, a literature review is an overview of what we know and what we do not know about a given topic. It is a critical discussion and summary of literature related to leadership preparation and development that is of general and specialized relevance to this particular area. Secondary data related to research studies concerning leadership development conducted mainly in South Africa were extracted. These research studies include Bush and Oduro (2006); Mestry and Singh (2007); Mathibe (2007); Bush, Duku, Glover, Kiggundu, Kola, Msila and Moorosi (2009); Bush, Kiggundu and Moorosi (2011); Moorosi and Bush (2011); Bush and Glover (2012); Msila and Mtshali (2013); Naidoo and Petersen (2015); Msila (2015); and Mestry (2017). These qualitative studies explored a leadership development programme for principals using an interpretivist paradigm.

Defining leadership preparation and leadership development

Day (2001: 582) explains that leadership involves preparing people for roles and situations beyond their current experience, whereas management development equips managers with the knowledge, skills and abilities to enhance performance on known tasks through the application of proven solutions. Leadership development is about building capacity in anticipation of unforeseen challenges. Bush (2010) argues that principals in the twenty-first century require specific leadership development and cites three reasons for this paradigm shift:

- The increase in the scope of leadership due to the decentralization of education from central authority to local communities;
- The increasing complexity of school contexts where principals are required to engage with their communities to lead and manage institutions effectively;
- The unfairness to appoint new principals without providing them effective preparation and induction.

Leadership preparation

There is a strong link between the preparation of school leaders to the effectiveness of leadership practices and overall school improvement (Moorosi and Bush, 2011). Various countries have specific requirements to ensure that aspiring principals are prepared for their leadership roles. For example, Singapore, the United Kingdom (UK) and the United States (US) have national qualification structures in place (Quong, 2006; Walker and Qian, 2006). In the United States, a teacher is only eligible to apply for the principal's post once he/she has completed the Master of Educational Administration degree (Tucker and Codding, 2002). In the United Kingdom, teachers who wish to continue up the career ladder first become senior teachers or deputy heads and work with the principal as a member of the senior management team. With an average of about five years' experience as a deputy, they can apply for headship posts (Weindling and Dimmock, 2006).

As previously mentioned, in South Africa, an applicant for a principalship post is only required to have a teacher's qualification and seven years' teaching experience. No other formal leadership preparation is required. Bush and Oduro (2006) explain that throughout Africa, there is rarely any formal leadership training, and principals are appointed on the basis of their teaching record rather than their leadership potential. Induction and support are usually limited and principals have to adopt a pragmatic approach. Providing principals with the necessary knowledge, skills, values and attitudes becomes increasingly important in relation to the difficulties faced by a dynamic and ever-changing educational culture. Bush et al. (2011) argue that, while there is an increasing body of evidence that leadership makes a significant difference, there is less agreement about what preparation is required to develop appropriate leadership behaviours.

Leadership development

High academic standards demand high professional measures for school leadership (Gallie and Keevy, 2014). People in leadership positions have to think about what they should do to become effective leaders. Thus, improving the capacity of principals through leadership development interventions is imperative to ultimately improve teaching and learning and hence student academic achievement in public schools (Bush, 2008; Slater and Nelson, 2013). Leithwood et al. (2006) identified leadership practices that will enhance the leadership of principals: setting direction, developing people, restructuring the organization and managing the instructional programme.

Wiehahn and Du Plessis (2018) aver that there is an urgent need to train and develop both existing and newly appointed principals to effectively lead and manage organizational structures and other facets of education management development, so that improvements in the quality of teaching and learning take place. Some professionals consider leadership development as training, a means of keeping abreast of developments or a way to build a career, while professional associations hold the view that leadership development is part of lifelong learning, a means of gaining career security, a means of personal development, a means of assuring the public that individual professionals are up-to-date, a method whereby professional associations can verify competence and a way of providing employers with a competent and adaptable workforce (Friedman and Phillips, 2004; Craft, 2000).

According to Guskey (2002), high-quality leadership development is a central component in nearly every modern proposal for improving education. Leadership development in school education consists of any educational activity which helps to maintain, develop or increase knowledge, problem-solving skills, technical skills or professional performance standards, all with the goal of providing quality education (Kennedy, 2005). Leadership development should be seen as a process by which principals review, renew and extend their commitment as change agents to the moral purposes of teaching, and by which they acquire and develop their knowledge, skills and attitudes (Mestry, Hendricks and Bisschoff, 2009). Craft (2000) avers that there are many reasons for principal leadership development. They include to improve their leadership and management skills; develop the professional knowledge and understanding of a principal in order to fulfil his/her instructional responsibilities more effectively; make staff feel valued; promote job satisfaction; develop an enhanced view of the job; enable teachers to anticipate and prepare for change, and to derive excitement from it; and make teachers feel willing and competent to contribute positively to the development of the school. Day and Sachs (2004) describe leadership development for principals as all the activities in which they engage during the course of their career which are designed to enhance their work performance. This professional development can involve any relevant learning activity, whether formal and structured or informal and self-directed.

It should be noted that leadership and management should be seen as a process whereby the development of education leaders and the achievement of organizational goals are synchronized (Mestry and Grobler, 2004). The process of development is mainly concerned with equipping principals to acquire and improve the necessary competencies to lead and manage their schools effectively (McClay and Brown, 2003). While proposed leadership development programmes vary widely in their content and format, most share a common purpose: to align the professional practices, beliefs and understanding of school principals with the achievement of school goals, namely, the improvement of student learning. Leadership development programmes are systematic efforts to bring about change in school leadership whereby new behaviours, attitudes and beliefs contribute to the educational outcomes of the institution and, invariably, the learning outcomes of students. According to Sullivan and Associates (2013), leadership development frameworks for principals enable them to focus on their responsibilities, tasks and characteristics that support effective learning.

Leadership preparation and development:
A South African context

Moorosi and Bush (2011) state that the discourse on effective leadership for school improvement brings under the spotlight the significance of leadership preparation and development and whether training programmes equip leaders with the necessary skills to address current and emerging school challenges. Thus, three critical questions have to be asked: How are school leaders prepared for the role? What type of leadership development do they receive? What impact does the training and development have? The first question has already been answered, and the two other questions are discussed here.

In 2007 the Department of Basic Education (DBE), in collaboration with non-governmental organizations (NGOs) and universities, introduced a threshold qualification for aspiring and practising principals as well as other school management team (SMT) members (heads of departments (HoDs) and deputy principals) to improve educational standards (Bush and Glover, 2012). The course, the Advanced Certificate in Education: School Leadership (ACESL), was intended to be an entry-level qualification for new principals and a leadership development programme for practising principals (novice and experienced). Based on research funded by the DBE, it was found that the delivery of the course benefitted principals (and other school leaders) significantly, thus making schools more effective. The success of the ACESL course led the DBE to replace the ACE with the Advanced Diploma in Education (ADE) as a qualification to raise the benchmark for principalship in South Africa. However, some teacher unions opposed the idea that this qualification should become an entry-level qualification for principals. Negotiations are still ongoing between the DBE and teacher unions to make this qualification entry-level for principals.

Since the ACESL course was not a compulsory qualification for principals, only selected principals in each province of the country were provided with bursaries to study this course at tertiary institutions. Structured leadership development was non-existent for those not selected. Where provincial departments of education offered mandatory leadership development programmes, these were usually 'one-size-fits-all' programmes that dealt mainly with curriculum changes. According to Mestry and Singh (2007), education district officials did not attach any importance to leadership development for principals. Most of the development programmes arranged by education districts dealt mainly with curriculum changes such as the National Curriculum Statement (NCS), Revised National Curriculum Statement (RNCS) and Curriculum Assessment Policy

Statement (CAPS). It was recorded that ad hoc development programmes such as SGB training workshops were provided. To improve their leadership practices, many principals chose to study the B. Ed. (Hon) or M. Ed. courses in leadership or collaborated with consultants from universities or NGOs to deliver leadership development workshops for themselves and/or for their teaching staff.

More recently, the DBE also introduced the Standard for Principalship, which explains the competencies required of principals to lead and manage schools effectively.

Policy on the Standard for Principalship

The DBE, acknowledging that principals play a pertinent role in school improvement and school effectiveness, introduced a policy on the South African Standard for Principalship (hereafter *Standard*) (South Africa, 2016). The Standard applies to principals in all South African schools and sets out key dimensions of the work to be undertaken by them. It also makes reference to the skills and qualities that are necessary for executing the duties of a school principal. The information provided in the Standard will assist in the recruitment, selection and appointment of principals and will help principals improve the leadership and management processes at their schools. It will also assist the DBE and provincial departments of education in designing training programmes that will promote leadership development. Thus, it is envisaged that all future leadership development programmes, including the ADESL course, should be underpinned by the Standard. The core modules of the ADESL course should integrate competencies required of principals as stated in the Standard. In fact, external agencies such as Bridge (NGO) (http://www.bridge.org.za/about-us/our-team/) and some higher education institutions have begun using the Standard to develop leadership development programmes for aspiring and practising school principals.

The Advanced Certificate in Education (School Leadership) as a leadership development programme

The ACESL course, offered as a two-year part-time leadership development programme, comprised of five core modules: Managing Teaching and Learning (Curriculum); Managing People; Managing Organizational Systems, Physical Resources and Financial Management; Managing Policy; and Understanding School Leadership in a South African context. Two foundation modules were included in the curriculum: Managing Information and Communications

Technology (ICT) and Demonstrating Effective Language Skills. In addition to assignments, tests and group presentations, principals were required to undertake a leadership project incorporating competencies gained from the core and foundation modules (South Africa, 2015).

The programme was designed to provide principals with the knowledge base and rigorous intellectual analysis experience that would equip them to harness the human and other resources necessary to ensure that educational institutions are highly effective. Principals should have insight into aspects dealing with school improvement, such as assessing school needs; the strategic direction and development of the school; teaching and learning; legislation and policy issues relating to schools; and empowering staff and allowing them to be involved in the development of the school (Mestry and Singh, 2007). The main thrust of the ACESL course as a leadership development programme was to provide principals with the necessary knowledge, skills, values and attitudes that would assist them to lead and manage educational institutions effectively. This course aimed to acquaint participants (principals) with theories and research in behavioural sciences that relate to studies of organizations. Within the framework of current developments in education theory and practice, it also aimed to provide principals with opportunities to analyse situations and formulate strategies for tackling leadership and management problems in education (Mestry and Singh, 2007).

The impact of the ACESL as a leadership development programme

In this section, the effectiveness of the ACESL course as a leadership development programme for principals will be examined. Research conducted by Bush et al. (2011), Msila (2015) and Mestry and Singh (2007) concluded that the ACESL programme was conceived as a practice-based programme and was intended to lead to enhanced leadership practice. Most principals claimed to have improved their leadership and management practice, and this was confirmed by district officials and by scrutinizing off-school policy documents. Areas of improvement included policy implementation, improved relationships with educators, more delegation to other SMT members, enhanced financial management and conflict management. The principals mentioned gains in several personal attributes, including enhanced confidence, improved self-control and better relationships with educators and SMTs. Some also claimed skill development, including ICT, problem solving, financial planning and better team work. However, an investigation of how the ACESL and other leadership development programmes positively impacted on school outcomes is not the focus of this chapter.

In the following discussion, we highlight some pertinent features of the ACESL development programme.

Instructional leadership

The core module on Managing Teaching and Learning aimed to develop the knowledge and skills of principals that would enable them to becoming effective instructional leaders. Instructional leadership includes, among other factors, ensuring that teachers have a good grasp of the subject matter, integrate educational resources in teaching, apply various learner assessment methods, co-ordinate the curriculum and monitor and evaluate learner outcomes. Although pertinent issues such as managing curriculum changes were dealt with, Naidoo and Petersen (2015) aver that principals should be provided with strategies to balance their administrative responsibilities with curriculum matters. Studies by Mestry and Singh (2007) and Naidoo and Petersen (2015) found that most principals used the distributed style of leadership to lead and manage teaching and learning. They delegated all the functions of managing curriculum to their deputy principals and HoDs and absolved themselves from instructional responsibilities (Mestry, Moonsammy-Koopasammy and Schmidt, 2013). To improve educational standards and student performance in schools, it is imperative for principals to be developed in curriculum matters so that they don't abdicate their instructional leadership role.

Creating collaborative networks

Research conducted by Bush et al. (2011) and Mestry and Singh (2007) revealed that the ACESL programme attended by principals promoted collaborative networks among peers in neighbouring schools. Schools benefitted from sharing resources, finding solutions to challenges and resolving conflicts through discussion networks and professional learning communities that were created as a result of the ACESL development programme. Most of the provinces had some form of network activity, usually initiated by mentors or the principals themselves. The survey findings were positive, with 76 per cent stating that developing networks was a great help (Bush et al., 2011). In their evaluation report, Bush and Glover (2012) indicated that networking was not fully established and was inclined to focus mainly on assignment preparation, and thus it did not provide a sustainable basis for collaborative working across schools. In a more recent research undertaken, Naidoo and Petersen (2015) found that many principals who completed the ACESL course were still collaborating with each other through different channels. For example, in one education district, principals meet frequently to discuss educational matters of common concern through an established principals' forum.

Cohort sessions

Bush et al. (2011) found that the delivery model of the ACESL appeared to produce different levels of satisfaction on the part of principals. Despite the aspirations of most lecturers, interaction was very limited in the larger groups (at least 200 participants in some cohorts), thus working against the philosophy of the programme. In practice, these sessions usually comprised content delivery rather than interactive learning. However, the findings of Msila and Mtshali (2013) and Mestry and Singh (2007) revealed that the ACESL course gave principals a coherent and sustainable approach to building leadership and management capacity. Principals who attended cohort sessions benefitted by gaining new insights into dealing with staff, students and parents. In these sessions, principals shared their experiences, challenges, struggles, frustrations, opinions, perspectives and practical ways in which they overcame their challenges and struggles (Mestry and Singh, 2007). These sessions helped them see problems from a different perspective, as it often came up during discussions that colleagues had had to deal with similar situations. The participants were happy to report on their enhanced leadership and management skills, their more rational approach to dealing with serious issues, their confidence in approaching problems and conflicts and their ability to maintain a disciplined and cooperative spirit in the school. They claimed competence in dealing with complex issues, and said that they now had the ability to deal with matters on a much more personal basis than before (Mestry and Singh, 2007).

Induction and mentorship

According to Msila (2012), many principals spoke about how helpless they were when they assumed their position without being given a formal induction. They were filled with considerable anxiety, frustration and professional isolation over the fact that they did not understand the nature of their leadership responsibilities before they got into 'the hot seat' (Walker and Qian, 2006). All the principals interviewed confirmed that the ACESL course had effectively promoted their professional growth and given them a better understanding of their role in the school. This course could serve as an induction as well as a leadership preparation programme.

According to Bush et al. (2011), mentoring was a distinctive and central feature of the ACESL programme, designed to facilitate the transfer of learning to principals. Effective mentoring provides strong potential for deep learning. Mentoring is about professional development, and professional development is about growth and advancement (Msila, 2011). Bush et al. (2011) and Bush and Glover (2012) raised some critical issues regarding mentoring. It would appear that mentors were responsible for a large number of principals (between 9 and 38) and the facilitation sessions took place in groups or 'cohorts', which did not match the generally accepted definition of mentoring, namely, a one-to-one relationship (Bush, 2008). In one of the provinces, the mentors made no school visits but rather resorted to mentoring principals during cohort sessions and through telephone conversations. The study conducted by Msila (2011) revealed that principals (mentees) did not feel comfortable being mentored by supervisors, although they stated that the mentors were good. They (the mentees) were always reluctant to open up and discuss their inadequacies because they learnt that the district office would soon know of their shortcomings. Msila (2011) found that mentors who emphasized vision were preparing their protégés for the future: how to adapt their schools to constant change. On the other hand, mentees need to mature professionally, to develop a sense of efficacy and independence.

A well-functioning mentoring programme would be a major asset for the programme and could contribute in a powerful way to developing school leaders and their schools. However, it was clear that there were two major constraints on the effective practice of mentoring: the cost of providing one-on-one mentoring, and the limited availability of well-trained and motivated professionals with good experience of leading township and rural schools, who were also free to visit principals' schools during the working day (Bush et al., 2011).

Assessments and major project

To be awarded the ACESL qualification, principals were required to complete a number of assignments for each module and one major leadership project based on the needs of their schools. Each principal was required to develop a project plan in collaboration with relevant role players and take a leadership role to compile a portfolio of evidence. The portfolio influenced the principals' ability to reflect on situations and account for activities taking place in their schools. The success of the project depended on the active involvement of all role players under the principal's leadership. From the projects received and assessed by both internal and external site-based assessors, it would appear that cooperation among role players existed (Mestry and Singh, 2007; Mestry and Schmidt, 2010). Bush, Duku, Glover, Kiggundu, Kola, Msila and Moorosi (2009) found that while the quality of principals' portfolios was variable, most portfolios were well organized and included school documents as well as school-based activities. However, very few of them showed evidence of reflection, despite 63 per cent of respondents saying that 'opportunity for reflection' was 'of great help' (Bush et al., 2009). It was clear from the analysis of portfolios that many principals found it difficult to go beyond description to adopt a reflective approach, leading to changes in leadership practice. The portfolio was regarded as an assessment chore rather than a starting point for school improvement (Bush et al., 2009). Participants complained that the ACESL programme had too many assignments and that the course was over-assessed (Bush et al., 2009).

Conclusion and recommendations

Leadership preparation and development for novice, experienced and aspiring principals is central to school effectiveness and school improvement. To cope with the demands of the twenty-first century, principals should be exposed to innovative leadership development programmes that will help them prepare for their broader roles and responsibilities and develop a deeper understanding of their purpose. Principals require the necessary leadership skills to provide strategic direction, develop school plans and set organizational goals. They should build networks among schools to stimulate innovation, develop diverse curricula, adapt teaching programmes to local needs, promote teamwork among teachers and engage in teacher monitoring, evaluation and leadership development. Three pertinent aspects regarding leadership development for principals should be considered: the Standard for Principalship, the professionalization of principalship and the implementation of leadership development programmes.

The Department of Basic Education (DBE) has taken strides to raise the professional standards and competencies of school principals by formulating the Standard for Principalship (South Africa, 2014). The DBE should provide strategies for effectively implementing the Standard for Principalship policy. While the DBE recognizes the current lack of a co-ordinated system to meet the identified needs of school leaders, it should seek to develop and implement a system of career pathing for education leaders and managers as well as a framework of leadership and management development processes and programmes. The Standard for Principalship policy can be integrated into the ADESL course. It is envisaged that the Standard for Principalship can be built upon an agreed understanding of the core purposes of leadership roles, the key functions within these, the values which underpin them and the personal and professional attributes required to carry them out.

The professionalization of principalship can be considered as the strategically most important process in the successful transformation of education. In keeping with international standards, the DBE should ensure that suitable candidates are appointed as principals by making the ADESL mandatory as a new entry requirement to qualify as school principal. Furthermore, all practising principals who only hold undergraduate qualifications should, within three years of this requirement becoming policy, obtain the ADESL qualification. Thus, this initiative will give recognition to those who obtain the ADESL as the entry-level qualification. The desired outcome of the ADESL course is that participants be provided with the relevant knowledge and skills to develop and implement school development plans, to draw appropriate policies in line with national legislation and regulations to guide their practices and to set up mechanisms to deal with issues across all aspects of school management and leadership. This ADESL qualification is practice-based and should be aimed at providing management and leadership support through a variety of interactive programmes to improve principals' practice, professional growth and ethos of leadership.

References

Bryman, A. and S. Lilley (2009), 'Leadership Researchers on Leadership in Higher Education', *Leadership*, 5 (3): 331–46.

Bush, T. (2008), *Leadership and Management Development in Education*, London: Sage.

Bush, T. (2010), 'Leadership Development', in T. Bush, L. Bell, and D. Middlewood (eds), *The Principles of Educational Leadership and Management: Second Edition*, London: Sage.

Bush, T. and D. Glover (2012), 'Leadership Development and Learner Outcomes: Evidence from South Africa', *Journal of Educational Leadership, Policy and Practice*, 27 (2): 3–15.

Bush, T., E. Kiggundu, and P. Moorosi (2011), 'Preparing New Principals in South Africa: The ACE: School Leadership Programme', *South African Journal of Education*, 31: 31–43.

Bush, T. and G. Oduro (2006), 'New Principals in Africa: Preparation, Induction and Practice', *Journal of Educational Administration*, 44: 359–75.

Bush, T., N. Duku, D. Glover, E. Kiggundu, S. Kola, V. Msila, and P. Moorosi (2009), *External Evaluation. Research Report of the Advanced Certificate in Education*, Pretoria: Department of Basic Education.

Craft, A. (2000), *Professional Development: A Practical Guide for Teachers and Schools*, London: Routledge.

Day, C. and J. Sachs (2004), *International Handbook on the Continuing Professional Development of Teachers*, Berkshire: Open University Press.

Day, D. (2001), 'Leadership Development: A Review in Context', *Leadership Quarterly*, 11 (4): 581–613.

Department of Basic Education (2014), *Report on the Annual National Assessments of 2014*, Pretoria: Department of Basic Education.

Dimmock, C. (2012), *Leadership, Capacity Building and School Improvement*, Oxon: Routledge.

Friedman, A. and M. Phillips (2004), 'Continuing Professional Development: Developing a Vision', *Journal of Education and Work*, 17 (3): 361–76.

Gallie, M. and J. Keevy (2014), *Standards Framework for Teachers and School Leaders*, London: Commonwealth Secretariat.

Goslin, K. G. (2009), 'Systems Thinkers in Action: A Field Guide for Effective Change Leadership in Education', *Canadian Journal of Education*, 32 (3): 660–3.

Guskey, T. R. (2002), 'Professional Development and Teacher Change', *Teachers and Teaching Practice*, 8 (3/4): 381–91.

Kennedy, A. (2005), 'Models of Continuing Professional Development: A Framework for Analysis', *Journal of In-Service Education*, 31 (2): 235–50.

Leithwood, K., A. Harris, and D. Hopkins (2008), 'Seven Strong Claims about Successful Leadership', *School Leadership and Management*, 28 (1): 27–42.

Leithwood, K., C. Day, P. Sammons, A. Harris, and D. Hopkins (2006), *Seven Strong Claims about Successful School Leadership*, London: DfES.

Leithwood, K., S. E. Anderson, B. Mascall, and T. Strauss (2010), 'School Leaders' Influences on Student Learning: The Four Paths', in T. Bush, L. Bell, and D. Middlewood (eds), *The Principles of Educational Leadership and Management: Second Edition*, London: Sage.

Mathibe, I. (2007), 'The Professional Development of School Principals', *South African Journal of Education*, 27 (3): 523–40.

McClay, M. and M. Brown (2003), 'Using Concept Mapping to Evaluate the Training of Primary School Leaders', *International Journal of Leadership Education*, 6 (1): 73–87.

Mestry, R. (2017), 'Empowering Principals to Lead and Manage Public Schools Effectively in the 21st Century', *South African Journal of Education*, 37 (1): 1–11.

Mestry, R. and B. R. Grobler (2004), 'The Training and Development of Principals to Manage Schools Effectively Using the Competence Approach', *International Studies in Educational Administration*, 32 (3): 2–19.

Mestry, R., I. Hendricks, and T. Bisschoff (2009), 'Perceptions of Teachers on the Benefits of Teacher Development Programmes in One Province in South Africa', *South African Journal of Education*, 29 (4): 475–490.

Mestry, R., I. Moonsammy-Koopasammy, and M. Schmidt (2013), 'The Instructional Leadership Role of Primary School Principals', *Education as Change*, 17 (1): 49–64.

Mestry, R. and M. Schmidt (2010), 'Portfolio Assessment as a Means of Evaluating the Professional Development of School Managers', *Education and Urban Society*, 42 (3): 352–73.

Mestry, R. and P. Singh (2007), 'Continuing Professional Development for Principals: A South African Perspective', *South African Journal of Education*, 27 (3): 477–90.

Moorosi, P. and T. Bush (2011), 'School Leadership Development in Commonwealth Countries: Learning across Boundaries', *International Studies in Educational Administration*, 39 (3): 59–72.

Msila, V. (2011), 'School Management and the Struggle for Effective Schools', *Africa Education Review*, 8 (3): 434–49.

Msila, V. (2012), 'Mentoring and School Leadership: Experiences from South Africa', *Social Sciences*, 32 (1): 47–57.

Msila, V. (2015), 'The Struggle to Improve Schools: Voices of South African Teacher Mentors', *Educational Management Administration & Leadership*, 44 (6): 936–50.

Msila, V. and J. Mtshali (2013), 'Getting Principalship Right? Piloting a Principal Professional Leadership Development Model', *International Journal of Education Science*, 5 (1): 47–54.

Mullis, I. V. S., M. O. Martin, P. Foy, and M. Hooper (2015), *PIRLS 2016. International Results in Mathematics*, Chestnut Hill: TIMSS & PIRLS International Study Center. Available online: http://timssandpirls.bc.edu/timss2015/international-results/wp-co ntent/uploads/filebase/full%20pdfs/T15-International-Results-in-Mathematics-Grade-8.pdf (accessed 19 April 2019).

Mullis, I. V. S., M. O. Martin, P. Foy, and M. Hooper (2017), *TIMSS 2015. International Results in Reading*, Chestnut Hill: TIMSS & PIRLS International Study Center. Available online: https://nicspaull.files.wordpress.com/2017/12/p16-pirls-internati onal-results-in- reading.pdf (accessed 19 April 2019).

Naidoo, P. and N. Petersen (2015), 'Towards a Leadership Programme for Primary School Principals as Instructional Leaders', *South African Journal of Childhood Education*, 5 (3): 1–8.

Quong, T. (2006), 'Asking the Hard Questions: Being a Beginning Principal in Australia', *Journal of Educational Administration*, 44: 376–88.

Shelton, S. V. (2011), 'Strong Leaders, Strong Schools: 2010 State Laws'. Available online: http://www.wallacefoundation.org/knowledge-center/school-leadership/ (accessed 21 March 2018).

Simkins, T. (2005), 'Leadership in Education: "What Works" or "What Makes Sense"', *Educational Management, Administration and Leadership*, 33 (1): 9–26.

Slater, C. L. and S. W. Nelson (2013), 'Awareness of Self and Others in Principal Preparation: An International Perspective', in C. L. Slater and S. Nelson (eds), *Understanding the Principalship: An International Guide to Principal Preparation*. Bingley: Emerald Books, Vol. 19: 291–314.

South Africa (1998), *Employment of Educators Act, No.76 of 1998*. Pretoria: Government Printers.

South Africa (2015), *Revised Policy on the Minimum Requirements for Teacher Education Qualifications*. National Qualifications Framework Act, 2008 (Act No. 67 of 2008). Pretoria: Government Printers.

South Africa (2016), *The South African Standard for Principals (In Terms of Section 3(4) of the National Education Policy Act of 1996)*. Pretoria: Government Printers.

Spaull, N. (2013), *South Africa's Education Crisis: The Quality of Education in South Africa 1994-2011*. Johannesburg: Centre for Development and Enterprise.

Spaull, N. (2015), 'Schooling in South Africa: How Low-Quality Education Becomes a Poverty Trap', *South African Child Gauge*, 34–41. Available online: http://www.ci.u ct.ac.za/sites/default/files/image_tool/images/367/Child_Gauge/South_African_Chi ld_Gauge_2015/Child_Gauge_2015-Schooling.pdf (accessed 19 August 2018).

Spaull, N. (2017a), 'Study Shows SA Kids "Can't Read for Meaning"'. Available online: https://www.huffingtonpost.co.za/2017/12/05/south-african-learners-worst-at-read ing-in-world-shows-international-study_a_23297219/ (accessed 24 August 2018).

Spaull, N. (2017b). 'The Unfolding Reading Crisis: The New PIRLS 2016 Results'. Available online: https://nicspaull.com/2017/12/05/the-unfolding-reading-crisis-the -new-pirls-2016-results/ (accessed 19 April 2019).

Steyn, G. M. (2002), 'The Changing Principalship in South African Schools', *Educare*, 31: 251–74.

Stronge, J. H., X. Xu, and L. M. Leeper (2013), *Principal Evaluation: Standards, Rubrics, and Tools for Effective Performance*, Virginia: Association for Supervision and Curriculum Development.

Townsend, T. and J. Macbeath (2011), *International Handbook of Leadership for Learning*, Glasgow: Springer.

Tucker, M. S. and J. B. Codding (2002), *The Principal Challenge*, San Francisco: Jossey- Bass.

van der Westhuizen, P. (2007), 'Professionalising Principalship in South Africa', *South African Journal of Education*, 27 (3): 431–45.

Walker, A. and H. Qian (2006), 'Beginning Principals: Balancing at the Top of the Greasy Pole', *Journal of Educational Administration*, 44: 97–309.

Weindling, D. and C. Dimmock (2006), 'Sitting in the "Hot Seat": New Headteachers in the UK', *Journal of Educational Administration*, 44: 326–40.

Wiehahn, J. and P. du Plessis (2018), 'Professional Development of Newly Appointed Principals at Public High Schools in Gauteng. Is Social Justice Served?' *KOERS – Bulletin for Christian Scholarship*, 83 (1): 1–11.

6

Framing the Context of School Leadership Preparation and Development in Kenya

Janet Mola Okoko

Introduction

Variation in the contexts within which school leaders work has led scholars and practitioners to advocate context-specific school leadership preparation and development (SLP&D) initiatives (Eacott and Asuga, 2014; Goldring et al., 2008; Hallinger, 2018). However, the elements, structures and concepts used to describe effective school leadership tend to be global (Bush, 2008; Darling-Hammond et al., 2010; Huber, 2004; Leithwood, 2007; Republic of Kenya, 2010). For instance, school leaders' work is nested in the hierarchy and bureaucracy of national or regional jurisdictions. The expectation that school leaders will carry out both leadership and management functions is a universal assumption (Bush, 2010; Nelson, De la Colina and Boone, 2008). They are therefore held responsible for creating a conducive environment for teaching and learning by managing related services and resources and maintaining bureaucratic order, as well as setting direction and pacing school improvement (Bush, 2010).

Previous studies have suggested that leadership development in Kenya, as in many other developing countries, tends to ignore contextual needs as it strives to fit in with global trends (Eacott and Asuga 2014; Onderi and Croll, 2008). Some authors have described SLP&D in Kenya as colonial, based on deficit thinking and attempting to compete in the global arena without considering contextual realities (Eacott and Asuga, 2014). Many other studies have cited deficiencies in the existing SLP&D in Kenya and have suggested ways that the initiatives could be improved (Abaya, 2016; Asuga and Eacott, 2012; Kitavi and van der Westhuizen, 1997; Okoko, 2018; Onguko, Abdalla and Webber, 2008;

Wanzare and Ward, 2000). This chapter refers to the aforementioned studies but essentially focuses on the author's study (Okoko, 2018, Okoko, Scott and Scott, 2015), wherein school leaders' experiences were used to explore and suggest a context-specific framework for school leadership preparation and development in Kenya.

School leadership in Kenya

The Government of Kenya (GoK) acknowledges that school leadership must be developed if the national goals of education are to be achieved (Republic of Kenya, 2014). School leadership in Kenya is structured to promote a collective responsibility where a Cabinet Secretary of Education, a bureaucrat, is mandated to manage schools through school boards of management (BoMs), with representatives from the Teachers Service Commission (TSC), the National Examinations Council (KNEC), and County Education boards, parents and communities (Republic of Kenya, 2017). The law that governs education, the 'Basic Education Act', defines the role and functions of each of these partnering bodies and prescribes how members should be appointed. It gives the cabinet secretary's office at the various jurisdictions the mandate to oversee and appoint members of the BoM for each public school (Republic of Kenya, 2017).

Positional leaders of primary schools (head teachers) and those of secondary schools (principals), as middle-level managers, are accountable to their BoM in the day-to-day leadership of schools. These school-based leaders work with assistance from a deputy, teachers and support staff. They are charged with quality assurance duties related to instruction, accounting for revenue and all other resources and maintaining an environment conducive for teaching and learning (Republic of Kenya, 2010; Teacher Service Commission, 2018). As agents of the teachers' employers (e.g. the TSC), they must be familiar with, and adjudicate, the respective teachers' code of regulations.

Even though the TSC now requires school leaders to have at least a bachelor's degree (Teacher Service Commission, 2018), they are not expected to have any formal leadership preparation before they are appointed. Most of them get to the leadership position through a seniority process whereby they move from being a classroom teacher to senior teacher/head of department (HoD), to deputy head teacher or deputy principal and then to head teacher or principal (Republic of Kenya, 2010; Teacher Service Commission, 2018). This model assumes that the knowledge skills and dispositions (KSDs) they acquire at the various levels are transferable to leadership. As classroom teachers, they manage students and resources, keep records of attendance, develop and organize teaching and learning material, plan lessons, assess students' progress, maintain discipline and instil moral values in students. These roles are elevated to school level when they move to a senior teacher position (e.g. maintain school's records of enrolment, resources, professional development initiatives). Similar designations at secondary school level, head of subject (HoS) and HoD, provide leadership for academic matters in their subject area. This includes curriculum planning, coordinating school-based professional development and keeping records of work and assessments. When they reach the position of deputy head teacher/ principal, they schedule instructional duties, co-ordinate both curricular and co-curricular activities and supervise teaching and non-teaching staff. They also manage all school supplies and facilities, are in charge of discipline in the school and stand in for the principal or head teacher in the latter's absence (Republic of Kenya, 2010). The movement from classroom teacher to head teacher takes an average of 19 years (Okoko et al., 2015).

At the head teacher or principal level, they account for finances and all the school resources and are responsible for the quality of teaching and learning. They are responsible for overall planning, procuring instructional material and the construction of physical facilities. They are also accountable for teacher development and skills upgrading, promoting the welfare of staff and students, guiding and counselling teacher trainees, inducting and mentoring new teachers, interpreting and implementing policy decisions, promoting linkages between the school community and other organizations and providing feedback to the Ministry of Education (MoE) and TSC (Republic of Kenya, 2010). Despite these responsibilities, the Basic Education Act and other related policies do not mention how school leaders should be prepared for their role. The available recommendations lean towards the establishment of partnerships in developing administrators at ministerial level and strengthening school BoMs (Republic of Kenya, 2014). An example of such a partnership is the Agile and Harmonized Assistance for Devolved Institutions (AHADI) programme, funded by the United States Agency for International Development, which focuses on building capacity for BoMs (Ministry of Education, 2018). The MoE also offers induction for school leaders when there are curriculum reforms, such as the change to a competency-based system from the structure oriented 8-4-4 system of education (Ministry of Education, 2018).

School leadership preparation and development

Formal SLP&D initiatives, especially the establishment of the Kenya Education Management Institute (KEMI) and then the Kenya Education Staff Institute (KESI), arose out of the government's realization that school leaders needed specific skills to carry out their roles (Eshiwani, 1993). Even with the establishment of KEMI, reviews of government staff development revealed how KEMI and other available initiatives did not meet the needs of a majority of teachers and school leaders (Wanzare and Ward, 2000). After various reviews, KEMI is now a full-time SLP&D institution that is mandated to offer need-based courses on school management and leadership-related topics (Republic of Kenya, 2010).

Efforts to improve SLP&D in Kenya have led the government to encourage development partners to invest in both formal and informal initiatives, including academic- and practice-based courses offered by the MoE, private institutions and non-governmental organizations (NGOs) (Asuga et al., 2015; Onguko, Abdulla and Webber, 2008). These courses are open to aspiring and practising school leaders who voluntarily decide to take them (Okoko et al., 2015; Okoko, 2018). The academic courses offered in the universities are mainly part of graduate degree programmes in educational administration (Onguko, Abdalla and Webber, 2008). Students doing a Bachelor of Education degree are also required to take a course in educational administration. These academic courses are structured to address theory, while practice-based courses are mainly in the form of professional development (PD) that is limited to private institutions or schools that have support from NGOs or donor funds (Waudo et al., 2002).

Despite these efforts, Kenya does not have a clear structure for SLP&D (Republic of Kenya, 2010, 2014). Not all leaders are assured of induction or PD after their appointment (Okoko et al., 2015). School leaders are encouraged to go through needs-based leadership development courses at KEMI, while a few pursue university degrees on their own initiative (Asuga and Eacott, 2014; Okoko et al., 2015). Various studies have also reported how related courses offered in the universities lack essential SLP&D content, including the requisite KSDs for addressing context-specific leadership-related issues. Onguko, Abdulla and Webber (2008) mentioned information technologies, gender, student leadership and HIV and AIDS, while Kitavi and van der Westhuizen (1997) mentioned a lack of basic facilities, poor living conditions for teachers, long distances travelled by students and inadequate financial support. Onguko, Abdalla and Webber (2008) also highlighted how most courses emphasize managerial rather than leadership skills. Many years later, such issues still hinder leaders' ability to manage schools in both rural and urban areas (Abaya, 2016; Okoko, 2018). Tribal clashes, displacement of families and student unrest are also among the contextual challenges to school leadership (Abaya, 2016; Oywa and Abuga, 2018).

The study by Onderi and Croll (2008) reported how priorities for training were dominated by pressures from externally driven agendas. They described how SLP&D initiated by government and donor-funded projects called for change to leadership strategies in a context where resources were scarce, without offering plans for sustainability (Onderi and Croll, 2008). Similarly, school leaders interviewed in the Okoko et al. (2015) study described some donor-funded SLP&D as fulfilling funders' interests rather than those of the targeted leaders. Eacott and Asuga (2014) described the proliferation of SLP&D courses in Kenya as focused on standardization, mainly driven by pressure from the increased competition for students and not focusing on the quality of leadership preparation.

Notwithstanding these criticisms, studies have revealed the usefulness of the existing leadership preparation experiences. More than 50 per cent of the participants in the Okoko study (Okoko 2018; Okoko et al., 2015) felt prepared for school leadership despite the lack of structure and the fragmented nature of their experience. This chapter focuses on findings relating to leadership preparation and development from the aforementioned study.

The study

Data used in the Okoko study were gathered between 2012 and 2013 from 116 leaders, 84 head teachers and 32 principals, using a questionnaire and interviews (Okoko et al., 2015; Okoko, 2018). The questionnaire was developed by the International Study of Principals Preparation (ISPP) team and adapted for the Kenyan context (Okoko et al., 2015; Webber et al., 2014). The questionnaire has 40 items that include a Likert scale on preparedness and problematic areas with regard to school leadership. Table 6.2 below has the aspects covered in the scale. The tool also has an item that required the participants to identify experiences that best characterize their SLP&D from a two-end scale (See Table 6.1).

Twenty-one out of the 116 school leaders who responded to the questionnaire were interviewed to corroborate data from the questionnaire and also ascertain the meaningfulness and clarity of results (Plano and Ivankova, 2016). These 21 respondents represented two levels of basic education (primary and secondary), two types of schools (public and private) and various socio-economic strata

Table 6.1 School Leadership Preparation Experiences

Informal and non-formal		Formal	
	% N=116		% N=116
My learning was by accident	19.8	My learning was planned	80.2
My course was a general teacher training course	79.3	The course was on the administration, leadership and management of a school	20.7
I learnt locally in my school (induction)	30.2	My learning was centralized at National/Provincial/District level	69.8
My learning was rushed/reactive	34.5	My learning was practical/proactive	65.5
My learning was informal/I did not attend a structured course	39.7	My learning was formal (I attended a structured course)	60.3
My learning was in bits and pieces (fragmented)	60.3	I attended a full course in a university or college (systematic)	39.6
I decided to learn on my own/ self-initiated	55.1	The course was initiated by the Ministry/my employer/TSC	44.8
I volunteered to learn/I was not required by my employer	46.6	I was required by TSC or my employer to do the course	53.4
The course I did was through workshops/seminar organized by either KESI/Kenya Institute of Management (KIM)/Kenya Institute of Education (KIE) or an NGO (semi-structured, not certified)	56.9	The course I did was part of my primary teacher education or university degree (structured and certified)	42.3

Source: J. M. Okoko, S. Scott, and D. Scott (2015), 'Perceptions of School Leaders in Nairobi about their Leadership Preparation and Development', *International Journal of Leadership in Education*, 18 (3): 287.

(schools serving low, middle and high-income communities). The leaders were guided to provide descriptions of how they became school leaders, the experiences that prepared them for leadership, the areas that remained problematic, what they wished they had learnt before their appointment to school leadership and what they thought was the best way to learn how to lead a school; they were also asked for any suggestions they had for developers and instructors of SLP&D programmes.

Findings

The findings identified views from leaders regarding their leadership preparation experiences, how they perceived the adequacy of the experiences that prepared them for school leadership and their insights for improving SLP&D in Kenya.

Leadership preparation experience

The SLP&D experiences garnered included formal courses from accredited universities, structured but short needs-based courses offered by the MoE through KEMI and the national centre for curriculum development, inductions, informal learning through proxy and mentorship as they moved through ranks within the school systems. Most of the leaders (more than 60 per cent) attended structured but fragmented courses, workshops, seminars and meetings organized by either their employers, professional associations (e.g. the Kenya Primary School Heads Association – KEPSHA; the Secondary School Principals Association – KSSPA) or the GoK and their development partners. The GoK-sponsored and professional association initiatives were centralized according to areas of the jurisdictions within the education system. Leaders from very low-income private schools missed out on most opportunities because they were not part of the public school system and could not afford to pay the fees required for private entries. A majority (79.3 per cent) of the participants considered components of their teacher education programmes as playing a role in preparing them for school leadership. Table 6.1 has descriptions of the dominant experiences and the percentage of participants who responded to them.

Interviews revealed how school leaders considered their leadership preparation experience as including the deliberate actions they took to pursue scholarly credentials like graduate degrees, personal experiences associated with cultural practices and inspiration from spiritual teachings. They illuminated the leaders' preference for formal SLP&D credentials that blended academic and practice-based components. The leaders were also appreciative of the mentorship they received as they moved through the ranks. The interviews also revealed how family situations influenced decisions about taking up leadership positions and committing to SLP&D. Factors such as the age of their children and financial situation influenced decisions about if and when participants, mostly female, became leaders or engaged in certain SLP&D initiatives. These factors also determined where they chose to attend courses and the mode of SLP&D they preferred.

Perceived preparedness for leadership

More than 50 per cent of the participants agreed that they had been prepared for leadership in all the areas identified in the Likert scale (see Table 6.2), while more than 70 per cent of the participants agreed that they had been adequately prepared in 19 out of the 25 items on the scale (Okoko et al., 2015).

Findings in Table 6.2 indicate that leaders felt more prepared for visible daily roles in the school community rather than the aspects related to their personal growth and the bureaucratic demands of the school system. This could be because of the experience they gained as they moved through the ranks. Meanwhile the subjective aspects such as managing emotions, pressure from

Table 6.2 Adequacy of School Leadership Preparation

School leadership responsibilities	% agreement (N=116)
Working with teachers to solve problems/create positive environment	86.4
Initiating school improvement (improving teaching and learning)	85.3
Guiding curriculum and teaching/instruction	85.3
Managing staff appropriately (timetabling, matching teachers to class or subjects)	81.9
Building positive relationships with staff and parents	81
Working with teachers to change teaching methods where students are not succeeding (addressing teachers' poor performance)	79.3
Managing time	79.3
Engaging/working with parents and the community to support students	78.5
Feeling credible as a leader	77.6
Handling conflict (among teachers, students, parents, etc.)	76.7
Applying policies/guidelines and directives from the MoE	75.9
Fostering teachers' professional development/capacity (for knowledge and skills in teaching)	75
Developing and communicating school vision	74.1
Understanding the culture of the community which the school is located	74
Developing relationships within the community in which the school is located	73.3
Acquiring appropriate resources (books, facilities, equipment)	70.7
Adjusting to the isolation of the position	70.7
Helping teachers develop goals for their practice and professional learning	70.1
Managing paperwork (returns to Ministry and records)	68.1
Achieving a work and life (personal) balance	62.9
Handling the pressure of being judged by others in my day-to-day work	62.9
Managing school budget	56.4
Negotiating a balance between Ministry, TSC and school community demands	52.6
Getting access to staff and teachers you need	50.8

Source: J. M. Okoko, S. Scott, and D. Scott (2015) 'Perceptions of School Leaders in Nairobi about their Leadership Preparation and Development', *International Journal of Leadership in Education*, 18 (3): 288.

being judged, feeling credible and adjusting to isolation of the position were not areas they were required to account for. One interesting finding from the questionnaire data was that the participants rated most of the areas identified in Table 6.1 as problematic (Okoko et al., 2015). This was also evident in the gaps they identified in the existing SLP&D initiatives, which are discussed in the next section as insights for improvement.

Insights for improving school leadership preparation and development

As documented in Okoko (2018), insights from the findings revealed specific competencies, systemic gaps and personal realities that needed to be attended to as part of SLP&D. The insights are listed in Table 6.3 and are discussed subsequently.

Competencies

Gaps in leadership competencies were revealed in the challenges leaders faced when offering instructional support to teachers who were performing poorly. The examination-oriented nature of the school system made it more difficult for leaders to discourage ineffective pedagogical habits associated with teaching to the examinations. Offering instructional support was also expressed as a

Table 6.3 Features for Consideration

Features	Considerations
Competencies	Instructional support
	Financial management
	Human resource management
	Legal matters
	Project management
	Community engagement
	Policies and systemic procedures
	Personal leadership
Systemic gaps	Quality assurance /accreditation and licensure
	Selection of candidates and instructors for SLP&D
	Funding
Personal realities	Family commitments
	Financial constraints
	Job security

Source: J. M. Okoko (2018), 'Framing SLP&D for Kenya: Context Matters' (*Educational Management Administration and Leadership*, 2018, 1, p. 7).

concern in cases where leaders worked with teachers who had similar or higher teaching and academic qualifications.

Managing finance was perceived as critical because of the pressure emanating from the implications for job security of mismanaging funds. Many of the leaders considered the efforts of the existing SLP&D initiatives to provide skills in finance management as insufficient. The sentiments expressed included those of the leaders who used personal resources to pay consultants for support (Okoko, 2018). Determining the required human resources and the distribution of workload was a challenge that leaders encountered with both teaching and non-teaching staff. Leaders also mentioned the need for KSDs in handling legal matters as they described disputes about child rights, labour laws and conflicts with the community over school property. Competency in project management was highlighted as transferable to other school leadership responsibilities and therefore a necessary content area for SLP&D.

The leaders also felt unprepared to nurture and utilize relationships with the community to handle contextual issues related to poverty, gender, drug dependency, lack of discipline, insecurity and the effects of domestic violence. Additionally, the socio-economic status (SES) of the schools' communities influenced the SLP&D needs of the leaders. Those who served low-income communities sought KSDs for engaging with unwilling parents, while those serving middle and high-income communities sought KSDs for meeting the demands of highly educated parents who also had more sophisticated professional qualifications.

Competencies for negotiating controversial policies with communities and clear procedures for relaying ministerial policies and directives to school leaders were also identified as gaps in SLP&D. The controversial policies mentioned include requirements that pushed leaders to excessive enrolment and banned the practice that allowed students to repeat classes to raise schools' mean score in national examinations. These policies forced some leaders to succumb to pressure from parent and school owners for fear of losing their jobs. Clarifying procedures and the flow of directives were seen as ways to mitigate misleading information that was occasionally passed on to new leaders by their predecessors.

The need for competency in personal leadership revealed itself in respondents' feelings of fear resulting from job insecurity, lack of confidence and uncertainty about their own credibility, especially in cases where they engaged with peers and parents with higher qualifications. Nepotism and differences in political or tribal affiliation were also reported as creating a sense of insecurity for some leaders, as were issues of work–life balance.

Systemic gaps

Most of the leaders were in favour of having a standard for school leadership practice as a quality assurance measure. Prominent suggestions included accreditation and licensing of the school leadership practice, with periodic appraisal. These were seen as ways to provide credibility and assure quality to the practice. A strategic approach to selecting SLP&D courses' participants and instructors was also proposed as a way of enhancing the quality of practice. The proposals for participant selection were in favour of practitioners who held formal leadership positions (senior teachers, HoDs and deputy principals/head teachers). Regarding instruction, some of the leaders felt that school leadership courses offered in the academic institutions had instructors who did not have experience of working in schools. They stressed the need for instructors with both theoretical knowledge and practical experience in school leadership.

The way SLP&D was funded came up as an area that needed attention. The academic options were out of reach for many head teachers because of the cost implications from tuition and modes of delivery (Asuga et al., 2015; Okoko, 2018). The participants from private schools and low socio-economic groups could not access courses organized by KEMI and the MoE because of the required fees. Donor funding was also deemed as problematic because it was unreliable. Engaging communities in fundraising for SLP&D was an option that some of the leaders suggested.

Personal realities

Several aspects of SLP&D posed challenges to family and personal life, such as location and the costs incurred during training. Some short courses were held in locations that required long-distance travel and separation from families. The costs associated with travel and sustenance were reported as inhibiting. Family needs and priorities also hindered some leaders from committing to leadership and SLP&D, for instance, the aforementioned situations where the age of their children and the financial situation of the family determined if and when some participants became leaders or participated in SLP&D.

Implications for school leadership preparation and development in Kenya

The insights gained from the study have programme and contextual features that warrant consideration if Kenya is to have context-specific SLP&D. The programme-related features include modes of preparation, the competencies that SLP&D needs to cover, suitable candidates and funding. Contextual features include socio-economic differences and personal and systemic realities.

Modes and strategies

The leaders favoured formalizing SLP&D with a credential that blended academic and practice-based components, with mentorship as an expectation. Such a process would allow for a prescribed curriculum, as well as informal career development and reciprocal learning through mentorship (Crawford and Earley, 2011). However, mentors must be knowledgeable and skilled to avoid instances where new leaders rely on practices that are ill informed (Bush, 2010).

There is value in the non-academic SLP&D initiatives in Kenya (i.e. short courses, workshops, professional associations and induction), even though the quality of content and facilitation is not always guaranteed. Initiatives by employers and professional associations are viewed as opportunities for leaders to acquire competencies for emerging issues and job-specific challenges, whereas the experiences gained from movement through ranks and mentorship constitute a significant link between SLP&D and practice.

The uncertainty about quality and inconsistencies in the available options for SLP&D could be the reason for the leaders' strong push for regulation and clearer policies. Providers of SLP&D programmes should also watch for quality and coherence in the curriculum. This could be done by maintaining the link between modes of delivery and content and by ensuring that the modes and strategies align with contextual needs (Kitavi and van der Westhuizen, 1997; Onderi and Croll, 2008; Eacott and Asuga, 2014; Okoko, 2018).

Competencies

Leaders advocated for competencies in instructional leadership and managing needs associated with socio-economic diversity, politics, discipline and drug abuse. Along with these context-specific areas were generic components such as finance and human resources management, law, public relations, project management and policies related to community engagement and partnerships. These competencies can be learnt through SLP&D programmes where appropriate curriculum, modes and strategies are used in complementary ways to meet contextual needs (Earley and Jones, 2009; Osterman and Hafner, 2009).

The concern about limited opportunities and dissatisfaction with the capabilities of some of the appointees to school leadership and the beneficiaries of SLP&D could be mitigated if SLP&D were to target both aspiring and practising school leaders. Based on the findings, a higher academic qualification should not be the ultimate requirement for admission to SLP&D programmes because it locks out teachers who hold formal leadership positions within the ranks but may not have the requisite academic qualifications. Teachers who hold leadership positions (e.g. HoD/HoS, deputizing school leaders), if considered, would create pools from which schools could draw well-equipped leaders in the future. Nonetheless, a recent decree now requires the heads of public schools to have a bachelor's degree (Teacher Service Commission, 2018).

The suggestion about having instructors with field-based experience is feasible through collaboration and partnerships. Research and clinical activities provide opportunities for school and SLP&D institutions to collaborate in exposing instructors to the field (Darling-Hammond et al., 2010). Experienced school leaders could also be engaged as instructors or resource persons for SLP&D programmes.

Funding

The extent to which funding remains a challenge in accessing SLP&D is more pronounced among leaders who served private schools in low-income communities. This is mainly because they are not eligible for government subsidies. Degree programmes are also not affordable for most leaders, and yet a bachelor's degree has now become a minimum requirement (Teacher Service Commission, 2018). The unpredictable nature of donor funding had led some leaders to consider the potential of partnering with the community for fundraisers. Other suggestions included policies that embrace training as part of the school leadership appointment process and encouraging governments to allocate budgets for school leadership preparation.

Policy and standard

The competitive nature of the position is pushing leaders into taking courses that are not designed for school leadership as they seek ways of improving their qualifications and competences. As was expressed in the study, the quality and usefulness of the existing SLP&D initiatives are not guaranteed. Harmonizing the initiatives into a context-specific standard is a sensible option for assuring quality and providing oversight. Findings from the Okoko study point to the need for a standard that covers the structure, competencies, modes and strategies of SLP&D and the selection of course participants, as well as the licensing and accreditation of school leadership practitioners (Okoko, 2018).

Context

The Okoko study affirmed Hallinger's (2018) argument that the socio-cultural, economic and institutional context of a school shapes the type of leadership practice and the requisite SLP&D. In the case of Nairobi, those who serve well-off communities and international schools have access to targeted SLP&D in local and international universities. They also have professional development support from a more socio-economically able community. Those who serve middle to lower SES have some support from the community and have more access to both government and donor-funded SLP&D at a cost because they serve public schools. They tend to belong to and benefit from professional association and union SLP&D initiatives. Yet leaders from private schools in extremely poor communities, who need SLP&D most because of their lower academic and professional qualifications, do not have access to most opportunities. The variations in working conditions, parental and community engagement and the culture of the schools across SES, tribal context and location (rural, urban) also calls for varied competencies (Abaya, 2016; Okoko, 2018; Onderi and Croll, 2008).

Personal realities

Findings illuminated how personal realities influence pertinent leadership development decisions, such as when individuals taking up leadership positions, the modes and location of SLP&D initiatives that they choose to engage in and what counts as meaningful content. This was more evident among women who most times found it difficult to stay away from their families in pursuit of SLP&D. This finding affirmed the importance of family support in the success of African women in positions of educational leadership (Johnson, 2014). Personal realities also influence the sense of security, intra- and interpersonal competencies leaders need as they provide support and a conducive environment for teaching and learning (Gardner, 1983; Osterman and Hafner, 2009).

A framework towards the delivery of School Leadership Preparation and Development in Kenya

Previous studies, including Abaya (2016); Asuga and Eacott (2014); Onderi and Croll (2008); Onguko, Abdalla and Webber (2008); Wanzare and Ward (2000); and Kitavi and van der Westhuizen (1997) are in line with the five features advocated for by Okoko (2018) as fundamental in framing of SLP&D in Kenya, namely a) quality and consistency, b) contextual foci, c) accessibility, d) community engagement and partnerships, and e) accreditation. These features should manifest in the selection of SLP&D participants, competencies provided for in the curriculum, modes of preparation and delivery, funding and quality assurance. The features are illustrated (see Figure 6.1) and discussed in the following section.

Quality and consistency

Harmonizing and regulating the fragmented SLP&D initiatives can assure quality and consistency. The regulation should be within a contextualized standard that cover competencies and the quality of candidates recruited for

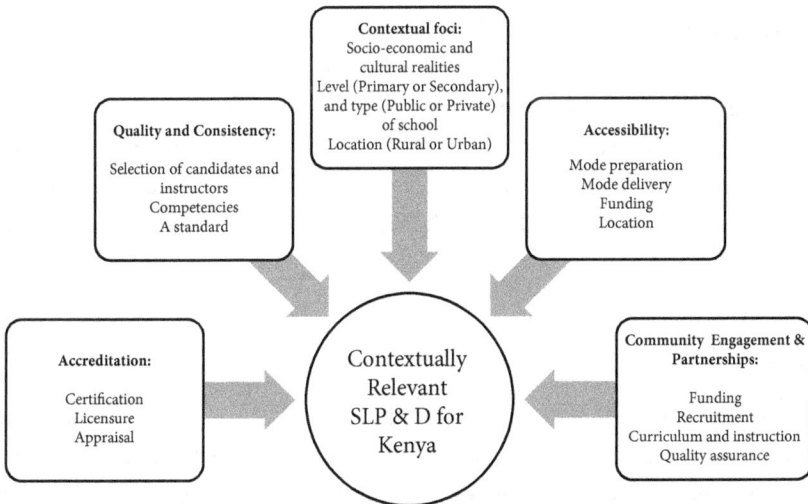

Figure 6.1 A contextually relevant framework for SLP&D in Kenya.

Source: J. M. Okoko (2018), 'Framing SLP&D for Kenya: Context Matters' (*Educational Management Administration and Leadership*, 1, p. 13).

SLP&D. The standard should equip leaders to nurture and work with the realities and potential within them, their communities and their education system. The standard ensure that leaders are equipped in the relevant leadership function (e.g. instructional leadership), as well as generic managerial competencies such as finance and human resource management, related law, policies and the emerging social, political and economic issues that affect schools (Osterman and Hafner 2009).

The criteria for selecting course participants and their instructors need to include academic qualifications, teaching and school leadership experience and personal attributes such as career aspirations and leadership potential (Darling-Hammond et al., 2010; Schleicher, 2012). This could be achieved through authentic means such as credible references, portfolios and personal statements.

Contextual foci

SLP&D initiatives need to accommodate all the daily realities that school leaders work with, their values, what they consider meaningful competencies and suitable SLP&D modes. This should include socio-cultural and individual value associated with gender roles, family and spiritual convictions. The realities associated with SES of the communities school leaders serve require context-specific competencies. For instance, KSD for managing issues related to poverty, parental engagement, discipline, drug abuse and family disputes vary in each community. Variations in types of school (public and private), levels of education (primary or secondary) and jurisdictions (rural and urban or conflict-prone areas) call for differences in SLP&D experience. The outcomes of SLP&D courses should match these contextual needs (Abaya, 2016; Kitavi and van der Westhuizen, 1997; Okoko, 2018; Onderi and Croll, 2008; Onguko, Abdalla and Webber, 2008).

Accessibility

Modes of preparation delivery and funding of SLP&D should be regulated to enhance access for all school leaders. This could be achieved by offering both academic and practitioner oriented learning that utilizes distance and online, onsite, in-service and pre-service modes of delivery. The frame should cover personal life situations such as family and aspirations, as well as the actions leaders take as individuals or as a collective towards SLP&D.

SLP&D should be accessible through certified programmes (degrees and short courses), formal and informal mentorship and experiences that use fora created by professional associations such as the KEPSHA, Kenya Secondary School Heads Association (KESSHA) and unions (Kenya National Union for Teachers). It should include approaches that accommodate those who may not be able to participate in cohorts due to financial, family or work-related commitments.

The sourcing of funds should encourage commitments from the participants themselves, school communities, employers/the government and other development partners. Since most of the funding for education is dependent on parents and communities, the Kenyan spirit of 'Harambee' (community fundraising) can be used to forge collaboration with the community for purposes of raising funds.

Community engagement and partnerships

The centralized nature of the school system in Kenya allows for institutions to collaborate and partner across government jurisdictions (divisional, county or national) and institutions (Universities and KEMI and schools). It also allows for coherence in SLP&D curriculum and quality assurance and paves the way for efficient recruitment of aspirants, affordable field experience, hiring and induction of new school leaders. As other studies have shown, such partnerships can also ensure that aspiring leaders are supported to develop as individuals and embrace professional growth (Darling-Hammond et al., 2010). The 'Harambee' culture can be utilized to develop SLP&D. Partnering with schools communities and experienced school leaders in field-based experiential activities such as internship, mentorship could mitigate the disconnect between SLPD initiatives and the reality in schools (Schleicher, 2012).

Accreditation

The centralized nature of the school system in Kenya also allows for a coherent accreditation process that can assure quality and standards for SLP&D. The process needs to be collaborative and could possibly engage a reputable institution with the capacity to constantly review SLP&D. Their mandate should include the certification, licensing and periodic assessment of school leaders. This proposal is attainable, considering the government's commitment to improving school leadership (Republic of Kenya, 2014, 2018).

Conclusion

It is evident from the existing SLP&D initiatives that the government and education practitioners in Kenya see the value of equipping school leaders for their work. However, there is no clear strategy towards attaining this goal. The existing options are fragmented and, in most cases, not context specific. This chapter highlights experiences that positional school-based leaders in Kenya consider as meaningful for their preparation and development, and it suggests insights for framing SLP&D for Kenya. It is based on a study that revealed opportunities that can be explored in delivering quality SLP&D. Potential lies in harmonizing the existing unregulated experiences, which include academic courses, components of teacher education, needs-based courses and workshops offered by the MoE and its development partners and mentorship through ranks. There are also opportunities in the gaps and suggestions provided for streamlining policies and procedures about the modes and strategies for delivering SLP&D, requisite context-specific competencies, selection of participants, funding and partnering with the community. The analysis of findings suggest that context-specific SLP&D could be achieved for Kenya if the framing of related policies and programmes focuses on the core elements of quality and consistency, contextual foci, accessibility, community engagement and partnerships and accreditation.

References

Abaya, J. (2016), 'School Leadership Challenges along Kenya's Borabu-Sotik Border', *Educational Management Administration and Leadership*, 44 (5): 757–74. doi: 10.1177/1741143214558581

Asuga G. and S. Eacott (2012), 'The Learning Needs of Secondary School Principals: An Investigation in Nakuru District', *Kenya International Journal of Education Administration and Policy Studies* 4 (5): 133–40. doi: 10.5897/IJEAPS11.073

Asuga, G., S. Eacott and J. Scevak (2015), 'School Leadership Preparation and Development in Kenya: Evaluating Performance Impact and Return on Leadership Development Investment', *International Journal of Educational Management*, 29 (3): 355–67, https://doi.org/10.1108/IJEM-10-2013-0158

Asuga, G. N. and S. Eacott (2014), 'School Leadership Preparation and Development in Kenya: Evaluating Performance Impact and Return on Leadership Development', *International Journal of Educational Management*, 29 (3): 355–67.

Bush, T. (2008), *Leadership and Management Development in Education*, London: Sage.

Bush, T. (2010), 'Leadership Development', in T. Bush, L. Bell and D. Middlewood (eds), *The Principles of Educational Leadership and Management*, 112–31, London: Sage.

Crawford, M. and P. Earley (2011), 'Personalised Leadership Development? Lessons from the Pilot NPQH in England', *Educational Review*, 63 (1): 105–18.

Darling-Hammond, L., D. Meyerson., M. LaPointe, M. Orr, and M. Barber, (2010), *Preparing Principals for a Changing World: Lessons from Effective School Leadership Programs*, New York: John Wiley & Sons.

Eacott, S. and G. N. Asuga (2014), 'School Leadership Preparation and Development in Africa: A Critical Insight', *Educational Management Administration and Leadership*, 42 (6): 919–34, http://dx.doi.org/10.1177/1741143214523013

Earley, P. and J. Jones (2009), 'Developing and Sustaining Leaders', in D. Brent (eds), *The Essentials of School Leadership*, 166–82, London: Sage.

Eshiwani, G. S. (1993), *Education in Kenya Since Independence*, Nairobi: East African Educational Publishers.

Gardner, H. (1983), *Frame of Minds: The Theory of Multiple Intelligence*, New York: Basic Books.

Goldring, G., J. Huff, J. H. May, and E. Camburn (2008), 'School Context and Individual Characteristics: What Influences Principals?' *Journal of Educational Administration*, 46 (3): 332–52.

Hallinger, P. (2018), 'Bringing Context Out of the Shadows of Leadership', *Educational Management Administration and Leadership*, 46 (1): 5–24.

Huber, S. (2004), *Preparing School Leaders for the 21st Century: An International Comparison of Development Programs in 15 Countries*, London: Routledge Falmer.

Johnson, A. T. (2014), 'Performing and Defying Gender: An Exploration of the Lived Experiences of Women Higher Education Administrators in Sub-Saharan Africa', *Educational Management Administration & Leadership*, 42 (6): 835–50.

Kitavi, M. and P. C. van der Westhuizen (1997), 'Problems Facing Beginning School Principals in Kenya', *International Journal of Educational Development*, 17 (13): 251–63.

Leithwood, K. (2007), 'What We Know about Successful School Leadership', in J. M. Burger, C. F. Webber and P. Klink (eds), *Intelligent Leadership: Construct for Thinking Educational*, 41–66, Dordrecht: Springer.

Ministry of Education Kenya (2018), 'Kenya Primary Education Development Project'. Available online: http://www.education.go.ke/index.php/programmes/kenya-primary-education-development-project (accessed 15 October 2018).

Nelson, S. W., M. G. De la Colina, and M. D. Boone (2008), 'Lifeworld or Systems World: What Guides Novice Principals?' *Journal of Educational Administration*, 46 (6): 690–701.

Okoko, J. M. (2018), 'Framing School Leadership Preparation and Development for Kenya: Context Matters', *Educational Management Administration and Leadership*, 1–18. Available online: https://doi.org/10.1177/1741143218792913 (accessed October 2018).

Okoko, J. M., S. Scott, and D. Scott (2015), 'Perceptions of School Leaders in Nairobi about Their Leadership Preparation and Development', *International Journal of Leadership in Education*, 18 (3): 279–304.

Onderi, H. and P. Croll (2008), 'In-Service Training Needs in an African Context: A Study of Head Teacher and Teacher Perspectives in the Gucha District of Kenya', *Journal of In-Service Education*, 34 (3): 361–73.

Onguko, B., M. Abdalla, and C. Webber (2008), 'Mapping Principal Preparation in Kenya and Tanzania', *Journal of Educational Administration*, 46 (6): 715–26.

Osterman, K. and M. Hafner (2009), 'Curriculum in Leadership Preparation: Understanding Where We Have Been in Order to Know Where We Might Go', in M. D. Young, G. M. Crow, and R. T. Ogawa (eds), *Handbook of Research on the Education of School Leaders*, 129–56, New York: Routledge Taylor & Francis Group.

Oywa, J. and E. Abuga (2018), 'Student Unrest Continues Unabated Standard Digital', 12 July. Available online: https://www.standardmedia.co.ke/article/2001287681/stud ent-unrest-continues unabated (accessed 15 August 2018).

Plano, V. and N. Ivankova (2016), *Mixed Methods : A Guide to the Field*, Los Angeles: Sage.

Republic of Kenya (2010), *Teachers Proficiency Course Manual*, Nairobi: Government Printers.

Republic of Kenya (2014), *National Education Sector Plan. Volume One: Basic Education Programme Rationale and Approach 2013/2014–2017/2018*. Available online: https://www.globalpartnership.org/content/education-sector-plan-2013-2018-kenya (accessed 15 August 2018).

Republic of Kenya (2017), *Laws of Kenya. Basic Education Act No.14 of 2013. The National Council for Law*. Available online: http://www.education.go.ke/index.php/ downloads/file/96-basic-education-act-no-14-of-2013 (accessed 4 August 2018).

Schleicher, A. (2012), 'Preparing Teachers and Developing School Leaders for the 21st Century: Lessons from Around the World', *OECD Publishing*. Available online http://dx.doi.org/10.1787/9789264174559-en (accessed 15 October 2018).

Teachers Service Commission (2018), 'Career Progression Guidelines for Teachers', May 10, Available online: https://www.tsc.go.ke/index.php/media centre/downloads/ category/97-career-progression-guidelines (accessed 4 August 2018).

Wanzare, Z. and K. Ward (2000), 'Rethinking Staff Development in Kenya: Agenda for the Twenty-First Century', *International Journal of Educational Management*, 14 (6): 265–75.

Waudo, J., M. Juma, A. Herriot, and C. Mwirotsi (2002), 'Head Teacher Support Groups Initiative with the Prism Project in Kenya', *East Africa Social Science Research Review*, 18 (1): 97–108.

Webber, C., K. Mentz, S. Scott, J. M. Okoko, and D. Scott (2014), 'A Cross-Cultural Analysis of Principals' Preparation in Kenya, South Africa and Alberta, Canada', *Journal of Organizational Change Management*, 27 (3): 499–519.

7

School Leadership Preparation in Tanzania

Mohammed Abdalla, Mweru Mwingi, Nicholas Wachira,
Janet Mola Okoko and Charles F. Webber

Introduction

There is consensus that educational leadership has a significant impact on learning outcomes in schools (Bush and Glover, 2014; Leithwood and Jantzi, 2008). This understanding is evident in Tanzania's long-term vision for education (Ministry of Education and Vocational Training, 2004; United Republic of Tanzania, 1999). Leadership preparation programmes offered by public and private colleges and universities aim to improve the quality of educational leadership in Tanzania, with the major providers being the University of Dar es Salaam, the Agency for the Development of Educational Management (ADEM), the Dar es Salaam University College of Education and the Aga Khan University Institute for Educational Development, East Africa.

Leadership preparation programmes in Tanzania range from academic degrees to diplomas to certificates and short courses. The training opportunities notwithstanding, most education leaders in Tanzania assume office without requisite leadership skills and, therefore, may not be in a position to execute their duties effectively (Onguko, Abdalla and Webber, 2012).

According to Kumba and Nkumbi (2008) and Lattus (2010), the mismanagement of resources, the inability by school leaders to motivate teachers and low student outcomes are concerns raised about the quality of educational leadership in Tanzania. Therefore, it is important for us to understand how school leaders are prepared and how that preparation influences their practice.

The following account offers insights into how educational leadership development programmes in Tanzania are structured and the extent to which they address leadership preparation needs. These insights are intended to inform educational stakeholders, including ministry of education personnel, leadership programme providers and researchers.

Context

School leadership preparation in Tanzania is undertaken in the context of increased demand for quality education, an unprecedented rise in student enrolment and a realization that school leadership plays a crucial role in determining student outcomes (UNESCO, 2010). While the *Declaration on Education for All*, adopted at the World Conference on Education for All in Jomtien, Thailand, in 1990 (UNESCO, 1990) contributed greatly to the expansion of education in Tanzania (Bongonko, 1992), the Musoma Resolution of 1974 was among the earliest changes introduced to accelerate access to education in Tanzania (Sabates, Westbrook and Hernadez-Fernade, 2012).

The population of Tanzania has more than doubled in the last three decades, from 25.4 million in 1990 to 59 million in 2018. There is also a significant 44 per cent of the population that is under the age of 15 (World Population Review, 2018). These demographic changes correspond to an increase in the number of primary and secondary schools (see Table 7.1).

Upsurge in demand for school leaders

Official policy requires that head teachers have a leadership qualification but, in practice, vacant positions are filled by promoting teachers based on their teaching experience (Kuluchumila, 2013). Kuluchumila (2013) found that a significant number of head teachers were promoted to the headship without prior experience in junior leadership positions. This highlights the potential challenges of the headship in the absence of adequate leadership preparation and underscores the need for training both for those currently in leadership positions and those seeking such positions.

Table 7.1 Number of Primary and Secondary Schools

Year	1990	2000	2003	2009	2013	2016
Primary	-	-	12,815	15,727	16,343	17,174
Secondary	365	927	1,083	4,102	4,576	4,759
Total	365	927	13,898	19,829	20,919	21,933

Sources: Government of Tanzania (2013), UNESCO (2010); United Republic of Tanzania (2016).

Policy provisions and mandate of school leaders

The management of education in Tanzania falls under various government ministries, the key ones being the Ministry of Education and Vocational Training (MoEVT) and the Prime Minister's Office of Regional Administration and Local Government (PMO-RALG). The PMO-RALG is in charge of operating pre-primary, primary and secondary schools. The MoEVT remains in charge of overall policy formulation, coordination, monitoring, standard-setting, quality assurance and quality control of educational leadership across the entire education system. Among the policies and regulations developed by MoEVT is a school leadership preparation guideline (Ministry of Education and Vocational Training, 2009) stipulating job descriptions for head teachers and education officers.

Tanzania provides for educational leadership development in various policy documents (e.g. Ministry of Education and Vocational Training, 2004), and preparation in terms of leadership knowledge, skills and values is required of those in headship:

> All education managers at national, regional, district and post-primary education and training institutions have a university degree, professional training in education and management, as well as appropriate experience. Education managers at ward and primary school levels have a certificate or diploma in education, as well as professional training in education management and administration from a recognized institution. (Ministry of Education and Culture, 1995: 29)

The policy assumes that leaders will be effective in their practice, which includes being 'responsible for the coordination of the planning, provision, management, administration and quality control of formal, informal and non-formal education and training in their areas of jurisdiction' (Ministry of Education and Culture, 1995: 30). In addition, they will comply with the job description of head teachers stipulated in the *Guidelines for School Supervision* (Ministry of Education and Vocational Training, 2009), including managing school resources, supervising curriculum implementation, managing relations among various school stakeholders, promoting staff development and conducting teachers' evaluations. Other responsibilities include addressing issues which relate to integration of information and communication technology, gender equality, special needs education and HIV and AIDS.

Conceptual overview

What follows is a description of educational leadership development programming offered in Tanzania by academic institutions and governmental agencies. The description highlights the dominant principles that underpin leadership development and their associated values. The organizational and theoretical infrastructure informing leadership development is also presented in relation to programming. As portrayed in Table 7.2, this report juxtaposes ideals related to the principles, values and infrastructure with the factors inhibiting the realization of those ideals.

For example, the formal and informal programming offered by public and private organizations in Tanzania is premised on the principle that school leaders strongly influence the levels to which students learn, teachers are effective, community expectations are met and government policies are implemented. Similarly, leadership development providers in Tanzania offer programmes that seek to be culturally and contextually relevant. However, application of the principles and achievement of ideals are influenced by inhibitors such as limited access to leadership development initiatives because of admission regulations, and by geographic and financial factors.

Educational leadership programmes in Tanzania manifest the belief that ethical professional practice is an ideal that they aspire to facilitate. It is clear that programme designers believe that educational leadership can be learnt. Nonetheless, several inhibitors stand in the way, including the long-standing practice of appointing head teachers based on primarily seniority, and the strong socialization processes within schools that cause head teachers to manifest behaviours contrary to academic theory and research.

Table 7.2 Conceptual Overview

	Ideals	Inhibitors
Principles	Leadership matters	Limited access
	Cultural relevance	Cultural borrowing
Values	Ethical professional practices	Appointment by seniority
	Leadership can be learnt	Socialization
Infrastructure	Instructional design drives engagement	Lectures endure
	Structured, systematic leadership preparation	Too few providers
	Continuous professional development	Admission requirements
	Rigorous theoretical base	Contextual relevance
	Official policy relevance	Inability to implement

Finally, this description of public and private programming underscores the theoretical, academic, pedagogical and policy ideals that shape the organizational and conceptual infrastructure for educational leadership development in Tanzania. It is evident that numerous inhibitors impact the infrastructure intended to support leadership development. Inhibitors include the enduring dominance of university lectures over active and engaged learning activities, too few providers relative to the demand for leadership preparation and admission requirements unsuited to the demographics of the intended clientele. Other inhibitors to infrastructure effectiveness are the too often weak relevance of leadership theory and research to the Tanzanian context and, finally, insufficient resources.

Review process

To understand school leadership preparation and development in Tanzania, a review of publicly available policy documents, course handbooks, research publications, websites and other leadership programme materials was undertaken. The information was considered within the following categories: programme provider, certification, aims, structure and mode of training, content, assessment, entry qualification and intended client. Analyses indicated that leadership preparation was embedded, to varying degrees, in pragmatic, competency-based and transformational leadership orientations.

Programming observations

Tanzania began to pay attention to educational leadership only in the last decade, and by 2008 there were only two major institutions providing educational leadership training, the Agency for the Development of Educational Management (ADEM) and the Aga Khan University Institute for Educational Development, East Africa (AKU-IED, EA), (Onguko, Abdalla and Webber, 2008). The number of providers has since increased, but the capacity of these institutions remains inadequate to meet the need that exists for trained school leaders.

Programme providers and clients

In recent years, there has been an increase in the number of educational leadership programme providers. In the public sector, ADEM is the main provider of educational leadership training in Tanzania. It is publicly funded, and its remit is to provide training for teachers, head teachers, school inspectors and district educational officers at zonal and district levels. Other key players in the public sector are the University of Dar es Salaam School of Education (UDSM), the Dar es Salaam University College of Education (DUCE) and, in the private sector, the AKU-IED, EA.

Collectively, these universities offer educational leadership training at the certificate, diploma, baccalaureate and postgraduate degree levels. UDSM and DUCE provide both pre-service and in-service training, while AKU-IED, EA and ADEM mainly target educators who are already in leadership positions (see Dar es Salaam University College of Education, 2018; University of Dar es Salaam, 2017, 2018). Both AKU-IED, EA and ADEM require that one should have at least two years of teaching experience for certificate courses and, for the diploma offered by ADEM, a teaching certificate and an undergraduate or graduate degree are required (Aga Khan University, Institute for Educational Development, East Africa, 2016a; Agency for the Development of Educational Management, 2018). The advantage of training for practising educators is that it enables programme participants to apply their learning to their professional practice. The disadvantage, however, is that participants, while training, are subject to ongoing socialization from peers who may support practices that are inconsistent with theory and research guiding their training. Leadership preparation training targets all head teachers and teachers, but it is common that those from rural areas are disadvantaged in terms of access.

A baseline study in six districts in Tanzania by Pettersson et al. (2015) found that only 10 per cent of primary school teachers had completed Form 6 (two years of advanced level secondary education) while 76 per cent had a Form 4 (four years of ordinary secondary level education) qualification while the remaining 14 per cent had only completed primary schooling. The presence of primary school graduates teaching primary school indicates that there may well be head teachers in primary schools with only a primary or secondary school education. While females comprise more than half of all teachers (55 per cent), only 16 per cent of head teachers in the study were female (Pettersson et al., 2015).

Programme structure and mode of training, aims, content and assessment

Training programmes in Tanzania are somewhat similar and reflect generic educational leadership content. Common content includes leadership and management concepts and resource management, plus administrative processes such as planning, coordination, communication, decision-making, problem solving and delegating.

Most of the programmes studied seem not to include content that addresses challenges widespread in Africa, such as curricula inherited from developed countries, population density, insufficient civil services, dramatic increases in demand for schooling, the rise of large cities with extensive populations living in unplanned informal settlements and widespread poverty (Wolhuter, Walt and Steyn, 2016). It is therefore imperative that leadership preparation programmes be both comprehensive and contextually relevant in terms of content to sufficiently equip leaders to deal with additional issues commonly encountered, such as gender inequality (Okkolin, Lehtomäki and Bhalalusesa, 2010), sexual exploitation and early pregnancies (McClealry-Sills et al., 2013) and special needs education (Tungaraza, 1994, 2014). Sexual exploitation and early pregnancies are endemic in both primary and secondary education in Tanzania. Mbelwa and Isangula (2012) noted that girls as young as ten years old engage in sexual activities. In 2012 alone, a total of 4,866 girls dropped out of primary and secondary schools in Tanzania because of pregnancy (United Republic of Tanzania, 2014).

The impact of the content in leadership training programmes is enhanced when the structure and mode of training engages programme participants. Leadership development providers in Tanzania all have face-to-face modes of delivery varying from 3 to 36 weeks. Postgraduate programmes require students to complete a dissertation. The AKU-IED, EA master's programme includes a four-week practicum. For undergraduate programmes, UDSM and DUCE widely use lectures and seminars. ADEM diploma and certificate programmes (Agency for the Development of Educational Management, 2018) similarly utilize lectures and seminars.

The aim of the above programmes is to develop leadership competencies, and so leadership programmes should engage participants beyond seminars and lectures. Well designed and meaningful practica with feedback should be central in school leadership preparation programmes. A balance between content, teaching activities and assessment practices is equally important if such programmes are to achieve their aim of developing leaders who are equipped to improve schools and enhance student learning outcomes.

Programme delivery and pedagogy in competencies development

The role of programme delivery is crucial if leadership development programme beneficiaries are to acquire envisioned knowledge, skills, competencies and values. Scott (2015) underscored the significance of participatory pedagogy, instead of lecturing and memorization, in the development of competencies. The review of the leadership development programmes conducted for this report showed that most of the programmes are of short duration and so the supervised transfer and reinforcement of learning is absent. The application of learning to context therefore is not guaranteed as training recipients apply to their context what they deem fit, but such application also depends on how practical the training was. AKU-IED, EA, through its three-tiered programme structure, offers course participants both theoretical and practical training in its six-month certificate course.

In the first tier, course participants learn about the basics of leadership and management theory, current critical issues in education and the principles and application of action research through face-to-face training. The second tier is the practicum phase where course participants undertake action research, which requires them to transfer and apply theory to practice over 3–4 months. Practica are monitored and supported and contain structures for peer support, wherein course participants from cluster schools meet once a month to discuss their successes and challenges with the implementation of action research. In addition, there is an online group offering virtual support plus two face-to-face workshops during the practicum. In the third tier, which is delivered face-to-face, learning from practice is consolidated and skills on planning, monitoring and evaluation are taught for the sustainability of change initiatives and the transformation process. Training includes the use of active pedagogy like cooperative learning strategies, presentations by course participants, reflective dialogue, interactive lectures, small-group and whole-class discussions, brainstorming and role plays (Aga Khan University, Institute for Educational Development, East Africa, 2016b, 2017b,c).

Programme entry qualifications and certification

Educational leadership preparation providers offer courses at certificate, diploma, undergraduate and postgraduate degree levels. Some are for professional development programmes and are not tied to a particular academic entry qualification.

Certificate

The minimum entry qualification into a certificate programme offered by ADEM is four years of secondary education, better known as an 'O' level certificate; a Grade 'A' teaching certificate, which is college-level training experience; and three years of teaching experience. In contrast, AKU-IED, EA requires a minimum of two years working experience. Leadership preparation for leaders without a professional qualification is more accessible in an AKU-IED, EA programme, which considers for admission those head teachers who may have no 'O' level certificate or Grade A teaching certificate.

Diploma

The minimum entry qualification into the diploma programme offered by ADEM is an 'O' level certificate and a certificate in education leadership and management. These mandatory entry requirements make leadership entry into the diploma programme a challenge.

Undergraduate degree

The minimum entry qualification into the degree programme offered by DUCE is six years of secondary education, better known as 'A' level or an equivalent qualification such as a diploma. The degree programme, compared to the diploma and certificate, has the smallest number of participants in Tanzania because the major leadership development providers, except for DUCE, do not currently offer undergraduate degree programmes. ADEM plans to introduce a bachelor's degree in education leadership, management and quality assurance.

Postgraduate degree

UDSM and AKU-IED, EA provide postgraduate degrees in education leadership and management (Aga Khan University, Institute for Educational Development, East Africa, 2016a; Aga Khan University, Institute for Educational Development, East Africa, 2017a; University of Dar es Salaam, 2018). The entry qualifications include a bachelor's degree, and AKU-IED, EA requires at least two years of relevant work experience. The postgraduate educational leadership programme is inaccessible to the majority of teachers and educational leaders in Tanzania because they lack the entry qualification.

This also implies that the majority of educational practitioners are constrained by policy from occupying leadership positions at the national, regional, district and post-primary education and training institutions levels, which require entrants to possess a university degree and professional training in education and management, as well as appropriate experience (Ministry of Education and Culture, 1995).

Orientations of leadership preparation

A leadership orientation is a position taken on what leadership is and how it is executed. It is a covert meaning-making system that influences the form, design and delivery of leadership preparation (Bolman and Deal, 1990, 2013). Meaning-making is informed by how providers perceive leadership and relate it to practice, success and outcomes. This positioning shapes and defines leadership preparation programme priorities, content and pedagogy. Three major leadership preparation models or orientations – the efficiency model, competency model and transformational model – appear to have been adopted in preparing school leaders in Tanzania (see Table 7.3).

The pragmatic model

Pragmatic leadership development focuses mainly on how leaders achieve institutional goals efficiently. Pragmatism in leadership is about setting specific targets and objectives, trying to avoid uncertainty, doing what is possible and ensuring that what is planned is done (Meyer and Meijersm, 2017; Mumford et al., 2008). This model focuses more on supervision, appraisal, control and direction-setting. The emphasis is on teaching leaders how to make sure that institutional goals are achieved. The pragmatic mode of training emphasizes content on institutional vision, mission, goals and objectives; financial and other resource management; office and records management; educational statistics; planning and job descriptions. The structure and orientation of this model aligns with the head teachers' job description in the School Supervision Guidelines (Ministry of Education and Vocational Training, 2009).

The pragmatic model assumes that all that is encapsulated in school leadership and schools is known – the context, the system, the tasks, the policies and the roles and responsibilities. Thus, the training model is directed towards assisting leaders to fit effectively in the known contexts and to accomplish the prescribed policies, tasks, roles and responsibilities. Consequently, this model may be less responsive to changing contexts and needs. It focuses more on the managerial aspects of bringing stability to institutions. Helping school leaders to maintain stability and to deal with the known should be seen as strengths of the pragmatic models, as in leadership, 'there are practices that are likely to remain constant' (Drysdale and Gurr, 2017: 131). However, preparing school leaders to deal with only maintaining stability and dealing with the known is inadequate because 'the capabilities that underpin these practices can change' (Drysdale and Gurr, 2017: 131). Moreover, school leadership is a changing landscape shaped by

Table 7.3 Summary of the Three Types of Leadership

Model	Focus	Assumptions and values	Required knowledge and skills
Pragmatic	Adherence to efficiency, institutional structural requirements and management systems Focus on functions, tasks and behaviours	Establishment of structures and management systems critical to leadership Commitment and adherence to systems required Facts, analysis and data highly valued	Management of systems and knowledge of job descriptions Institutional vision, mission, goals and objectives Finance and resource management, planning
Competency	Leader equipped to perform duties and develop skills in others	Leadership is about empowerment Development of competencies results in effective leadership and productivity Self-development and competences valued	Human resource management, continued learning, team building, communication, networking and decision-making
Transformational	Leader equipped to initiate change and develop others' knowledge, skills and values	Leadership is about embracing change Integrity, inclusion, fairness, and justice Loyalty to change process valued	Change management, critical thinking, problem solving, practitioner research Visioning, monitoring and evaluating

constant changes and challenges in both the internal and external environments (Leithwood and Riehl, 2005). A pragmatic orientation to school leadership preparation is inclined to the management of schools; however, while it empowers school leaders to execute their formal management roles, it falls short of equipping them with the skills required to continually improve their schools.

The competency model

The competency model tends to focus on developing essential leadership competencies such as a set of related knowledge, skills and attitudes that enable one to be effective in undertaking one's leadership role (Spencer and Spencer, 1993).

Though the content is similar to that in the pragmatic model, the competencies are not tagged necessarily to head-teacher job descriptions. Rather, leadership is assumed to be most effective when the leader has competencies to harness resources, particularly human resources. This model emphasizes the importance of people and endorses the view that a good fit between people working together is important to the overall success of the leader and the organization (Tucker and Au, 2016). A good leader is one who is both facilitator and participative manager, as well as supportive and empowering of others. Coaching, participation, motivation, teamwork and good interpersonal relations are key in this model.

The overall goal of training within the competency model is to shape participants' behaviour so they can act in ways that demonstrate competencies necessary for effective performance. Such training is premised on the belief that the behaviour of individuals is strongly related to their levels of competency, and so if they are trained to take up certain behaviours, then their competencies will be improved and workplace productivity will rise. Critical reflection and action research constitute important programme content. Other aspects emphasized in the competency model include communication, networking, listening and decision-making skills.

The postgraduate programmes reviewed had the highest level of competency-related approach in the preparation of educational leaders, while the certificate courses had the lowest. This suggests that while development of skills may be a focus for leadership training in Tanzania, the focus on real-life skills development is situated in the diploma, degree and masters programmes, all of which are not easily accessible to the majority of teachers and educational leaders because of entry qualifications.

The transformational model

The transformational model of leadership preparation focuses on empowering and equipping programme participants to encourage, inspire and motivate their followers to engage with change. This assumes that leadership is about continuously initiating change and managing it by motivating followers to adopt and accept the change (Leithwood and Beatty, 2007). Transformational leadership is about leaders facilitating positive change among followers and creating environments whereby they take care of each other's interests and work for the interests of the whole group and institution. It is about engaging followers for self-development and greater-than-expected accomplishments through changing their attitudes, values and beliefs and aligning them with those of the organization (Bass, 1998; Bass and Avolio, 1994). Content is focused on reflecting on their leadership practice, identifying interventions for school improvement, team building, planning for managing change and change management.

The underlying assumption for this model is that leaders need consistently to improve their schools. The goals, aims, objectives and content of leadership preparation programming in Tanzania suggest that both certificate and master's qualifications contain the highest number of approaches associated with the transformational model. While the transformational approach was found across all leadership preparation programmes, it is at the certificate level where there is focus on change management through, for example, mentoring and peer coaching, monitoring and evaluation.

A transformational orientation within leadership programmes assumes preparation of leaders for change, innovation and versatility. With new schools being established throughout Tanzania because of educational expansion, there are teachers being appointed as head teachers with minimal teaching experience and little or even no leadership experience.

Informal leadership preparation

Most educational leadership preparation in Tanzania begins as informal, workplace-embedded learning. Onguko, Abdalla and Webber (2012) and Kuluchumila (2014) noted that informal preparation of educational leaders is too often ad hoc and unstructured. While such modes of preparation allow for the immediate transfer of what is learnt to actual practice, the disadvantage is that the leader is restricted to what the role model or mentor knows and does.

Bierne, Titka, Cerkovskis and Lasmane (2017) underscored the need for alignment of course components for meaningful development of competencies to occur. The programmes all aim to equip leaders to take on challenges. However, for the majority of the programmes, the course structure, content, mode of delivery and assessment seem insufficiently relevant to the knowledge, skills and values requisite for leadership transformation in Tanzanian schools.

Discussion and implications

The context of professional development in Tanzania is under resourced. Despite there being policy support for the development of school leaders, progress is slow regarding the number of training providers and the scope of training. There is little on offer for aspiring school leaders when most are left to learn how to lead on their own or on the job. Yet, for decades, school leaders have been expected to thrive in challenging circumstances such as those found in developing countries (Ngcobo and Tikly, 2010; Retallick, 2009). The development of a successful repertoire of school leadership knowledge, skills and values is continuous and is drawn from job experience but, more importantly, from training that is both consistent and relevant. The leadership development programmes currently offered in Tanzania demonstrate that there are divergent perceptions of school leadership, which, in effect, determines how school leaders are trained. In an environment with inadequate resources for implementing professional development that effectively supports official policy, the form, structure and content of school leadership training is determined largely by the providers of the training.

Tanzania has official education policies that are supportive of the preparation and continued professional development of head teachers (HakiElimu, 2005). However, Kumba and Nkumbi (2008) reported that professional development was not an area that was given a strategic emphasis by institutions responsible for professional development in Tanzania. For example, AKU-IED, EA leadership development programming indicates that the training was the first of its kind for the school leaders who attended, despite all of them having at least two years of experience in school leadership positions (Onguko, Abdalla and Webber, 2012).

Soko (2014) argued that initial teacher education is never enough to equip teachers with the necessary knowledge and skills for teaching. Therefore, continuous professional development is necessary for improving practice. Further, Soko (2014) found a disconnect between the knowledge and skills leaders had and what they actually required. There is high demand for leadership training for master's degree programmes in education leadership and management in Tanzania, but there are few providers. Other leadership development offerings vary in terms of content, outcomes and duration. Ad hoc training does not suffice to support continuous leadership development.

In summary, despite an increase in the number of providers of leadership preparation programmes, the dominant mode of acquiring leadership skills and knowledge, especially for new appointees or those who are not yet in leadership positions, is informal and school based. Pragmatics dominate, as leaders want to be equipped with skills that enable them to function in their lines of duty. Practicality includes learning how to improve communication with staff or to establish a school feeding programme or an income-generating project. Such learning is specific to the context of Tanzania, and it is informal in how it is communicated and acquired. Currently, informal training holds promise for leadership development in Tanzania because it is schoolbased, accessible and low-cost.

Conclusion

Further study of school leadership preparation and its impact on leadership practice in Tanzania is needed. Sound data are required to inform current practice and policy decision-making. With free primary and secondary education, practitioners and policy-makers in Tanzania know that an increase in school enrolment and the number of schools is under way. This means that it is imperative that there be more providers of programming at certificate and diploma levels which is the level accessible to existing and aspiring leaders.

Existing policy is supportive of the professional development of school leaders but requires the support of expanded avenues for leadership development, including informal school-based training. The integration of ICT into leadership preparation initiatives would enhance the learning of ICT skills, which, for many leaders in this context, are underdeveloped. Such a relatively low-cost design would expand accessibility in remote areas, making it a sustainable model of continuous learning for school leaders.

An ongoing concern about the content of school leadership preparation programming is the application of theory to leadership practice. Courses that are practical by design address the urgent knowledge and skills gaps that currently exist among school leaders in Tanzania, and leadership development providers should emphasize pragmatics in the design of leadership courses. In particular, the use of the case study is recommended, as this method can help to present course participants with real-life scenarios whereby they can apply and integrate knowledge, skills, theories and experience. The case study or problem-based approach promotes critical thinking and decision-making, helping current and aspiring school leaders to understand and solve complex issues and equipping them with the skills needed to execute day-to-day duties in informed and strategic ways. In addition, school-based projects that are embedded in action research allow leaders to engage with and interrogate an array of critical issues such as teacher truancy, resource management, large classes, gender equality, inclusion, special needs education and even the impact of HIV and AIDS on teachers and learners.

References

Aga Khan University, Institute for Educational Development, East Africa (2016a), *Master of Education*, Dar es Salaam: AKU-IED, EA. Available online: https://www.aku.edu/iedea/academics/Pages/m-ed.aspx

Aga Khan University, Institute for Educational Development, East Africa (2016b), *Certificate in Educational Leadership and Management Course Handbook*, Dar es Salaam: AKU-IED, EA.

Aga Khan University, Institute for Educational Development, East Africa (2017a), *Graduate Programmes Student Handbook*, Dar es Salaam: AKU-IED, EA. Available online: https://www.aku.edu/admissions/Documents/graduate-handbook.pdf

Aga Khan University, Institute for Educational Development, East Africa (2017b), *Educational Leadership in Practice Course Handbook*, Dar es Salaam: AKU-IED, EA.

Aga Khan University, Institute for Educational Development, East Africa (2017c), *Educational Leadership Course Handbook*, Dar es Salaam: AKU-IED, EA.

Agency for the Development of Educational Management (2018), *Invitations for Application*. Available online: https://shulezetu.or.tz/agency-development-educati onal-management-adem-invitatons-applications/

Bass, B. M. (1998), *Transformational Leadership: Industry, Military, and Educational Impact*, Mahwah: Erlbaum.

Bass, B. M. and B. J. Avolio (1994), 'Introduction', in B. M. Bass and B. J. Avolio (eds), *Improving Organizational Effectiveness through Transformational Leadership*, 1–9, Thousand Oaks: Sage Publications.

Bierne, J., J. Titka, E. Cerkovskis, and A. Lasmane (2017), 'Advanced Teaching Methods for Students' Competencies Development', *Society Integration Education*, 1: 63–72.

Bogonko, S. N. (1992), *Reflections on Education in East Africa*, Nairobi: Oxford University Press.

Bolman, L. G. and T. E. Deal (1990), *Leadership Orientations Instrument*, San Francisco: Jossey-Bass.

Bolman, L. G. and T. E. Deal (2013), *Reframing Organizations: Artistry, Choice and Leadership*, 5th edn, San Francisco: Jossey-Bass.

Bush, T. and D. Glover (2014), 'School Leadership Models: What Do We Know?' *School Leadership & Management*, 34 (5): 553–71.

Dar es Salaam University College of Education (2018), *Dar es Salaam University College of Education: A Constituent College of the University of Dar es Salaam*, Dar es Salaam: DUCE. Available online: https://duce.ac.tz/

Drysdale, L. and D. Gurr (2017), 'Leadership in Uncertain Times', *International Studies in Educational Administration*, 45 (2): 131–59.

Government of Tanzania (2013), *Basic Education Statistics (BEST)*, Dar es Salaam: Government Printers.

HakiElimu (2005), *Three Years of PEDP Implementation: Key Findings from Government Reviews*, Dar Es Salaam: HakiElimu. Available online: http://www.tzonline.org/pdf/threeyearsofpedpimplementation.pdf

Kuluchumila, R. C. (2013), 'The Implementation of Secondary Education Development Planning Tanzania: A Case Study Of Community Secondary School Heads in Shinyanga', *Journal of Education and Practice*, 14 (12): 198–216.

Kuluchumila, R. C. (2014), 'Preparation and Development of Secondary School Heads: What Should Be Done in Tanzania?' *British Journal of Education and Practice*, 2 (2): 9–39. Available online: http://www.eajournals.org/wp-content/uploads/Preparatio n-and-Development-of-Secondary-School-Heads.pdf

Kumba, W. L. and E. Nkumbi (2008), 'Teacher Professional Development in Tanzania: Perceptions and Practices', *Journal of International Cooperation in Education*, 11 (3): 67–83.

Lattus, A. (2010), '"Quiet Corruption" Undermining African Development', *DW: Made for Minds*, 18 March. Available online: https://www.dw.com/en/quiet-corrupt ion-undermining-african-development/a-5365508

Leithwood, K. and B. Beatty (2007), *Living with Teachers' Emotions in Mind*, Thousand Oaks, CA: Corwin.

Leithwood, K. and C. Riehl (2005), 'What We Know about Successful School Leadership', in W. Firestone and C. Riehl (eds), *A New Agenda: Directions for Research on Educational Leadership*, 22–47, New York: Teachers College Press.

Leithwood, K. and D. Jantzi (2008), 'Linking Leadership to Student Learning: The Contributions of Leader Efficacy', *Education Administration Quarterly*, 44 (4): 496–528. Available online: https://doi.org/10.1177/0013161X08321501

Mbelwa, C. and K. G. Isangula (2012), 'Teen Pregnancy: Children Having Children in Tanzania', *SSRN Electronic Journal*, DOI: 10.2139/ssrn.2028369. Available online: https://www.researchgate.net/publication/255699050_Teen_Pregnancy_Children_ Having_Children_in_Tanzania

McClealry-Sills, J., Z. Douglas, A. Rwehumbiza, A. Hamisi, and R. Mabala (2013), 'Gendered Norms, Sexual Exploitation and Adolescent Pregnancy in Rural Tanzania', *Reproductive Health Matters*, 21 (41): 97–105.

Meyer, R. and R. Meijers (2017), *Leadership Agility: Developing Your Repertoire of Leadership Styles*, Rotterdam: Center for Strategy and Leadership. Available online: https://www2.deloitte.com/content/dam/Deloitte/nl/Documents/humancapital/de loitte-nl-hc-leadership-agility-summary-booklet.pdf

Ministry of Education and Culture (1995), *Education and Training Policy*, Dar es Salaam: Government Printers.

Ministry of Education and Vocational Training (2004), *Secondary Education Development Plan (SEDP): 2004–2009*, Dar es Salaam: Government Printers. Available online: http://www.tzonline.org/pdf/educationsectordevelopmentprogra mme2009.pdf

Ministry of Education and Vocational Training (2009), *Guidelines for School Supervision*. Available online: http://www.tzdpg.or.tz/fileadmin/documents/dpg_int ernal/dpg_working_groups_clusters/cluster_2/education/School_Supervision_gu idelines.doc

Mumford, M. D., A. L. Antes, J. J. Caughron, and T. L. Friedrich (2008), 'Charismatic, Ideological, and Pragmatic Leadership: Multi-Level Influences on Emergence and Performance', *The Leadership Quarterly*, 19: 144–60.

Ngcobo, T. and L. P. Tikly (2010), 'Key Dimensions of Effective Leadership in Change: A Focus on Township and Rural Schools in South Africa', *Educational Management, Administration and Leadership*, 38 (2): 202–8.

Okkolin, M., E. Lehtomäki, and E. Bhalalusesa (2010), 'The Successful Education Sector Development in Tanzania – Comment on Gender-Balance and Inclusive Education', *Gender and Education*, 22 (1): 63–71. DOI:10.1080/09540250802555416

Onguko B., M. Abdalla, and C. F. Webber (2008), 'Mapping Principal Preparation in Kenya and Tanzania', *Journal of Educational Administration*, 46 (6): 715–26.

Onguko B., M. Abdalla, and C. F. Webber (2012), 'Walking in Unfamiliar Territory: Headteachers' Preparation and Experiences in Their First Year in Tanzania', *Educational Administration Quarterly*, 48 (1): 86–115.

Pettersson, G., G. Rawle, R. Outhred, S. Brockerhoff, G. Wills, D. Nugroho, P. Jasper, A. Kveder, and A. Beavis (2015), *Impact Evaluation of Education Quality Improvement Programme in Tanzania: Final Baseline Technical Report*, Dar es Salaam: EQUIP-Tanzania.

Retallick, J. (2009), 'Successful Schools: What Can We Learn from Them?' in R. Qureshi and F. Shamim (eds), *Schools and Schooling Practices in Pakistan: Lessons for Policy and Practice*, 188–210, Karachi: Oxford University Press.

Sabates, R., J. Westbrook, and J. Hernadez-Fernade (2012), 'The 1977 Universal Primary Education in Tanzania: A Historical Base for Quantitative Enquiry', *International Journal of Research & Method in Education*, 35 (1): 55–70.

Scott, C. L. (2015), *The Futures of Learning 3: What Kind of Pedagogies for the 21st Century?* Paris: UNESCO. Available online: http://unesdoc.unesco.org/images/00 24/002431/243126e.pdf

Soko, M. V. (2014), *Professional Development: Experiences Among Primary School Teachers in Tanzania*, Åbo: Åbo Akademi University Press.

Spencer, S. M. and L. M. Spencer (1993), *Competence at Work: Models for Superior Performance*, New York: John Wiley and Sons.

Tucker, J. and A. Au (2016), 'New Competency Leadership Theory', *International Journal of Advanced Educational Research*, 1 (4): 1–5. Available online: http://www .educationjournal.org/download/34/1-3-18-972.pdf

Tungaraza, F. D. (1994), 'The Development and History of Special Education in Tanzania', *International Journal of Disability, Development and Education*, 41 (3): 213–22.

Tungaraza, F. D. (2014), 'The Arduous March Toward Inclusive Education in Tanzania: Head Teachers and Teachers' Perspectives', *Africa Today*, 61 (2): 108–23.

UNESCO (1990), *World Declaration on Education for All: Framework for Action to Meet Basic Learning Needs*, Paris: Paris: United Nations Educational, Scientific and Cultural Organization. Available online: http://unesdoc.unesco.org/images/0012/00 1275/127583e.pdf

UNESCO (2010), *World Data on Education: VII Ed. 2010/11: United Republic of Tanzania*, Paris: United Nations Educational, Scientific and Cultural Organization.

Available online: http://www.ibe.unesco.org/fileadmin/user_upload/Publications/ WDE/2010/pdf-versions/United_Republic_of_Tanzania.pdf

United Republic of Tanzania (1999), *The Tanzania National Development Vision 2025*, Dar es Salaam: Office of the President and the Planning Commission, Government Printer. Available online: http://www.mof.go.tz/mofdocs/overarch/vision2025.htm

United Republic of Tanzania (2016), *Basic Education Statistics in Tanzania (BEST)*, Dar es Salaam: Government Printer.

University of Dar es Salaam (2017), *Postgraduate Prospectus for the Academic Year 2017/2018*. Available online: https://postgraduate.udsm.ac.tz/index.php/prospect us-2012-2014-2015.html?download=83:postgraduate-prospectus

University of Dar es Salaam (2018). *Admission into Postgraduate Programmes for 2018/2019 Academic Year*. Available online: http://www.udbs.udsm.ac.tz/images/D ocs/pg_courses_2018_19.pdf

Wolhuter, C., H. van der Walt, and H. Steyn (2016), 'A Strategy to Support Educational Leaders in Developing Countries to Manage Contextual Challenges', *South African Journal of Education*, 36 (4): 1–9. DOI: 10.15700/saje.v36n4a1297

World Population Review (2018), *Tanzania Population 2018*. Available online: http:// worldpopulationreview.com/countries/tanzania-population/

8

Leadership and Management Preparation and Development of School Leaders in Cameroon

Frederick Ebot-Ashu

Introduction

The 52 years that have passed since the independence of Cameroon have seen an increasing international interest in leadership development courses and programmes for school leaders. The idea of intervening to develop the leadership and management ability of school leaders derives from two core beliefs which now have wide international currency. The first of these is that the quality of leadership makes a significant difference to the effectiveness of both schools and educational systems by deepening the knowledge, expertise and behaviours of school leaders (Ebot-Ashu, 2014).

This belief that schools require effective leaders if they are to provide the best possible educational opportunities is common across both developed and developing countries and goes hand-in-hand with a concern about perceived leadership inadequacies among school leaders. The model for addressing these inadequacies is underpinned by the second core belief, namely, that the personal professional learning of leaders (Ebot-Ashu, 2014) is a fundamental precondition for the creation of a learning community (Day, 2001; Weindling, 2003; Lumby, Crow and Pashiardis, 2008).

This chapter will explore this belief that schools require effective leaders if they are to provide the best possible educational opportunities (Ebot-Ashu, 2014). Indeed, a 1996 report by the Commonwealth Secretariat showed that there is broad international agreement about the need for schools and educational systems to enhance their capacity to improve the development of schools and school leaders. However, proponents of investment in leadership and management development in an education context, especially in developing countries, where needs are most acute and yet resources and global engagement are most scarce, often lack direct empirical evidence for the effectiveness of such training.

The chapter provides an overview of current scholarship with respect to the importance of school leadership and management training. It draws in particular on a recent study in Cameroon, which sought to address the need for the central educational systems and communities to enhance their capacity in order to improve the development of schools and school leaders (Ebot-Ashu, 2014). There has been a clear trend towards the adoption of formal management and leadership training programmes for school leaders and, as Ebot-Ashu (2014) has recently predicted, expenditure on school leadership development will continue to grow throughout the next decade as still more educational systems recognize the shortage of talented leaders and the need to broaden viewpoints in order to compete globally (Hallinger and Heck, 1999). In respect to Cameroon and many other African countries, however, the provision of leadership education still lags far behind the demand for that education among aspiring school leaders (Ebot-Ashu, 2014; Akoulouze et al., 1999; Republic of Cameroon, 2005; Bush and Oduro, 2006; Bush and Jackson, 2002; GESP, 2010; MINEDUC, 2011).

The purpose of this chapter is to address two research questions:

1 How do school leaders in Cameroon perceive their own development opportunities, specifically in preparing them to become good head teachers?
2 How are school leadership and management development processes in Cameroon preparing prospective leaders to become effective school leaders?

Background and significance

As noted above, there is increasing emphasis around the world on leadership learning through formal development and training programmes as an element in the enhancement of school effectiveness.

In many African countries, however, and particularly in Cameroon, there is more dependence on in-service training opportunities for school leadership development (Commonwealth Secretariat, 1996; Bush, 2008; GESP, 2010) as opposed to pre-service. For example, Ebot-Ashu (2014), citing the Commonwealth Secretariat (1996), explains that this is certainly a problem in much of Africa where: without the necessary skills, many heads are overwhelmed by the task … strategies for training and supporting schools heads are generally inadequate throughout Africa. (Ebot-Ashu, 2014: 418)

In Cameroon, this in-service training typically includes a variety of leadership development experiences, such as mentoring, job assignments, feedback systems, on-the-job experience, peer observations and developmental relationships, but it features only very limited formal structured training (Ebot-Ashu, 2014; Commonwealth Secretariat, 1996).

While the variety of tasks and challenges encountered on the job are a major source of learning for aspiring head teachers, there remains a void in respect to what is known about effective methods of school leadership training and the management development of aspiring head teachers in Cameroon and about the factors that enhance aspiring heads' knowledge, performance, expertise and behaviours in creating effective schools and educational systems (Ebot-Ashu, 2014; Commonwealth Secretariat, 1996). Researchers have noted for some time that more empirical studies are needed to enable a more complete assessment of effective school leadership and management development approaches in an African context (Ebot-Ashu, 2014; Bush and Oduro, 2006).

This project, therefore, starts from the position that there is an inherent justification for the research in the apparent disjunction between the international trend towards formal leadership development processes and programmes for aspiring school leaders and the less structured approach in Cameroon.

It should be emphasized, however, that the mere fact that school leadership development in Cameroon, as in much of Africa, is less structured than in the developed world is not, in itself, evidence that this approach is less effective in preparing successful school leaders. It may be that, within the broader social and economic context prevailing in Cameroon, structured programmes could be less effective, or a less efficient use of scarce resources, than in developed countries. The Commonwealth Secretariat, for example, found that formal training programmes were expensive and inadequate in that they could only cater for a tiny proportion of the total number of current or prospective head teachers (Ebot-Ashu, 2014). It could also be that there are cultural influences which encourage the informal transfer of knowledge in preference to formal training programmes.

On the other hand, it might be that the creation of formal training programmes for school leadership, tailored to the needs and the social and economic realities of developing countries, does have the potential to address the chronic weaknesses in leadership training in Africa identified by the Commonwealth Secretariat (1996) and, more recently, by Ebot-Ashu (2014) with regard to Cameroon.

It is therefore currently very important to assess the various merits of formal and in-house leadership development processes and the extent to which these approaches offer both measurably positive outcomes, both for leadership and for school effectiveness, and whether these outcomes are delivered efficiently and in a manner that is able to be resourced in a sustainable way over the long term within a developing economy.

This chapter, therefore, applies an international theoretical perspective, and a rigorous data survey and analysis approach, such as that utilized by Ebot-Ashu, to the Cameroonian school leadership-training context. It thereby seeks, on the one hand, to develop the body of scholarly understanding of the issues facing school leadership development in Africa and, on the other hand, to inform the Cameroonian Ministry of Higher Education, and other education professionals in Cameroon, in regard to the development and dissemination of good practice in managing school leadership development structures and processes.

Continuous professional development (CPD) in Cameroon

Cameroon, like many other African countries, has few formalized procedures for preparing and developing school leaders. Most educational systems in Africa seem to work on the belief that a successful classroom teacher essentially makes an effective school administrator (Ebot-Ashu, 2014; Bush and Oduro, 2006). As a consequence, heads are frequently appointed on the foundation of a successful record as teachers, on the assumption that this offers a sufficient starting point for school leadership (Ebot-Ashu, 2014; Lumby, Crow and Pashiardis, 2008; Bush and Oduro, 2006). The selection and recruitment of head teachers is, therefore, mostly based on a teacher's seniority in rank and teaching experience (Ebot-Ashu, 2014).

The Commonwealth Secretariat (1996) and Bush and Jackson (2002), while they stress the importance of school leaders in Africa, also point to the difficulties of managing schools and educational systems in such a difficult context. Bush and Oduro (2006) note that little is known about school leadership in developing countries, and they are critical of the current inadequate arrangements and resources to support the development of aspiring heads. Despite the importance of school leadership, the means by which most school leaders in developing countries like Cameroon are trained, selected and inducted are ill-suited to the development of effective and efficient school managers (Bush, 2008; Lumby et al., 2008).

There is little evidence about the quality of school leaders' informal training in Cameroon. Two of the few sources are Ebot-Ashu (2014) and Akoulouze et al.'s (1999) guide for primary head teachers, which provides a detailed in-service training resource for head teachers. The guide gives pragmatic advice in relation to several aspects of in-service training, notably:

- pedagogical management
- functions of head teachers
- management of teaching and learning
- human resource management
- resource management
- personnel management
- financial management
- learning and assessment
- school relationship management
- learning development
- the school within its environment
- performance management
- self-development of leaders
- health and safety
- research in education
- leadership in education

The authors highlight how skills in the management of physical facilities and financial management need to be improved, especially in the context that the central education authority has devolved a significant proportion of such tasks to the school level, including budgeting, fundraising and fee setting (MINEDUB, 2001; GESP, 2010; MINEDUC, 2011).

Research design

Case study research forms the core of the research that underpins this chapter. These case studies have been designed and analysed in such a way as to ensure that, taken as whole, the chapter will utilize a qualitative-mixed (interpretive) methodology. Thus, the subjective and interpretative case study approach is supplemented by quantitative data collection methods. Initial data collection, therefore, utilized a small Leadership and Management Development Questionnaire (LMDQ), and this was supported through semi-structured interviews across a purposive sample of 25 school leaders from 13 case-study schools, along with documents from the Cameroon Ministry of Basic Education, in order to develop a deeper understanding of the training processes, leadership performance data and learning logs (LMDQ, interviews, documents) and to enable data analysis.

These methods aimed to provide breadth and depth, while ensuring the collection of rigorous and replicable data on school leaders' performance.

LMDQ data analysis

Research question one aimed to bring together evaluative data concerning the compulsory leadership and management training programmes in Cameroon that enhance the prospect of leaders becoming effective school leaders. The research utilized the LMDQ, which is a self-assessment form, completed by both aspiring heads and head teachers, that documents perceptions of leadership and management development attainments. For the collection of data, I have employed a paper self-administered LMDQ in the form of a checklist, plus semi-structured interviews and field document analysis. The LMDQ is an effective tool for aspiring head teacher's self-evaluation and development.

Prior to analysing the data, completed LMDQs were checked to ensure that respondents had complied with instructions for completing each LMDQ. Each respondent was allocated a unique code that identified their gender, age, job role, experience and type of school and entered into an excel spread sheet.

The extent to which the expectations of the few leadership development programmes were met was assessed in order to gain an indication of informal on-the-job training outcomes. Participants' views regarding the leadership and management development programmes, as well as further opportunities for headship development, were analysed with the use of mostly descriptive methods (frequencies and mean). Differences in teachers and head teachers' views according to personal features (such as job role, gender, age, experience in role and type of school) were also examined.

Descriptive statistics were used to identify any emerging differences between the main variables and the key issues that emerged from the analysis, linked to the research questions. The leadership and management learning attainments data were analysed in order to evaluate the extent to which

- School leaders were able to achieve leadership and management development targets
- The LMDQ was potentially an effective tool for aspiring head teachers' self-evaluation and development.

For the analysis of the LMDQ data, Ebot-Ashu's (2014) Rating Scale Model, which applies to Likert scale surveys, was used to analyse the data regarding the usefulness of the 30 units of study in the context of respondent informal on-the-job training. Codes are used to represent data sources. The first part of the code identifies the organization or school where the meeting took place and the town from which the quote was taken. Thus, CMBEMYUtt117-Utt122 refers to field document analysis from the Cameroon Ministry of Basic Education (CMBE), meeting (M) in Yaounde (Y), Utterance 117 to Utterance Utt122.

Findings and discussion

This section presents the main findings and discussions of this chapter. It begins by analysing the findings of the LMDQ – the main quantitative tool used in this study. This analysis will help to identify some of the issues to be explored through the qualitative methods later in the chapter.

Leadership and Management Development Programmes

This section provides statistical information derived from the data collected in the LMDQ from 190 school leaders (47 head teachers and 143 aspiring head teachers). The LMDQ serves to provide background data on perceptions of leadership and management development programmes, which can in turn be broken down by role type. The 30 aspects of management and leadership covered in the LMDQ are a composite from typical areas of study in both international school leadership and management development programmes and from the Cameroonian context of in-service training for aspiring school leaders. Table 8.1 illustrates the interpretation of the level of agreement in respect to each of the 30 leadership development aspects, according to the mean of the scores assigned by respondents on the 5-point Likert scale.

Table 8.1 Mean Score Interpretation

Mean Score	Interpretation – Level of Agreement
1.00–1.49	Strongly disagree
1.5–2.49	Disagree
2.5–3.49	Neutral
3.5–4.49	Agree
4.5+	Strongly agree

Aspiring heads and head teachers – background factors

Findings from the LMDQ (by mean score in descending order) are presented separately to enable some comparisons to be made between aspiring heads and head teachers' assessment of each aspect of leadership development (see Table 8.2 and 8.3). It should be noted, however, that 75 per cent of the sample was made up of aspiring head teachers; this will be accounted for in the analysis.

Table 8.2 shows that aspiring heads broadly agreed that they had been prepared with respect to the 30 aspects of leadership development.

Particularly strong levels of agreement were registered for curriculum and pedagogic management practices (e.g. on improving learning, improving teaching, learning and assessment) and organizational leadership practices (e.g. on health and safety, research in education, human resources management), indicating that these were seen as the most useful areas of development for their everyday roles and responsibilities as prospective head teachers. The fact that these developmental aspects of their role were given high priority by aspiring heads might suggest that they are often mainly responsible for administrative issues and have limited wider leadership responsibilities.

In the last, more discursive, section of the LMDQ, aspiring heads suggested that additional areas that could be included in their training were leadership skills in education, professional ethics in education, moral education and human rights and the management of extra-curricular activities.

Table 8.3 summarizes the results from the head teachers and indicates that they hold a slightly different range of views regarding the usefulness of the 30 aspects of leadership development, with curriculum and pedagogic management emotional intelligent (e.g. on learning development) found extremely relevant to their leadership development.

The head teachers also identified that the aspects of leadership development related to personal management (e.g. the self-development of leadership skills), organizational leadership practices (e.g. on financial management, strategic management in schools and the introduction to public policy in Cameroon)

Table 8.2 Mean Scores of Aspiring Head Respondents Views

Units of Studies	Aspiring Heads	Mean	Mean Scores
Human Resources Management	143	4.7	Strongly agree
Improving Learning	143	4.7	Strongly agree
Improving Teaching	143	4.6	Strongly agree
Health and Safety in School	143	4.5	Strongly agree
Research in Education	143	4.5	Strongly agree
Learning and Assessment	143	4.5	Strongly agree
Accountability	143	4.4	Agree
Quality Management in Education	143	4.4	Agree
Learning Development	143	4.3	Agree
ICT Management	143	4.3	Agree
Sharing Vision	143	4.3	Agree
Strategic Planning	143	4.2	Agree
Financial Management	143	4.2	Agree
Self-Development of Leaders	143	4.2	Agree
History of Education in Cameroon	143	4.1	Agree
Function of Headship in Education	143	4.1	Agree
Managing Interpersonal Skills	143	4.1	Agree
Managing Professional Development	143	4.1	Agree
Distribution Leadership	143	4.1	Agree
Leadership in Organization	143	4.1	Agree
School Community Relationship Management	143	4.1	Agree
Performance Management	143	4.1	Agree
Working With other Agencies	143	4.1	Agree
Strategic Management in School	143	4.1	Agree
Career and Counselling Management	143	4	Agree
Introduction to Public Policy in Cameroon	143	3.9	Agree
Change Management	143	3.9	Agree
Using Data to Raise Achievements	143	3.9	Agree
Policy Creation	143	3.6	Agree
Legal Aspects in School Management	143	3.6	Agree

and community management practices (e.g. on school community relationship management) were less useful in preparing them as effective head teachers. This may reflect the fact that these form a significant part of head teachers' responsibilities and that they felt under-prepared to operate effectively in these areas.

If the LMDQ results are broken down by job role (i.e. head teachers and aspiring head teachers) it is evident that there was a clear progression in the results from the more practically oriented areas of teaching practice (curriculum and pedagogic management) to the more policy oriented areas, with those that were progressively more policy oriented (organization management and administration) scoring progressively lower. This tends to conform to the other evidence presented in literature regarding the prominent role of on-the-job training as a mechanism for

Table 8.3 Mean Scores of Head Teacher Respondents Views

Units of Studies	Head Teacher Respondents	Mean Scores	Mean Scores Interpretations
Improving Learning	47	4.6	Strongly agree
Learning and Assessment	47	4.6	Strongly agree
Learning Development	47	4.5	Strongly agree
Improving Teaching	47	4.5	Strongly agree
Leadership in Organization	47	4.4	Agree
Research in Education	47	4.4	Agree
Health and Safety in Schools	47	4.3	Agree
Accountability	47	4.3	Agree
Quality Management in Education	47	4.3	Agree
History of Education in Cameroon	47	4.2	Agree
Function of Headship in Education	47	4.2	Agree
Strategic Planning	47	4.2	Agree
Using Data to Raise Achievements	47	4.2	Agree
Managing Professional Development	47	4.2	Agree
Human Resources Management	47	4.2	Agree
Performance Management	47	4.2	Agree
Working with other Agencies	47	4.2	Agree
Change Management	47	4.1	Agree
Managing Interpersonal Relationships	47	4.1	Agree
Distribution Leadership	47	4.1	Agree
Financial Management	47	4.1	Agree
School Community Relationship Management	47	4.1	Agree
Strategic Management in School	47	4.1	Agree
Self-Development of Leaders	47	4.1	Agree
Introduction to Public Policy in Cameroon	47	4	Agree
Sharing Vision	47	4	Agree
Legal Aspects in School Management	47	4	Agree
ICT Management	47	4	Agree
Career and Counselling Management	47	4	Agree
Policy Creation	47	3.7	Agree

leadership development in Cameroonian schools (Ebot-Ashu, 2014; Akoulouze et al., 1999). Scholarly research suggests that on-the-job training tends to favour the development of practical skills and that, while African educational systems tend towards an on-the-job training model, higher-level organization skills tend to suffer in this approach (Ebot-Ashu, 2014; Akoulouze et al., 1999; Bush and Oduro, 2006; Lumby et al., 2008). Similarly, Ebot-Ashu (2014) suggests that there is a need for schools and educational systems in African countries to encourage more distributional leadership, and these areas of practice also scored relatively less well compared to the rest of the study units.

Overview of the LMDQ findings

In many respects, the results from the LMDQ, however they are broken down, present a consistent picture. Each of the 30 aspects of leadership development contained in the questionnaire is recorded as useful, to greater or lesser degrees, by respondents, however those respondents are categorized. That said, if we investigate a little deeper, some interesting conclusions can be drawn. Consistently, the most highly ranked leadership development aspects were those relating to teaching and learning, learning and assessment, health and safety and research in education. In this regard, both head teachers and aspiring head teachers appeared to particularly value training that they saw as developing their skills in direct teaching activities and in obvious pastoral responsibilities (e.g. health and safety responsibilities). In contrast, a range of other leadership development aspects appeared to be less highly valued. These aspects included distributed leadership, change management, policy creation, using data to raise achievement, quality management in education, financial management, career and counselling management, introduction to public policy in Cameroon and legal aspects in school management.

What is striking about these findings is that although Cameroon's school system is operating in a time of fast-changing resources, responsibilities and expectations, many current and aspiring school leaders apparently retain a relatively narrow understanding of the skills required to be an effective school leader. In this respect, the findings from the LMDQ suggest that it would be worthwhile exploring the more qualitative research tools; the extent to which school leaders recognize that modern school leadership requires a much broader portfolio of skills than simply good teaching and pastoral skills; and how this broader portfolio might be developed in a context such as in Cameroon.

Perceptions of current development opportunities

Perceptions of the central government agencies as to their role in the leadership development process

There were three major findings in relation to how the central agencies saw their input into leadership development: that they saw their role as being primarily one of distributing information and generally facilitating leadership development opportunities; that they were engaged to some extent in sharing knowledge and best practice; and that they were also increasingly involved in organizing seminars to bring school leaders together and to expose school leaders to other professionals in a way which represents a tentative step towards the establishment of a national framework for leadership development.

Distributing information and facilitating leadership development opportunities

In this regard, the meeting with the national inspectorates of primary and nursery education identified that the national centre, the Ministry of Education, plays an important role in school leaders' development.

Akoulouze et al. (1999) recognize the importance of central agencies collating and distributing information. In terms of the role of central agencies in facilitating a culture of leadership development, the approaches vary between a context in which there is a centrally organized leadership development programme and one in which there is no such programme and instead a reliance on on-the-job training (such as in Cameroon). In regard to the latter scenario, Ebot-Ashu (2014) and Lumby et al. (2008) have argued that the central educational system is responsible for distributing clear definitions about leadership performance to encourage a systematic, results-oriented approach to management and leadership for high-performing communities, schools, head teachers and aspiring heads at local levels. The role of a good central educational system, as explained by Growth and Employment Strategy Paper GESP) (2010), is to help individual stakeholders, schools and communities engage in good learning habits (Day, 2001) as well as responding to stakeholders' feedback.

The Service Head of Nursery and Primary Education explained that the most important mission of the educational authority is to:

> develop a vision and strategy that encourages transformational and distributional leadership regarding the internal and external factors that drive the decisions of the educational system. (CMBEMYUtt106-Utt115)

Ebot-Ashu (2014) and Lumby et al. (2008) also argue that it is the duty of the educational system to provide services to support head teachers to create a shared vision and strategic plan. Bush and Jackson (2002) and Bush (2008) recommend that it is the duty of a central educational system to support head teachers to create a functional team in order to improve performance within efficient learning communities (see also Commonwealth Secretariat, 1996). Bush and Oduro (2006), meanwhile, specifically in an African educational context, say that it is the centre's responsibility to encourage school leaders to build effective and efficient schools in collaboration with others.

Encouraging an informal network of school leaders to share best practice

The evidence gathered from the central government agencies also demonstrated that

> successful school leaders learn to work together in the setting and achieving of ambitious, challenging goals and targets that support the development of schools. (CMBEMYUtt61-Utt64)

This implies an informal network of school leaders sharing best practice, and this is an idea that is further implied elsewhere in the evidence. Exploring the nature of leadership support in more detail with staff from the CMBE, it was discussed that

> the most effective programmes are school based, provide experience in authentic contexts, use mentors and cohort groupings and are structured to enable collaborative activity between the programmes and school, although there is as yet very limited empirical evidence to support this claim. (CBMEMYUtt136-Utt141)

As Akoulouze et al. (1999) show, there is good evidence that effective leadership programmes are school based and support participants to be committed to their own continuing professional development in their own context (Ebot-Ashu, 2014; Bush and Oduro, 2006; Hallinger and Heck, 1999).

The evidence supports the central agency's encouragement of an informal network of school leaders to share best practice since there are small formal and informal networks already in Cameroon. The central agencies can help the different systems and schools to share ideas, issues and best practice in learning initiatives at all levels of the system and in school communities.

Engaging system leaders in a variety of seminars and workshops

The suggestions from staff at the CMBE also provided evidence that school leaders in Cameroon are engaging in a variety of seminars and workshops designed at international, national, regional and divisional level to learn about different aspects of school management and leadership. Furthermore, the director of Human Resources at the CMBE added:

> Our policy documents tend to assume that the right personnel to support head teachers' in-service training are pedagogy advisers. That is why they have pedagogy seminars in which they learn about their role as a headmaster. Most head teachers have attended financial management training, then teaching and learning seminars that have a large part to play in the learning development of young people, assessment for learning and ICT are other important areas for

head teachers' development. These seminars enable our head teachers to carry out their duties effectively. (CMBEMYUTT291-UTT301)

The importance of seminars and workshops for the development of school leaders has been discussed by Ebot-Ashu (2014) and Lumby et al. (2008). Seminars are useful for bringing together professionals working in similar areas to pool ideas and experiences (Ebot-Ashu, 2014; Weindling, 2003), but they also serve to expose teachers to new ideas from educational professionals and researchers. This combination of general encouragement to share best practice through informal networks and the use of seminars and workshops, if taken together with the research literature, does demonstrate some real commitment to leadership development on the part of the central agencies in Cameroon that would be recognizable in an international context.

Perceptions of school leaders' roles in the leadership development process

The findings presented below outline the perceptions of school leaders regarding their role in, and opportunities for, leadership development, reinforcing the idea that school leaders, and particularly the head teacher, play a central role in pushing forward leadership development in the Cameroonian educational system.

Head teachers' roles in the leadership development process

The participant school leaders outline how the issues discussed above are reflected at the local level and, in particular, they comment on leadership development opportunities within schools.

Thus, in School K, one respondent discussed how

the head teacher is chiefly responsible for building capability across schools and for establishing a culture of professional and personal development in schools around the region. In fact, both the head teachers are good at identifying the development needs of aspiring heads and know how best to address their development once a structured framework is provided. (SKMUtt332-Utt341)

In School G, school leaders considered head teachers as instrumental to leadership development, describing them as

sympathetic leaders avoid stereotyping or judging too quickly, and they live their lives in an open, honest way; people with strong social skills are characteristically team players. Rather than concentrate on their own achievements, they assist others to grow and stand out. (SGMUtt228-Utt234)

These passages triangulate the information from the central documentation suggesting that head teachers are the central figures in ongoing leadership development activities. In these two schools, the head teachers are instrumental in pushing forward a leadership development agenda through identifying needs, distributing leadership responsibility and establishing informal best-practice networks. Ebot-Ashu (2014) and Lumby et al. (2008) considered the implications of sharing leadership across schools and the central educational system's responsibilities for transforming the role of head teachers and aspiring school leaders so as to build leadership capacity, manage resources and raise standards within and across educational organizations (GESP, 2010). The above understanding has parallels with the suggestion that school leaders *share* responsibility and are required to monitor the mission across the school community, including focus groups with children, taking initiatives and risks, through ongoing relevant opportunities and by working collaboratively with the central educational systems.

The findings, therefore, provide some examples of good practice, with a number of respondents describing head teachers as being good at identifying the development needs of others and of being able to promote leadership development in a supportive and non-judgemental way. Indeed, the kind of good practice highlighted by Ebot-Ashu (2014), Lumby et al. (2008), Weindling (2003) and Day (2001) can all be discerned from the findings. As Ebot-Ashu (2014) shows, when head teachers work well in this area, the results can be inspirational and can unleash real restructuring, cultural change and a turnaround in school fortunes. However, other scholars writing about the educational system in Cameroon have been sceptical, with both Akoulouze et al. (1999) and Tchombe (1998) arguing that head teachers routinely fail in the task of developing others because they do not have the personnel skills, emotional intelligence or leverage to alter behaviours like organization management skills.

Opportunities for on-the-job training experience

Respondents revealed a strikingly wide range of opportunities for on-the-job training experience in the findings, spanning organizational skills of various kinds, teaching skills and community engagement. For example, there is a mix of on-the-job training experienced by school leaders in Cameroon:

> The on-the-job training that I have received deals with a wide range of situations, like complex human resources issues; reorganisation of staff roles; recruitment; retention and staff capability performance issues. (KHT1Utt7)

On-the-job training has enabled me to develop fundraising skills to raise money for the school and carry out my administrative duties like assessing teachers' lesson plans, check their classrooms management skills and whether teaching and learning is effective; carry out peer assessments and hold departmental meetings to update myself on strategies for the smooth running of the school. (AHT1Utt18)

The formats for this training appear to include one-to-one meetings and peer support, together with broader school meetings. Overall, many of the strategies suggested by Ebot-Ashu (2014) in respect to on-the-job training appear to be utilized in Cameroon, and the literature from Cameroon itself also suggests that it is appropriate for central agencies to empower head teachers to provide management and leadership training (MINEDUB, 2001; Republic of Cameroon, 2005; GESP, 2010; MINEDUC, 2011).

Akoulouze et al. (1999) provide a strategic framework, which has been adapted for supporting on-the-job training for future school leaders. Ebot-Ashu (2014) states that peer support is a useful form of on-the-job training, and formal on-the-job training programmes in Cameroon are typically conducted by experienced head teachers who can effectively use one-on-one instructional techniques and who have superior technical knowledge and skills for building capability across schools and for establishing a culture of professional and personal development in schools around the region.

These school leaders are perceived to be good at identifying the development needs of aspiring heads and know how best to address their development, once a structured framework is provided. Ebot-Ashu (2014) emphasizes that management and leadership is not developed by specifically designed training programmes or organizing seminars and workshops, but forces managers to be taught new skills in the context of their daily practices (Bush and Jackson, 2002; Lumby et al., 2008). For these reasons, Ebot-Ashu (2014) argues that on-the-job training provides an opportunity for successful managers and leaders to make the most of their leadership knowledge, expertise and behavioural development potential. Contained within on-the-job training are the job-instruction technique, succession planning, apprenticeships, mentoring and coaching (Weindling, 2003).

Seminars and workshops

Seminars and workshops were also shown to play a prominent role in the leadership learning opportunities provided for school leaders in Cameroon. As school leaders HHT1 and HAH2 reported, these were mostly organized by the educational authority. Generally, such seminars are aimed at offering an authentic insight into the complexity and variety of school leadership (Ebot-Ashu, 2014; Weindling, 2003). Ebot-Ashu contends that seminars and workshop learning within communities are each focused on transformational leadership principles and on developing school leaders' assumptions or beliefs regarding the way children develop curriculum and pedagogic management and organizational leadership skills.

Ebot-Ashu (2014) also explains why seminars and workshops are an important forum in which school leaders are able to share their visions and acquire the capability and the competence to govern effective schools. The use of seminars and workshops for leadership development is well set out by Weindling (2003), who supposes that the leadership learning voyage takes the cohort through five ascending developmental stages: support, security, friendship, acquisition of knowledge, development and preliminary realization of each member's personal dream. This can be particularly useful in developing nations (Commonwealth Secretariat, 1996). In Cameroon, the distinctive feature of these seminars is that they draw attention to the strengths and weaknesses of participants, conceptual pluralism, the separation of leadership from management, the adaptation of the training and assessment processes and the inevitable pressure to cover content (GESP, 2010; MINEDUC, 2011). Problems with international, national, regional, divisional and local organized seminars in Cameroon, however, include funding, accounting for the different educational traditions, taking account of prior learning, the pressure on professionals' lives and on their schools and appropriate diversity among aspiring head teachers (GESP, 2010; MINEDUC, 2011).

The extent to which leadership development opportunities for school leaders in Cameroon occur in contexts outside of school

Several respondents reported developing their leadership skills in diverse contexts such as community, tribal group meetings and church groups and parent–teacher association (PTA) forums.

> Outside the professional setting, teachers and head teachers must serve as leaders for student learning. They also must be able to permit and encourage teachers to exercise leadership outside the classroom. (MAH1Utt42)
>
> I have similarly developed my leadership skills in my tribal or neighbour meetings. In one of my social gathering meeting I am the president, in other meetings I am the financial secretary and in other meetings the minutes secretary. (AHT2Utt43)

In the literature, Ebot-Ashu (2014) and Weindling (2003) outline the benefits of undertaking leadership learning in community contexts, suggesting that such learning forms part of a socially consistent activity structure that emphasizes shared authority for learning, opportunities for collaboration and teamwork. Additionally, community-based learning reflects a trend towards closer collaboration between schools and the different local learning communities. Some of the positive effects of community-structured learning experiences include enhanced feelings of group affiliation and acceptance, social and emotional support, motivation, persistence, group learning and mutual assistance (Ebot-Ashu, 2014; Weindling, 2003; GESP, 2010; MINEDUB 2001; MINEDUC, 2011).

Other school leaders (HHT1, IHT1 and EAH1) recommended that community group learning could help learners build group and individual knowledge, think creatively and restructure problems from multiple perspectives. Lumby et al. (2008), and Weindling (2003), for example, described community group learning models as being the type of team-building learning experience that is increasingly common in both developed and developing countries. Indeed, community learning does not require significant resources and is therefore particularly appropriate in the context of a developing country (Ebot-Ashu, 2014; Akoulouze et al., 1999; Bush and Oduro, 2006).

Two leaders (HHT1 and DHT1) also support the work of Ebot-Ashu (2014) in suggesting that learning in the community establishes a cycle of feedback in which people bring knowledge and experience from their line of work to community meetings, while simultaneously encouraging developmental opportunities for those same people to experience leadership and thus take new leadership skills back to their workplace.

Conclusions and recommendations

This chapter reports data from an evaluative multiple case study that contributes to the existing body of knowledge pertaining to how school leaders in Cameroon perceive their own development opportunities, specifically in preparing them to become good head teachers. In particular, it greatly extends the current knowledge relating to school leadership preparation in Cameroon and makes recommendations as to how the leadership skills of aspiring heads and head teachers in Cameroon could be better developed. A tentative framework for the improvement of management and leadership development arrangements in Cameroon, derived from the findings of this research, is also presented. This study represents a second attempt to employ a LMDQ methodology in a Cameroonian (and African) context – providing valuable lessons as to the benefits and flaws of this approach in this cultural context.

The outcomes of the LMDQ demonstrated relatively few significant differences in the data when it was analysed by age group, experience in role and school type factors. Overall, although there were limitations in the use of the particular LMDQ design employed in this study (which, we argue, was a consequence of the cultural context), the LMDQ results do contribute to overall knowledge in that they show the need for central agencies to design, deliver and administer structures that engage school leaders into a leadership culture; and that the needs of the participants of those programmes may vary according to their experience and gender. In particular, the LMDQ showed that in Cameroon currently, most school leaders identified more with practical outcomes as opposed to organizational and policy outcomes in leadership development programmes, and this suggests that consideration needs to be given to how the latter could be made more relevant to participants.

This study has provided the first in-depth insight into the nature of current leadership development opportunities in Cameroon. This insight complements the work of Ebot-Ashu (2014) in surveying leadership development approaches in Africa, but it is new (in Africa) in terms of its focus on a single system and its attempt to take in the entirety of that system. In particular, it has collated evidence to show the central role of head teachers themselves in pushing forward leadership development in Cameroon and also the important role played by on-the-job opportunities and by seminars; it has also been able to provide a unique insight into the extent to which community and out-of-school development opportunities are perceived by school leaders in Cameroon as having been useful in their leadership development. In each of these areas, this research has extended existing knowledge and provided a basis for scholars to explore further.

References

Akoulouze, R., L. Ongbwa, C. Salla, J. Ndjie, E. Kenne, J. Coadou, M. Ngoube, I. Soucat, M. Itoe, D. Mongue, M. Molinier, C. Martin, J. Tchakou, M. Tondji, M. Morand, A. Eppoh, R. Mouaze, O. Hayatou, S. Kamga, G. Husson, P. Noa, C. Edjang, and J. Martin (1999), *A Guide for Primary School Head Teachers*, Yaounde: Ministry of National Education, CEPER S.A.

Bush, T. (2008), 'From Management to Leadership: Semantic or Meaningful Change?' *Educational Management Administration & Leadership*, 36 (2): 271–88.

Bush, T. and D. Jackson (2002), 'A Preparation for School Leadership: International Perspectives', *Education Management and Administration*, 30 (4): 417–29.

Bush, T. and G. Oduro (2006), 'New Principals in Africa: Preparation, Induction and Practice', *Journal of Educational Administration*, 44 (4): 359–75.

Commonwealth Secretariat (1996), *Better Schools: Resource Materials for Heads: Introductory Module*, London: Commonwealth Secretariat.

Day, D. V. (2001), 'Leadership Development: A Review in Context', *Leadership Quarterly*, 11 (4): 581–613.

Ebot-Ashu, F. (2014), *Effectiveness of School Leadership and Management Development in Cameroon: A Guide for Educational Systems, Schools and School Leaders*, Newcastle Upon Tyne: Cambridge Scholars Publishing.

GESP (2010), *Growth and Employment Strategy Paper. Reference Framework for Governmental Action over the Period (2010–2020)*, Yaounde: Prime Minister Office.

Hallinger, P. and R. Heck (1999), 'Can Leadership Enhance Effectiveness?' in T. Bush, L. Bell, R. Bolam, R. Glatter and P. Ribbins (eds), *Educational Management: Redefining Theory, Policy and Practice*, 178–90, London: Paul Chapman.

Lumby, J., G. Crow, and P. Pashiardis (2008), *International Handbook on the Preparation and Development of School Leaders*, New York: Routledge.

MINEDUB (2001), *Budget Implementation Measures for State Primary Schools*, Yaounde: Circular 21/A/135/MINEDUB/CAB.

MINEDUC (2011), *Completing Circular 21/A/MINEDUC/CAB of on Budget Implementation Measures for State Primary Schools*, Yaounde: Circular 33/A/135/MINEDUC/CAB.

Republic of Cameroon (2005), *Draft document of the Sector-wide Approach to Education*, Yaounde: Presidency of the Republic.

Tchombe, T. (1998), *Progressive Transformative Teacher Education in Cameroon*, Yaounde: Cameroon. [online]. Available from: http://www.ejournal.aiaer.net/vol22 210/5.T.M.%20Tchombe.pdf (accessed December 2010).

Weindling, D. (2003), *Leadership Development in Practice: Trends and Innovations. A Review of Programme Literature Carried Out for the National College for School Leadership*, Nottingham: National College for Teaching and Leadership.

9

A Focus on Craft Knowledge in the Preparation of School Heads in Ghana

Michael Amakyi and Alfred Ampah-Mensah

Introduction

School heads occupy a unique position in the running of educational institutions. They play a defined role in the actualization of the mission of the school and the attainment of educational goals. The defined role of the school head is to ensure that ultimately, learning takes place in the classroom. This critical role is expected to manifest itself through the daily duties of the school head: mobilizing and managing key resources to achieve goals. Through normative leadership and management functions, school heads carry out their role. The expectations of the role of the school head in Ghana are prescribed by *the Ghana Education Service HeadTeachers' Handbook* (2010). The handbook delineates two broad roles for the school head. The first role behoves the school head to manage the school by having proficiencies in managing people, instructional time, co-curricular activities, teaching and learning resources and school finances. The second role places a responsibility on the school head to improve the quality of learning by having proficiencies in increasing school intake and attendance, assessing pupil performance, assessing teacher performance, facilitating staff development and improving relations between school and community.

In addition to the *HeadTeachers' Handbook*, the Ghana Education Service (GES) appraisal instrument for evaluating the performance of school heads provides insight into the role expectations of school heads (Zame, Hope and Respress, 2008). School heads are evaluated on their management activities, instructional supervision practices, staff development activities, record-keeping practices, relationship with the school community and communication skills.

When the role expectations and the performance deliverables of school heads, as spelled out in the handbook and captured in the performance appraisal instrument, respectively, are taken together, the overarching role expectations of school heads tend to align with the tenets of the Educational Reforms of 2007. The salient elements of the reforms demand greater accountability from schools, improved student achievement, increased community involvement in schools and partnership with non-governmental organizations. The school head is thus expected to lead and manage schools for effective teaching and learning to take place.

It is logical that in order to meet the stated role expectations, school heads should possess the competencies to address problems of practice. Every job requires the mastery of certain ideas and processes embedded in its professional knowledge base. Such mastery of the essentials of the profession in educational administration puts school heads in a pole position to carry out daily leadership and managerial activities. The knowledge base (theoretical and craft) acquired by the school head determines the ability to define and frame problems of practice and subsequently informs the level of readiness to address the problems. However, the lingering question is 'How does one acquire mastery of the essentials of a profession?'

Career path to pre-tertiary school headship in Ghana

The opportunity to serve as a pre-tertiary school head is at the basic education level or at the second-cycle education level. The current structure of the education system emerged from the Education Reforms of 2007, in which the basic education level consists of two years of kindergarten, six years of primary school and three years of junior high school (Education Act 2008 [Act 778]). After junior high school, students are expected to take a national standardized test, the Basic Education Certificate Examination (BECE). The students' performance in the BECE is used to place them into the various categories of second-cycle institutions (WAEC, undated).

With regard to second-cycle education, even though Act 778 prescribed four years for the duration of second-cycle education, the number of years was reverted to three years in 2009 and has remained the same to date. The second-cycle education is made up of a two-track system of senior high school or technical education. Technical education is designed to prepare students for a career as middle-level engineers and technicians for industries, while the senior high-school education focuses on college or university preparation (MoE, 2012).

Ordinarily, there is a single school head for the kindergarten and the primary school and a different school head for the junior high school. However, there are instances where there is a single school head for the kindergarten, the primary school and the junior high school. This situation usually occurs when the student population is not too large and the various sections (kindergarten, primary, junior high school) are in contiguous school buildings. The senior high school or the technical school is assigned a single school head.

Those who are appointed school heads in Ghana are usually selected from the ranks of teachers. They are not required to complete a professional standardized preparatory programme in educational administration prior to their appointment. The GES – the body empowered by the Constitution of Ghana to conduct pre-tertiary education – has no requirement for a prospective school head to complete specified academic preparatory programmes in educational administration or related areas. The circular advertising for the position of school head by the GES Council over the years, seeking prospective school heads, show the eligibility criteria as being silent on any requirement for a formal preparatory programme involving the completion of specified academic courses. An example of the requirements to qualify as a second-cycle school head contained in one of these circular letters is presented:

1. Be a professional graduate teacher with satisfactory work history and conduct within the GES.
2. Have served at the rank of deputy director for at least 2 years.
3. Have served as an assistant headmaster/mistress, unit head at the headquarters, or an equivalent position for at least 3 cumulative years.
4. Not be over the age of 55 years at the time he or she applies for the position.

(Ghana Education Service Council [ESC], 2016)

The requirement to be of the rank of deputy director changes to principal superintendent for prospective basic school heads.

Teachers in the GES go through a rank system where years of teaching experience are the determining factor for progression. Progression through the ranks occurs after the teacher has completed at least three cumulative years at each rank and has successfully passed an interview conducted by a panel of eminent educationists. Principal superintendent is the entry rank into GES for professional teachers with a bachelor's degree. Alternatively, for those without a bachelor's degree, this rank is attained after a minimum of 12 years of teaching experience and going through various ranks – assistant superintendent, superintendent and senior superintendent. Beyond the rank of principal superintendent, the ranks of assistant director II, assistant director I and deputy director exist in the GES.

Eligibility to become a school head comes with being a professional teacher with several years of teaching experience. The extent of teaching experience thus becomes a pre-requisite for becoming a school head. The criteria for appointing school heads in Ghana emphasize teaching experience and rank over academic preparation in educational administration. The criteria have remained the same over the years. Oduro (2003) noted that the processes of pre-service, selection, appointment and on-the-job training of school heads in Ghana have not changed. A study conducted by Bush and Oduro (2006) on the nature of preparation to become school heads in Africa concluded that the preparation received is inadequate throughout Africa. Focusing on Ghana, Bush and Oduro pointed out that most heads are appointed without any specific preparation (e.g. management training) and few receive appropriate on-the-job training following their appointment. A feature article by Zubeviel in 2012 highlights the emphasis Ghana's education system puts on long service in teaching as main qualification to become a school head. The writer observes that in Ghana, school heads are either appointed or rise to such positions by virtue of long service, and no conscious efforts are made to prepare teachers, either by way of special educational qualification or some form of induction and initiation into such professional (headship) roles. The closest a prospective school head gets to any experience in school leadership is the requirement to have served in certain positions in the school or education office alluded to earlier on. It is revealing to note that even though the Report of the President's Committee on Review of Education Reforms in Ghana (RPCRERG) in 2002 noted that the introduction of new policies and subsequent changes in the education system placed additional responsibilities on school heads so they need to be prepared for the new challenges, the call for a change in policy with regard to school head preparation was not heeded.

Ghana's eligibility criteria for appointing school heads seem to suggest that the GES has an operating assumption that good teachers can become effective school heads without specific academic preparation in administration. It is important to note that after teachers assume the position of the school head, they engage very little in the technical aspects of teaching that earned them the position (Oduro and Bosu, 2010). The skills needed to effectively function as school head and the outcomes by which the school head's success is judged are so different that one literally leaves teaching when appointed as school head and enters a new and different occupation.

The absence of the requirement for aspiring school heads to take prescribed courses in educational administration cannot be ascribed to the non-availability of opportunities to enrol in school administrator preparatory programmes. Ghana can boast of at least two well-established universities (i.e. the University of Cape Coast and University of Education, Winneba) that have institutes that offer programmes in educational administration. For example, the Institute for Educational Planning and Administration (IEPA) at the University of Cape Coast was established with the mandate to specifically undertake research in educational leadership and management (ELM) and to provide training and facilitation to improve the leadership and managerial capabilities of educational administrators and planners (IEPA, 2016). The IEPA runs a competency-based master's of education in school administration, which is essential for teachers who intend to pursue a career in school governance and leadership. The master's of education in school administration provides teachers with the opportunity to move into school leadership positions in basic education (KG – JHS) or second-cycle education (SHS or TVET). Oduro (2003) observes that because of the emphasis on experienced and long-serving teachers, graduates from IEPA or other related institutions are not considered for headship positions based on their qualifications but have to go through the ranks to meet the long-serving teacher criterion.

Reliance on craft knowledge

The absence of emphasis on research or theoretical knowledge in school administration leaves the school head with a reliance on artistry or craft knowledge to function. Craft knowledge offers school heads the opportunity to engage in reflective practice towards a reality-based understanding of their role as school heads. It equips the school head with the competencies to cope with the job as it exists but not how to transform it, especially to carry out protracted school improvements. The reliance on craft knowledge drives heads of schools to develop relationships with one another in order to learn from each other. School heads in Ghana belong to the Conference of Heads of Assisted Secondary Schools (CHASS) or Conference of Heads of Basic Schools (COHBS). The conferences offer them the platform to engage in peer assessment. The school heads learn from each other and use the feedback provided by peers to inform their own learning. In the absence of any clearly defined orientation and induction programmes for school heads, peer assessment has become a useful device for supporting the socialization into school leadership of novice heads and the continuing development of practising heads because of its focus on dialogue and shared interpretations of events (Amakyi and Ampah-Mensah, 2014).

There are two sides to the situation of heads learning from each other. The downside is that novice school heads will learn practices to just stay afloat and maintain the status quo – learning how to stay out of trouble. The positive side is that novice school heads will learn best operating practices to improve their schools. The difficulty for the novice school head in this scenario is to discern between wholesale adoption of a school's best operating practice or context adaptation of the best practice.

The findings of the study by Zame, Hope and Repress (2008) that heads of basic schools lacked leadership proficiencies because of the absence of school leadership preparation programmes can be ascribed to a reliance on craft knowledge. They posit that heads of basic schools lack professional preparation in leadership, and that they practice management rather than leadership. The researchers go on to make recommendations to policy-makers to institute educational reform that addresses head teachers' leadership in basic schools.

Implications for practice

The GES policy of not having specified studies in educational administration as a pre-requisite for appointment as school head suggests that school administration is viewed more as a non-science in Ghana. The absence of theoretical knowledge in school administration as a pre-requisite for the position of school head leaves the school head with a sole reliance on artistry or craft knowledge when addressing problems of practice. There is little interest in learning theory and applying it to running schools. School heads rely more on intuition to make important decisions. Both theoretical and craft knowledge are important segments of the knowledge base of school administration, and successful school heads apply them to inform critical decisions. Such administrators, over time, interface theoretical and craft knowledge to develop the skills and disposition that enable them to adequately address unique problems of practice that defy textbook solutions.

Woodruff (2008) writes that problems of practice are perceived difficulties in performing a professional responsibility, regardless of cause. School heads in Ghana report problems of practice mainly emanating from two major areas: (a) having to operate in a rigid hierarchical structure in which reforms are pursued in the context of political-coercive strategy (i.e. the reforms are determined by government officials, and heads are mandated to implement them); and (b) inadequate funding to effectively run the school due to delinquent national government fiscal distributions to schools (Amakyi, 2017). A study conducted by Amakyi (2012) puts problems of practice into three broad categories: *leadership-related*, which refers to what needs to be done and why; *management-related*, which refers to how and when emerging problems are to be addressed; and *political-related*, which pertains to emerging problems involving competition for scarce and limited resources. Major findings reported in a follow-up study by Amakyi (2017) on the readiness of school heads to address problems of practice showed that there was statistically significant differences in the readiness of respondents (different categories of school heads) to address problems of practice. Respondents who had taken graduate-level courses in educational administration showed more readiness to address problems of practice than those who had not taken such courses. The study further showed that the difference in readiness to address leadership-related problems was more pronounced.

Amakyi (2017) intimated that the findings showing less readiness on the part of respondents who have not taken courses in educational administration or leadership to address leadership-related problems may be associated with inadequate knowledge and skills in educational administration or leadership. According to Woodruff and Kowalski (2009), school heads who have not been prepared to assume certain responsibilities may not be able to recognize and define problems related to those responsibilities. School heads in Ghana may be limited in addressing leadership-related problems of practice.

Leadership literature (e.g. Bush and Glover, 2016; Cardno, 2003) points to a strong need for professional development of head teachers to prepare them to manage the problems they face in their work situations. Theoretical knowledge is an important segment of the knowledge base of school administration (Amakyi and Ampah-Mensah, 2013), and successful school heads apply this to inform critical decisions. The GES perpetuates a policy for the appointment of school heads that appears to be incongruent with demands for school heads to lead school improvement. This assertion is driven by two main factors. First, educational reforms (i.e. Free Compulsory Universal Basic Education of 1995

(MoE, 1996); Educational Reforms of 2007, (MoE, undated)) in Ghana demand greater accountability from schools, improved student achievement, increased community involvement in schools and partnership with non-governmental organizations. Second, the role expectations of the school head as outlined by the GES include (a) leading and managing the school and (b) improving the quality of learning. The demands of the reforms and the role expectations require a school head who possesses the knowledge and core technical skills of leadership and management. On-the-job training alone is more likely to equip the school head with the competencies to cope with the job as it exists but not how to transform it, especially to meet the demands of the reforms (Amakyi and Ampah-Mensah, 2013).

Implications for policy

Attempts for post-employment preparation of school heads have not been carried out in a consistent manner. The absence of policy does not augur well for continuous programmes. Post-employment preparation mostly takes place through projects conducted by the universities, development partners and the GES. Once the project duration has elapsed, the preparatory programme for the school heads comes to an end. One such project is reported by the IEPA, University of Cape Coast, whose partnership with Cambridge University and the GES resulted in the post-employment preparation of basic school heads through the *Leadership for Learning (LfL)* project (IEPA, 2016). The focus of the LfL project was to improve leadership and learning in basic schools in Ghana. The LfL uses research outcomes to improve students' learning through enhancing the leadership capacity of school heads. According to the IEPA report, the institute conducted capacity-building workshops and monitoring visits to schools and offered support to school heads. The IEPA also engaged in the publication of the LfL Ghana Newsletter, outlining best operating practices, and researching and documenting Leadership for Learning activities in Ghana. The LfL principles were adopted by the GES and were used as the basis for school heads' professional development for the period the project lasted (MacBeath et al., 2013).

The knowledge base of the school head (theoretical knowledge in educational administration and craft knowledge) is paramount to meeting the demands of stakeholders. The professional preparation programmes (both pre-employment and post-employment) are designed to equip school heads with the relevant knowledge, skills and dispositions for the position. Lashway (2006) sees a period of formal preparation as a crucial socialization tool that enables aspiring school leaders to consciously confront the issues they will face as school heads. He identifies the period of formal preparation as providing the opportunity for focused reflection on school leadership dilemma, because once on the job, school heads or leaders will find reflective opportunities to be much rarer.

The gap in adopting best practices for the preparation of school heads has prompted the Ministry of Education (MoE) to act. The MoE has mooted the idea of implementing a policy to introduce a professional leadership course for school heads. According to the MoE, the initiative would help build the capacity of school heads to be abreast of current developments in the management of schools. All school heads would be required to undertake leadership training (MoE, 2018).

In tandem with the recognition that for a policy to work, there must be corresponding structures to support its implementation, the MoE announced a partnership between the Ministry and the Varkey Foundation, aimed at improving the skills of thousands of school leaders across Ghana. The partnership is to support the Ministry's priority of training all in-service and aspiring school leaders to be able to manage their schools effectively. The Varkey Foundation is mandated to develop core training modules which are designed to create leaders with the skills and competencies to drive continuous school improvement (MoE, 2018).

Implementing such a policy is laudable, and hopefully the intended purpose of the training will facilitate the provision of opportunities and structures for school-based educators to engage in continuous study, reflection, dialogue and learning to increase their effectiveness. A policy to transform the approach to school leadership that shows the readiness to address problems of practice by challenging existing models and improving the quality of the learning community in schools should be approached with the urgency it deserves. Such a policy is consistent with best practices in school leadership in many countries (e.g. Bush and Oduro, 2006; Dònkor, 2015).

Conclusion

The nature of today's school environments places new demands on school heads. They are expected to both lead and manage schools to produce students who have the essential knowledge and skills to function in information and a technologically oriented society. The school heads are to lead and manage schools, to engage in continuous school improvements and to dramatically improve student achievement. It is imperative that preparatory programmes for school heads be structured in such a manner as to enable practitioners to meet the demands of their job. Broader responsibilities and incessant pressures for deep and lasting reforms require the school head to be well prepared for the job.

The appointment of school heads in Ghana on the basis of their teaching record rather than their leadership potential and exposure to theory and practice in educational administration is arguably problematic. One cannot ascertain whether school heads are adequately prepared to carry out protracted school reforms and improvements. Professions commonly stipulate that practitioners must possess necessary knowledge, skills and abilities (Kowalski, 2008). And these are maximized with a combination of theoretical knowledge through structured academic programmes and craft knowledge through experience.

References

Amakyi, M. (2012), 'Perceptions of Problems of Practice of Heads of Senior High Schools in South West Ghana', *International Journal of Educational Leadership*, 4 (4): 274–9.

Amakyi, M. (2017), 'Profiles of High School Heads and Readiness to Address Problems of Practice', *Journal of Education and Practice*, 8 (27): 114–19.

Amakyi, M. and A. Ampah-Mensah (2013), 'Preparation of School Heads in Ghana: Making a Case for Theoretical Knowledge', *Journal of Education and Practice*, 4 (23): 154–8.

Amakyi, M. and A. Ampah-Mensah (2014), 'Reflective Practice in Teacher Education in Ghana', *International Journal of Education and Practice*, 2 (3): 42–50.

Bush, T. and D. Glover (2016), 'School Leadership in West Africa: Findings from a Systematic Literature Review', *African Education Review*, 13 (3–4): 80–103.

Bush, T. and G. Oduro (2006), 'New Principals in Africa: Preparation, Induction and Practice', *Journal of Educational Administration*, 44 (4): 359–75.

Cardno, C. (2003), 'Emerging Issues in Formalizing Principal Preparation in New Zealand', *International Electronic Journal for Leadership in Learning*, 7 (17). Available online: http://iejll.synergiesprairies

Donkor, A. K. (2015), 'Basic School Leaders in Ghana: How Equipped Are They?' *International Journal of Leadership in Education: Theory and Practice*, 18 (2), 225–38.

Ghana Education Service (2010), *Headteachers' Handbook*, Accra: Ghana Education Service.

Ghana Education Service Council (2016), 'Application for Appointment as Headmaster or Headmistress of Senior High School in the Ghana Education Service', *ESC*, 73 (3): 121.

IEPA (2016), *Institute for Educational Planning and Administration Students' Handbook*, Cape Coast: University of Cape Coast Press.

Kowalski, T. J. (2008), *Case Studies on Educational Administration*, 5th edn, Boston: Allyn and Bacon.

Lashway, L. (2006), 'The Landscape of School Leadership', in S. C. Smith and P. K. Piele (eds), *School Leadership: A Handbook for Excellence in Student Learning*, 18–37, Thousand Oaks: Corwin.

MacBeath, J., S. Swaffield, G. K. T. Oduro, and A. Ampah-Mensah (2013), 'Building Leadership Capacity, Enhancing Learning and Teaching in Ghanaian Basic Schools', in J. MacBeath and M. Younger (eds), *A Common Wealth of Learning: Millennium Development Revisited*, 49–60, London: Routledge.

MoE (undated), *Education Reforms at a Glance*. Available online: https://planipolis.iiep. unesco.org/sites/planipolis/files/ressources/ghana_education_reform_2007.pdf

MoE (1996), *Free Compulsory Universal Basic Education (FCUBE)*, Accra: Ministry of Education.

MoE (2012), *Education Strategic Plan 2010–2020*, Accra: Ministry of Education.

MoE (2018), 'School Leaders to Undergo Training in New MoE-Varkey Partnership'. Available online: http://moe.gov.gh/index.php/school-leaders-to-undergo-traini ng-in-new-moe-varkey-partnership/

Oduro, G. (2003), 'Perspectives of Ghanaian Headteachers on Their Role and Professional Development: The Case of KEEA District Primary School', Doctoral diss., University of Cambridge, Cambridge.

Oduro, G. and R. Bosu (2010), 'Leadership and Management of Change for Quality Improvement', EdQual – Ghana policy brief No. 5. Available online: https://www.edqual.org/publications/policy-briefs/pb5.pdf/at_download/file.pdf

WAEC (undated). *Basic Education Certificate Examination for School Candidates*. Available online: https://www.waecgh.org/bece

Woodruff, S. B. (2008), 'Perceptions of Ohio Novice High School Principals Regarding Problems of Practice', *Dissertation Abstracts International*, 69 (2). (UMI No.3302610).

Woodruff, S. B. and T. J. Kowalski (2009), 'Problems Encountered by Novice High School Principals: Implications for Academic Preparation and State Licensing', Paper Presented at the Annual Meeting of the American Education Research Association, San Diego, CA.

Zame, M. Y., W. C. Hope, and T. Respress (2008), 'Educational Reform in Ghana: The Leadership Challenge', *International Journal of Educational Management*, 22 (2): 115–28.

Zubeviel, T. (2012), 'Improving Educational Outcomes: The Leadership Imperative', *Feature Article of Saturday*, 17 March 2012. Available online: https://www.ghanaweb .com/GhanaHomePage/features/Improving-Educational-Outcomes-The-Leaders hip-Imperative-232940?channel=D1

10

A Review of Preparation and Development of School Leaders in Nigeria

Raphael Isibor Imoni

Introduction

Obiakor (2004) argues that leadership in Africa is mostly a borrowed concept. He also expresses the need for African countries to develop their own educational philosophies. This implies that African nations develop attitudes that would produce authentic leadership. He states the need 'for the institutionalization of a pragmatic system of African-centered education that opens concrete rooms for African experiments and African experiences and fosters the use of the African body, mind, and soul' (Obiakor, 2004: 404). Hallinger (2017: 16), supports the need for 'diversifying the global knowledge base' in relation to research from Africa, with a view to exploring new areas in educational leadership and management. The implication here is that good leadership preparation will lead to good practice. Thus, a well-balanced education might serve as the basis for this preparation. This chapter focuses on the nature of leadership preparation and development in Nigeria.

Nigeria National Policy on Education

The Nigeria National Policy on Education provides a framework for education from primary to tertiary levels. This framework stipulates leadership preparation and development. The policy states that 'education shall continue to be highly rated in the national development plans ... education and training facilities shall continue to be expanded in response to societal needs' (FRN, 2004: 4). The National Policy (FRN, 2004) identifies the broad goals of secondary education.

It includes national development through education and the acquisition of skills and ability for personal development. Furthermore, the National Policy also makes 'provision in teacher education programmes for specialization in early childhood education' (FRN 2004: 7) and that 'all teachers ... shall be encouraged to undergo training in methods and techniques of teaching' (op cit: 25) and should be 'regularly exposed to innovations in their profession' and 'regular in-service training programmes for teachers and headteachers' (op cit: 28–29). Arguably, self-development includes the development of those who aspire to leadership and management of educational institutions.

However, many commentators (e.g., Arikewuyo, 2009a) lament the lack of political will by the government in the implementation of this policy. Arikewuyo suggested that leadership preparation and development of school leaders would contribute towards solving educational problems (Arikewuyo, 2007). Despite this policy, Humphreys and Crawfurd (2014: vii) claim that the 'overall evidence base on the outcomes of basic education in Nigeria is weak. There is no nationally institutionalised system for the regular measurement of learning outcomes. However, those measures that do exist suggest very low learning levels'.

Headship and school leadership preparation

Principals and heads provide school leadership at the secondary and primary school levels (Imoni, 2018; Adeniyi, 2014; Iwu and Iwu, 2013; Ololube, 2006). It is recognized that effective principals and heads of schools are needed to realize organizational goals and objectives. The principal serves as the coordinating agent in collaboration with other staff. Adeniyi (2014) believes that the managerial competence of the school principal links to personality traits. Arguably, school leadership in Nigeria differs from that in the rest of the world. For example, while distributed leadership is advocated in some Western countries, it is mostly allocative distributed leadership in Nigeria's highly centralized system (Imoni, 2018). This suggests the need for specific leadership development suitable for leadership practice in Nigeria (Adegbemile, 2011).

There is little preparation for leadership in Nigeria (Arikewuyo, 2007; Nakpodia, 2012; Ikegbusi, 2016). Nakpodia (2012: 94) argues that the 'quality that any educational institution in a country looks for in terms of effective administration and management is leadership skills'. He claims that leadership skills are lacking in Nigerian schools. Ikegbusi's (2016) survey of 100 principals from the South East geopolitical zone of Nigeria, involving five states – Abia, Anambra, Ebonyi, Enugu and Imo – shows the lack of adequate training and preparation of school principals and other staff in leadership positions. Similarly, Uwakwe's (2017) survey of 162 principals and 1,077 teachers drawn from three states – Anambra, Ebonyi and Enugu – suggests a lack of leadership preparation. These authors recommend the preparation of those appointed to a leadership position to equip them for effective school management.

Following a study carried out in South East Nigeria, Uwakwe (2017: 16510) argues that 'it is obvious that principals who were appointed to manage the schools are incompetent and lacked the required capacities to effectively cope with the myriads of students' personnel management roles'. He further states that principals from South East Nigeria need highly skilled and trained school leaders to achieve high-quality teaching and learning and effective school management. In a review of the basic literature on education in Nigeria, Humphreys and Crawfurd (2014) link poor teaching and the overloaded curriculum to the lack of proper training of teachers. They argue that teachers need support and mentoring. Similarly, Arikewuyo (2009a) investigates the assessment of the training needs of principals newly appointed to junior secondary schools from Rivers and Bayelsa states (south-south), as well as in Lagos and Ogun (south-west) geopolitical zones in Nigeria. The study includes 485 principals: 120 from Bayelsa State, 105 from Rivers State, 140 from Lagos State and 120 from Ogun State. The study shows that all the principals were evaluated during several workshops organized for principals of secondary schools in Nigeria between 2006 and 2007. The study concludes that the 'training needs of principals are still at a low ebb in Nigeria' (Arikewuyo (2009a): 101). The author argues that school leaders, particularly principals, agreed that they need some form of training in leadership and management to effectively achieve the goals and objectives of their organizations.

Teacher leadership and development

There are several studies linking school leadership practice with teacher development. Moorosi and Bush (2011) distinguish between categories of leadership preparation. They note that 'while leadership development is often used as a generic term for both pre-service and in-service leadership training, leadership preparation and development are deliberately distinguished in this paper to give sufficient focus to each type of training' (Moorosi and Bush, 2011:

60). The view that specific leadership training should be provided is supported by Eacott and Asuga (2014), who see leadership preparation and development in Africa as 'hot topics' in the scholarship of educational leadership, management and administration. Similarly, Bush and Oduro (2006) highlight the challenges faced by school principals in Africa, ranging from the poor working environment to untrained staff. They also note that the appointment of principals is based on years of experience rather than formal training. Bush and Jackson (2002) point to the now widely accepted notion that teachers need both initial training and in-service development in order to be effective classroom practitioners. In the same breath, they advocate for the need for continuing professional development for principals throughout their careers. In their systematic review of the literature on West Africa, Bush and Glover (2016) uncover a number of practices within the region that pertain to lack of preparation for leadership. They argue that specific preparation is needed by principals to articulate current leadership practices. Their review shows

> the challenges faced by principals in improving and developing their teachers. Classroom practice is the most significant variable influencing learner outcomes (leadership is second) and in-service professional development is essential to enhance subject knowledge, pedagogic skills, and classroom management. This is one of the most important roles for principals, but … being aware of development needs is only the starting point and many principals do not have access to high-quality training opportunities for their teachers (or even for themselves). (Bush and Glover 2016: 93)

Moja (2000) discusses the establishment of centres for the training of teachers in Nigeria. She argues that the National Commission for College Education (NCCE) is responsible for teacher professional training and observes the lack of focus on the developmental needs of managers. Arikewuyo (2009b: 80) argues that 'the professional training of school administrators, particularly principals of secondary schools, has not been given any serious attention in Nigeria's educational policies'.

Presently, Nigeria has 58 colleges of education. The NCCE is responsible for setting up guidelines for the training of teachers. The National Policy on Education stipulates the minimum requirement for graduates of colleges of education, which is the National Certificate of Education (NCE). It follows that graduates from colleges of education could only teach in primary and secondary schools. However, those who aspire to teach at secondary school level are required to have a university degree in education.

Teacher on-going professional development

Moja (2000) presents imperatives for training administrators and school leaders for self-development aimed at effective school leadership:

> The development of human resource capacity for the delivery of an effective education is critical. There are human resource needs for administration, management, research and teaching, as well as for support and technical staff. Lack of well-trained human resources is a problem in almost every area of education. There is an urgent need for capacity building in the various Commissions charged with responsibility for governing and managing different aspects of education. (Moja, 2000: 39)

The importance of leadership training for school leaders was also underscored by Akinola (2013):

> Principals' leadership skills are crucial in ensuring academic achievement of students. The poor academic performance of south western Nigerian public secondary school students in external examinations cast doubts on the possession of leadership skills by their principals This study, therefore, seeks to find out if the principals of public secondary schools in south western Nigeria possess leadership skills and the relationship between the leadership skills they possess or lack and school effectiveness. (Akinola, 2013: 28)

Akinola (2013) also argues that, even though school principals in South West Nigeria possessed some leadership skills, there was much room for improvement. The Nigerian policy on education indicates that 'all teachers in educational institutions shall be professionally trained. Teacher education programs shall be structured to equip teachers for the effective performance of their duties' (FRN, 2004: 39–40). However, there is no mention of the professional development of principals, leaving the individuals to develop themselves. This may be because principals are appointed based on competence and experience, which is why individuals strive to attain the highest academic standard (Imoni, 2018). This practice of appointing principals on the basis of experience, rather than their qualifications and training, appears to have contributed to the falling standard in the quality of leadership provided in secondary schools (Oladipo, Adebakin and Iranloye, 2016; Arikewuyo, 2009b). Arikewuyo (2009b: 80) notes that, 'despite the enormous expectations of school principals, many are poorly prepared for the task'. Nakpodia (2012) advocates the training of principals to acquire appropriate leadership skills.

The government's reform strategy

To address the training of principals, the federal government of Nigeria set up a reform strategy in 2002 (Saint, Hartnett and Strassner, 2003). The reform process involves the establishment of a National Education Support Strategy for Nigeria. The body focused on school improvement from 2006 to 2015. To address this programme, the federal government of Nigeria approved agencies and parastatals to focus on education development and improvement by the year 2020. The agency has the remit to develop a new vision for schools. The role of the agencies included starting a process of reform to equip teachers and school leaders with adequate knowledge appropriate for school leadership. The Federal Ministry of Education also established other agencies with responsibility for teacher quality, standards and accountability (Federal Ministry of Education, 2008). The agencies were announced in 2009 and include a wide range of bodies:

> The [*sic*] Federal Ministry of Education (FMOE) and State Ministries of Education (SMOEs), UBE Commission, National and State Legislatures, State Universal basic Education Boards (SUBEBs), Local Government Education Authorities (LGEAs), Host Communities of Basic Education Institutions, Traditional rulers/community leaders and, Schools (their Administrators and School Management Committees). Others are Parents, Teachers, Learners (Basic 1–9), Judiciary and law enforcement Agencies, Private Sectors/corporate organizations, Non-Governmental organizations (NGOs), Community Based Organizations (CBOs), Civil Society Organizations (CSOs including Faith Based Organizations [FBOs]), and the Media. (Amuche and Kukwi, 2013: 159–60)

During this period, the government discovered that reforms cannot be achieved without highly qualified, competent and motivated school leaders. This led to the setting up of the National Institute for the training of teachers and for professional development (FME, 2008). However, there seems to be no follow-up to this laudable plan, as most principals rely on personal self-development rather than well-structured training provided by the government. Okoro (2011) is critical of the ineptitude and failure of Nigeria's school system. He argues that there is a failure by the government and stakeholders to meet the needs and aspirations of the Nigerian public. He states that the policy on universal primary education 'was widely regarded as a failure as it was marred by inadequate planning, insufficient infrastructure and unqualified teachers' (Okoro, 2011: 7). This view is supported by Okoroma (2006) and Nwagwu (2002), who blame policy failure on lack of adequate planning. The authors further attribute this apparent setback to poor leadership.

Leadership models

Having discussed some issues affecting leadership, and the need for training principals and other staff in leadership responsibilities, it is important to highlight some leadership models that might form part of their training and development as educational leaders. This might be helpful to those already employed as principals and school heads, or those aspiring to such roles. Uwazurike (1991) points to the need for educational leadership and theories of management for Nigerian schools. This view is reinforced by Ofoegbu, Clark and Osagie (2013), who argue that leadership preparation is a recurring challenge in the Nigerian school system. The following leadership models are likely to be helpful to understanding and enacting leadership in Nigerian schools.

Managerial leadership: Adegbesan (2013: 16) argues that the key element in managerial leadership is the 'ability to lead effectively, coordinate a complex situation and shows concern for both the human and material resources available'. He further notes the need for coordination and effective performance of interdependent leadership roles that seem difficult in the work environment, where important decisions have to be made on a systematic and continuing basis (Adegbesan, 2013). Gberevbie et al. (2017) reinforce the notion of accountability for effective school management, as seen also in the hierarchical model presented here. Adeyemi (2010) notes the effects of supervision and mentoring to elicit better job performance among teachers. However, he argues that school heads can sometimes be more effective when they employ the autocratic leadership model (Adeyemi and Bolarinwa, 2013). Othman, Mohammed and D'Silva (2013) claim that managerial leadership can bring about organizational commitment. This claim is reinforced by Bush and Glover (2016). Their study shows that there is no specific leadership preparation in West Africa, including in Nigeria, but that the main leadership style tends to be managerial. The study recommends the development of specific programmes for current and aspiring principals (Bush and Glover, 2016).

Instructional model: The primary aim of this model is to improve school development through pedagogy (Adeogun, 2015; Salo, Nylund and Stjernstrøm 2015). Principals and school heads provide direction for learning and progress. Leithwood et al. (2004) believe that teachers' behaviour positively affects student outcomes when they engage in activities that directly affect the growth of students. Arikewuyo (2009a, 2009b) notes the link between teacher leadership and learning as well as that between teacher leadership and curriculum leadership (Spillane and Diamond, 2007; Timperley, 2005). Several studies support this notion. For example, principals provide the direction for collaboration for teaching and learning by motivating teachers (Olujuwon and Perumal, 2015; Okoroji, Anyanwu and Ukpere, 2014; Duze, 2012). This is because 'the accomplishment of school aims and objectives depends highly on teachers being the prime movers in the implementation of curriculum and teaching/learning' (Duze, 2012: 155–66). This suggests a demand for effective teacher training programmes for the Nigerian teachers of the twenty-first century (Ololube, 2006a; Obanya, 2004). Duze (2012: 112), for example, claims that 'the role of instructional leadership for school principals … is a relatively new concept of the early 1980s which called for a shift of emphasis from principals being managers or administrators to instructional leaders'.

Transformational leadership: 'Transformational leadership is a comprehensive model in that it provides a normative approach to school leadership which focuses primarily on the process by which leaders seek to influence school outcomes, rather on the nature or direction of those outcomes' (Bush, 2011: 85). Critical to this model is the quality of leadership, and a positive school climate for principals, students and the entire school (Leithwood et al., 1999). Benwari and Dambo (2014: 405) link transformational leadership to the process of change and greater productivity. They imply that transformational leaders encourage change, leading to greater efficiency. In this model, it is the responsibility of the principal to create a conducive school climate by creating school goals and building its vision, as well as offering support to individuals. Ofoegbu et al. (2013) believe that school leaders engage in bringing about change in their organizations. The model advocates that the principal's duty is to promote learning and teaching (McCarley, Michelle and John, 2016). Hallinger (2017) note the emerging literature on leadership transformation in Africa, including in Nigeria.

Corroborating the notion of transformational leadership in Nigeria, Olujuwon and Perumal (2018: 77) note that, in Nigeria, the 'principal's leadership style and behaviour plays an important role in enhancing teacher's morale and effectiveness in achieving goals', suggesting a transformational approach. The study suggests that principals exercise influence on teachers by developing working relationship with subordinates as colleagues. In this way, principals create a participative environment for leadership by enabling teachers to articulate the direction of teaching and learning. Their study recommends that principals see teachers working in partnership to achieve school goals and objectives. Akomolafe (2012) suggests many ways in which teachers benefit from transformational leadership in Ekiti State, Nigeria. Such benefits include being motivated by school principals, being curriculum leaders and building a school vision collaboratively. The principal's transformational leadership style also suggests rewards for good behaviour and excellence by the principal as incentives for hard work to teachers (Akomolafe, 2012).

Participative leadership: The participative leadership model recognizes leadership qualities in other members of staff. It recognizes and utilizes the 'input of others' (Amanchukwu, Stanley and Ololube, 2015: 8). School heads utilize the participative model to encourage contributions from individuals to address the goals and objectives of the school. It 'encourages participation and contributions from group members and helps group members to feel relevant and committed to the decision-making process' (Amanchukwu, Stanley and Ololube, 2015: 8). The participative leadership approach is conceived as a model that empowers individuals to be involved in a collaborative partnership for the benefit of the school. It creates a sense of ownership in the process of leadership (Imoni, 2018). For example, vice principals, teachers and heads of departments acknowledge participation in various decision-making processes as a sense of belonging and a means to participate in school leadership. Moreover, participation in leadership eases the burden of leadership on school heads (Imoni, 2018). Imoni (2018) shows that this was evident in his study of distributed leadership in Nigeria, for example, in the frequency of school meetings where principals encouraged staff input. Participation in the school's decision-making processes also created a sense of ownership by teachers and principals, as shown in Imoni's (Imoni, 2018) research. Amanchukwu et al. (2015: 10) link decision-making to a democratic process in which 'team members tend to have high job satisfaction and are productive because they are more involved'. As Stegall and Linton (2012: 63) note, the nature of decision-making forms a core element in participative leadership:

> For teachers to become effective leaders, administrators must create the appropriate environment. This includes providing opportunities for teachers to make appropriate instructional decisions for the school, processes for building trust and rapport, opportunities to collaborate with peers in order to build shared capacity, and occasions to make decisions regarding resource allocations and school processes.

Distributed leadership: This model has been described as the 'normatively preferred leadership model in the twenty-first century, replacing collegiality as the favoured approach' (Bush, 2011: 88). Gronn (2000: 333) says that it is 'an idea whose time has come'. Harris (2008) argues that distributed leadership does not mean that everyone leads but that everyone has the potential to lead under the right circumstances. She also suggests that 'distributed leadership has captured the imagination of those in educational leadership and is appealing to policymakers, researchers and practitioners alike' (Harris, 2007: 315). Lumby (2013) argues that distributed leadership is popular because it is more inclusive than other models of leadership, while Harris and Muijs (2003: 438) say that distributed leadership helps 'teachers to develop expertise by working collaboratively'.

In Nigeria, teachers have been seen to adapt themselves to school conditions to achieve organizational goals and objectives (Onyekuru and Ibegbunam, 2013). As Obadara (2013: 73), notes, 'schools need to adopt a distributed leadership model because school organizations are so complex and tasks so wide-ranging that no one person can manage all'. Imoni's (2018) study of distributed leadership in Nigeria suggests notions of allocative distributed leadership in the form of leadership delegation in a highly centralized school system.

> The growing popularity of distributed leadership has led to various interpretations. These include allocative distributed leadership, which seems particularly well suited to centralised countries such as Nigeria, where distributed leadership assumes the form of leadership delegation, informed by accountability within a hierarchical school system. The concept is relatively new in Nigeria, and the pattern of distribution appears to be top-down, linked to the emerging theme of allocative distributed leadership. (Imoni, 2018: 57)

Imoni's (Imoni, 2018) findings indicate that teachers are predominantly assigned tasks to perform to achieve school objectives. He argues that 'distributed leadership should be promoted as a lens for leadership practice in the Nigerian educational system. Allocative distributed leadership has the potential to enhance leadership within schools in Nigeria given that participants regard it as a fluid approach to leadership' (Imoni, 2018: 268–9).

The above leadership approaches might appear normative or prescriptive. However, they illustrate what might form part of a curriculum for leadership preparation and development. As Bush (2010: 112) notes, 'the argument that leadership does make a difference is increasingly, if not universally, accepted, [but] there is an ongoing debate about what preparation is required to develop appropriate leadership behaviour'. As noted here, there is emerging evidence that Nigerian school leaders enact a range of leadership practices. It is imperative that effective training, including awareness of leadership models, be developed for current and future school leaders to prepare them for the complex role of school leadership in Nigeria.

Conclusion

Nigerian principals provide direction for schools within the hierarchy of the Ministry of Education (MoE). Their power and control are limited, and they need the support of other staff. The MoE is ultimately responsible for school management, while the principal remains the immediate link between government, the school board and the staff. It is important, therefore, for principals to acquire basic knowledge and skills to deal with the complex school environment. There is increasing evidence of parents' involvement in schools, often through parent–teacher associations (Imoni, 2018; Ajayi, 2008). This body is presided over by an elected member of the association. The principal is present at any meeting, and this further emphasizes the need for the principal to engage more fully in school leadership through professional development. Such training is likely to assist in facilitating school improvement. There are likely to be positive outcomes if principals engage in formal leadership preparation and continuous professional development, including greater efficiency and better school outcomes.

References

Adegbemile, O. (2011), 'Principals' Competency Needs for Effective Schools' Administration in Nigeria', *Journal of Education and Practice*, 2 (4): 15–23.

Adegbesan, S. O. (2013), 'Effect of Principals' Leadership Style on Teachers' Attitude to Work in Ogun State Secondary Schools, Nigeria', *Turkish Online Journal of Distance Education – TOJDE*, 14 (1): 14–28.

Adeniyi, W. O. (2014), 'Personality Traits and Administrative Effectiveness of Secondary School Principals in Southwestern Nigeria', *Advances in Social Science Research*, 1 (8): 198–206.

Adeogun, A. O. (2015), 'Reconceptualizing the Music Teacher Education Curriculum for the Colleges of Education in Nigeria', *SAGE Open*, 8 (2): 1–12.

Adeyemi, T. O. (2010), 'Principals' Leadership Styles and Teachers' Job Performance in Senior Secondary Schools in Ondo State, Nigeria', *Journal of Education Administration and Policy Studies*, 2 (6): 83–91.

Adeyemi, T. O. and R. Bolarinwa (2013), 'Principals' Leadership Styles and Student Academic Performance in Secondary Schools in Ekiti State, Nigeria', *International Journal of Academic Research in Progressive Education and Development*, 2 (1): 187–98.

Ajayi, H. O. (2008), 'Early Childhood Education in Nigeria: A Reality or a Mirage?' *Contemporary Issues in Early Childhood*, 9 (4): 375–80.

Akinola, O. B. (2013), 'Principals' Leadership Skills and School Effectiveness: The Case of South Western Nigeria', *World Journal of Education*, 3 (5): 26–32.

Akomolafe, C. O. (2012), 'Principals' Leadership Capacities as Perceived by Teachers in Secondary Schools in Ekiti State, Nigeria', *European Scientific Journal*, 8 (22): 28–38.

Amanchukwu, R. N., G. J. Stanley, and N. P. Ololube (2015), 'A Review of Leadership Theories, Principles and Styles and Their Relevance to Educational Management', *Scientific & Academic Publishing*, 5 (1): 6–14.

Amuche, C. I. and I. J. Kukwi (2013), 'An Assessment of Stakeholders' Perception of the Implementation of Universal Basic Education in North-Central Geo-Political Zone of Nigeria', *Journal of Education and Practice*, 4 (3): 158–67.

Arikewuyo, M. O. (2007), 'Teachers' Perception of Principals' Leadership Capacities in Nigeria', *Academic Leadership Journal*, 5 (3): 1–8.

Arikewuyo, M. O. (2009a), 'An Assessment of the Training Needs of Newly Appointed Principals of Junior South-South and South-West Regions of Nigeria', *Research in Education* 82: 100–6.

Arikewuyo, M. O. (2009b), 'Professional Training of Secondary School Principals in Nigeria: A Neglected Area in the Educational System', *Florida Journal of Educational Administration & Policy*, 2 (2): 73–84.

Benwari, N. N. and B. I. Dambo (2014), 'Improving Secondary Schools Management through Transformational Leadership Approach and Management Information Systems', *Journal of Educational and Social Research MCSER Publishing*, 4 (6): 401–6.

Bush, T. (2010), 'Leadership Development', in T. Bush, L. Bell and D. Middlewood, *The Principles of Educational Leadership and Management*, 2nd edn, London: Sage.

Bush, T. (2011), *Theories of Educational Leadership and Management*, 4th edn, London: Sage.

Bush, T. and D. Glover (2016), 'School Leadership in West Africa: Findings from a Systematic Literature Review', *Africa Education Review*, 13 (3–4): 80–103.

Bush, T. and D. Jackson (2002), 'A Preparation for School Leadership: International Perspectives', *Educational Management & Administration*, 30 (4): 417–29.

Bush, T. and G. Oduro (2006), 'New Principals in Africa: Preparation, Induction and Practice', *Journal of Education Administration*, 44: 359–75.

Duze, C. O. (2012), 'The Changing Role of School Leadership and Teacher Capacity Building in Teaching and Learning', *Journal of Emerging Trends in Educational Research and Policy Studies (JETERAPS)*, 3 (1): 111–17.

Eacott, S. and G. N. Asuga (2014), 'School Leadership Preparation and Development in Africa: A Critical Insight', *Educational Management Administration & Leadership*, 42 (6): 919–34.

FME (2008), The Development of Education National Report of Nigeria by The Federal Ministry of Education for the Forty-Eight Session of the International Conference on Education (ICE) Theme: Inclusive Education: The Way Future Geneva, Switzerland, 25–8. Available at www.ibe.unesco.org/fileadmin/user.../National_Repo rts/ICE_2008/nigeria_NR08.pdf

FRN (2004), *Federal Republic of Nigeria, National Policy On*, 4th edn, Abuja: NERDC Press.

Gberevbie, D., S. Joshua, N. Excellence-Oluye, and A. Oyeyemi (2017), 'Accountability for Sustainable Development and the Challenges of Leadership in Nigeria, 1999–2015', *SAGE Open*, 7 (4): 1–10.

Gronn, P. (2000), 'Distributed Leadership: A New Architecture for Leadership', *Educational Management Administration and Leadership*, 28 (3): 317–38.

Hallinger, P. (2017), 'Surfacing a Hidden Literature: A Systematic Review of Research on Educational Leadership and Management in Africa', *Educational Management Administration & Leadership*, 1–23.

Harris, A. (2007), 'Distributed Leadership: Conceptual Confusion and Empirical Reticence', *International Journal of Leadership in Education: Theory and Practice*, 10 (3): 315–25.

Harris, A. (2008), 'Distributed Leadership: According to the Evidence', *Journal of Educational Administration*, 46 (2): 172–88.

Harris, A. and D. Muijs (2003), Teacher Leadership – Improvement through Empowerment? An Overview of the Literature, *Educational Management & Administration*, 31 (4): 437–48.

Humphreys, S. and L. Crawfurd (2014), *Review of the Literature on Basic Education in Nigeria: Issues of Access, Quality, Equity and Impact*. Available online: https://ed orennigeria.files.wordpress.com/2014/07/review-of-the-literature-on-basic-educat ion-in-nigeria-june-2014-3-1.pdf (assessed on 24 September 2018).

Ikegbusi, N. Gloria. (2016), 'Management Competency Needs of Principals for Effective Administration of Secondary Schools in Nigeria', *International Journal of Advanced Research in Education & Technology (IJARET)*, 3 (3): 61–7.

Imoni, R. I. (2018), 'Leadership Distribution in Government Secondary Schools in Nigeria: Fact or Fiction?' (Unpublished thesis), University of Nottingham.

Iwu, C. G. and I. C. Iwu (2013), 'Factors Inhibiting Effective Management of Primary Schools in Nigeria: The Case of Ebonyi State', *Journal of Social Science*, 35 (1): 51–60.

Leithwood, K., D. Jantzi and R. Steinbach (1999), *Changing Leadership for Changing Times*, Buckingham: Open University Press.

Leithwood, K., K. S. Louis, S. Anderson and K. Wahlstrom (2004), *How Leadership Influences Student Learning. Review of Research. Wallace Foundation*.

Lumby, J. (2013), 'Distributed Leadership: The Uses and Abuses of Power', *Educational Management Administration & Leadership*, 41 (5): 581–97.

McCarley, T. A., L. P. Michelle, and M. D. John (2016), 'Transformational Leadership Related to School Climate: A Multi-Level Analysis', *Educational Management Administration & Leadership*, 44 (2): 322–42.

Moja, T. (2000), *Nigeria Education Sector Analysis: An Analytical Synthesis of Performance and Main Issues*, Washington DC: The World Bank.

Moorosi, P. and T. Bush (2011), 'School Leadership Development in Commonwealth Countries: Learning across Boundaries', *International Studies in Educational Administration*, 39 (3): 59–75.

Nakpodia, E. D. (2012), 'Leadership Development Skills: A Nigeria Educational Institution Review', *Global Business and Economics Research Journal*, 1 (2): 93–110.

Nwagwu, N. (2002), 'From UPE to UBE: Some Basic Planning Considerations for Effectiveness'. Lead paper presented at a conference organized by the National Institute of Educational Planning and Administration, Ondo May 30–31.

Obadara, O. E. (2013), 'Relationship between Distributed Leadership and Sustainable School Improvement', *International Journal of Education and Science*, 5 (1): 69–74.

Obanya, P. (2004), *The Dilemma of Education in Africa*, Ibadan: Heinemann Educational Books.

Obiakor, F. E. (2004), 'Building Patriotic African Leadership through African-Centered Education', *Journal of Black Studies*, 34 (3): 402–20.

Ofoegbu, F. I., A. O. Clark, and R. O. Osagie (2013), 'Leadership Theories and Practice: Charting a Path for Improved Nigerian Schools', *International Studies in Educational Administration*, 41 (2): 67–76.

Okoro, M. (2011), 'Funding Teacher Education: A Catalyst for Enhancing the Universal Basic Education in Imo State of Nigeria', unpublished thesis, Seton Hall University Dissertations and Theses (ETDs). Paper 436.

Okoroji, L. I., O. J. Anyanwu, and W. I. Ukpere (2014), 'Impact of Leadership Styles on Teaching and Learning Process in Imo State', *Mediterranean Journal of Social Sciences*, 5 (4): 180–93.

Okoroma, N. S. (2006), 'Educational Policies and Problems of Implementation in Nigeria', *Australian Journal of Adult Learning*, 46 (2): 243–63.

Oladipo, S. A., A. B. Adebakin, and O. F. Iranloye (2016), 'Mentoring and Succession of Administrators: Critical Issues in Public and Private Secondary Schools in Lagos State, Nigeria', *Bulgarian Journal of Science and Education Policy (BJSEP)*, 10 (1): 19–38.

Ololube, N. P. (2006), 'The Impact of Professional and Non-Professional Teachers' ICT Competencies in Secondary Schools in Nigeria', *Journal of Information Technology Impact*, 6 (2): 101–18.

Ololube, N. P. (2006a), 'Teachers Instructional Material Utilization Competencies in Secondary Schools in Sub-Saharan Africa: Professional and Non-Professional Teachers' Perspective', *Conference Proceedings of the 6th International Educational Technology Conference* EMU, 19–21, North Cyprus.

Olujuwon, T. and J. Perumal (2015), 'Promoting Teacher Leadership in Nigerian Public Secondary Schools', *Conference: 59th World Assembly of the International Council on Education for Teaching at Naruto*, Japan, 59.

Olujuwon, T. and J. Perumal (2018), 'Exploring the Tools of Leadership by Education Leaders in Public Secondary Schools in Lagos', Conference Paper, International Council on Education for Teaching: Expanding Access and Exploring Frontiers: Laredo, Texas. Available online: https://www.researchgate.net/publication/328290254

Onyekuru, B. U. and J. O. Ibegbunam (2013), 'Teaching Effectiveness of Secondary School Teachers in Emohua Local Government Area of Rivers State, Nigeria', *European Scientific Journal*, 9 (28): 1857–81.

Othman, J., K. A. Mohammed, and J. L. D'Silva (2013), 'Does a Transformational and Transactional Leadership Style Predict Organizational Commitment among Public University Lecturers in Nigeria?' *Asian Social Science*, 9 (1): 165–70.

Saint, W., T. Hartnett, and E. Strassner (2003), 'Higher Education in Nigeria: A Status Report', *Higher Education Policy*, 16: 259–81.

Salo, P., J. Nylund, and E. Stjernstrøm (2015), 'On the Practice Architectures of Instructional Leadership', *Educational Management Administration and Leadership*, 43 (4): 490–506.

Spillane, J. P. and J. B. Diamond (2007), *Distributed Leadership in Practice*, New York: Teachers College Press.

Stegall, D. and J. Linton (2012), 'Teachers in the Lead: A District's Approach to Shared Leadership', *Phil Delta Kappan*, 93 (7): 62–5.

Timperley, H. S. (2005), 'Distributed Leadership: Developing Theory from Practice', *Journal of Curriculum Studies*, 37 (4): 395–420.

Uwakwe, I. S. (2017), 'Capacity Building Needs of School Principals for the Effective Students' Personnel Services in Secondary Schools In South East, Nigeria', *International Journal of Development Research*, 7 (11): 16508–24.

Uwazurike, C. N. (1991), 'Theories of Educational Leadership: Implications for Nigerian Educational Leaders', *Educational Management and Administration*, 19 (4): 259–63.

11

How Does Africa Compare to the Rest of the World?

Tony Bush

Introduction

Leadership is widely understood to be the second most important factor influencing student outcomes (Leithwood et al., 2006: 5). There is also compelling evidence that specific leadership behaviours are more likely be effective in promoting student learning. Transformational leadership has been advocated for more than 20 years because of the research showing that it has positive effects on student outcomes. Leithwood et al. (2006) also stressed the importance of distributed leadership, describing this claim as 'compelling'. However, Robinson, Hohepa and Lloyd (2009) concluded that instructional leadership is more powerful than transformational leadership in promoting student learning:

> The impact of pedagogical (instructional) leadership is three to four times that of transformational leadership. The reason for this is that transformational leadership is focused on the relationships between leader and follower rather than on the educational work of the school. (Robinson, Hohepa and Lloyd, 2009: 201)

This brief review shows that transformational, distributed and instructional leadership models all have their advocates, supported by some convincing empirical evidence (Bush, 2018). A fundamental question is, how school leaders acquire the knowledge, understanding and skills to practice as effective leaders, deploying any or all of these models? The logical answer is that these dimensions should be included in principal preparation and development programmes. However, principal preparation is neglected in many countries, including most of Africa, where a teaching qualification and teaching experience are considered to be sufficient requirements for new principals, as noted in most of the chapters in this book. Bush and Oduro (2006: 362) comment that the preponderance of views among African national and local administrators is that good classroom teachers will become effective school leaders without specific preparation. Such policies fail to recognize that being a principal is a different role from classroom teaching and requires specific preparation (Bush, 2008, 2018; Crow, Lumby and Pashiardis, 2008).

The case for leadership preparation

The case for specific preparation is linked to the evidence that the quality of leadership is vital for school improvement and student outcomes, as noted above. In most countries, school leaders begin their professional careers as teachers and progress to headship via a range of middle and senior leadership and management roles. Principals often continue to teach following their appointment, particularly in small primary schools. This leads to a widespread view that teaching is their main activity, and that a teaching qualification and teaching experience are the only requirements for school leadership. Bush and Oduro (2006: 362) note that 'throughout Africa, there is no formal requirement for principals to be trained as school managers. They are often appointed on the basis of a successful record as teachers with the implicit assumption that this provides a sufficient starting point for school leadership'. However, as shown in several chapters in this volume, specific preparation is required to enhance the quality of leadership. As Pansiri and Majwabe note, in respect of Botswana, 'leadership cannot be left to chance'. Similarly, Mestry argues that in South Africa, 'leadership preparation … is central to school effectiveness and school improvement'. Imoni claims that there is a lack of adequate training and preparation of school principals in Nigeria.

The case for trained leaders is underpinned by four overlapping considerations:

The expansion of the role of school principal.
Devolution to school level.
Recognition that preparation is a moral obligation.
Recognition that effective preparation and development make a difference.

(Adapted from Bush, 2008, 2018)

The expanded role of school leaders

The additional responsibilities imposed on principals in many countries make great demands on post holders, especially those embarking on the role for the first time (Walker and Qian 2006). These demands often relate to the accountability pressures facing principals. Governments, parents and the wider public expect a great deal from their schools, and most of these expectations are transmitted via the principals. The pressures facing leaders in developing contexts are even more onerous than those in the world's richest countries. In many countries in Africa, principals manage schools with poor buildings; little or no equipment; untrained teachers; a lack of basic facilities such as water, power and sanitation; and learners who are often hungry (Bush and Oduro, 2006).

Ofoegbu, Clark and Osagie (2013: 67) undertook research with 237 people undertaking school leadership training in Nigeria to ascertain their expectations of skills to be developed in meeting their potential leadership roles. In a powerful critique, they conclude that

> the Nigerian school of today is different and much more complex than that of some decades ago. There is very little semblance between the earlier schools and today's in terms of population, infrastructure and technology, particularly communication technology ... Leadership in schools is therefore very different and more difficult today than it was two or more decades ago ... standards of teachers' performance and students' academic performance are very much below expectations.

Devolution to school level

One of the main global policy trends is the devolution of powers to site level. In many countries, the scope of leadership and management has expanded as governments have shifted responsibilities from local, regional or national bureaucracies to school principals. The inevitable consequence of such changes is an increase in leadership scope as heads, principals and other leaders have to exercise functions – notably financial management and staffing issues – that were previously undertaken outside the school. There is less evidence of devolution in Africa, as most countries retain the centralized and bureaucratic structures inherited from the colonial powers. However, even modest and tentative shifts towards decentralization have implications for the scope of leadership and the responsibilities imposed on school principals.

Leadership preparation as a moral obligation

The additional responsibilities imposed on school leaders increase the need for principals to receive effective preparation for their demanding role. Being qualified only for the very different job of classroom teacher is no longer appropriate. While competence as a teacher is necessary for school leaders, it is certainly not sufficient. As this argument has gained ground, it has led to the view that offering preparation opportunities is a moral obligation (Bush, 2008, 2018). Requiring individuals to administer schools, lead teaching and learning, manage staff and care for children without specific preparation is foolish as well as being manifestly unfair for the new incumbent. As Bush and Heystek (2006) note, in respect of South Africa, requiring principals to embark on such a demanding career without specific preparation is a recipe for personal stress and system failure, with serious ethical implications. Kitavi and van der Westhuizen (1997) show that novice principals in Kenya feel considerable anxiety, frustration and professional isolation.

Effective leadership preparation makes a difference

The belief that specific preparation makes a difference to the quality of school leadership is underpinned by research on the experience of new principals. Sackney and Walker's (2006: 343) study of beginning principals in the United States found that they were not prepared for the pace of the job, the amount of time it took to complete tasks and the number of tasks required. They also felt unprepared for the loneliness of the position. Daresh and Male's (2000: 95) research with first year principals in England and the United States identified the 'culture shock' of moving into headship for the first time. Without effective preparation, many new principals 'flounder' (Sackney and Walker 2006: 344) as they attempt to juggle the competing demands of the post.

The challenges often faced by new principals lead to a view that systematic preparation, rather than inadvertent experience, is more likely to produce effective leaders. Novice principals lack a reservoir of experience and confidence to sustain them through the most challenging times (Montecinos, Bush and Aravena, 2018). This argument is supported by the findings from a longitudinal study of the effects of a national principal development programme in South Africa (Bush, Kiggundu and Moorosi, 2011). Bush and Glover (2012: 14) found that schools with at least one graduate from this programme improved their school leaving examination results faster than schools with no such graduate. They conclude that 'there is every reason to believe that such favourable outcomes could be replicated in other countries' (2012).

Identity and socialization

As teachers embark on their training and professional practice, they become socialized as teachers and develop and hone their professional identity. However, moving into the very different role of principal is likely to lead to new socialization processes and a change in identity (Bush, 2018).

Heck (2003) uses the concepts of professional and organizational socialization as a lens to examine the impact of preparation. Professional socialization includes formal preparation, where it occurs, and the early phases of professional practice. Organizational socialization involves the process of becoming familiar with the specific context where leadership is practised. Crow (2006: 321) suggests that 'a traditional notion of effective socialization typically assumes a certain degree of conformity ... a "role-taking" outcome where the new principal takes a role conception given by the school, district, university or community'. He argues that the greater complexity of leadership contexts requires a 'role-making' dimension, whereby new principals acquire the attributes to meet the dynamic nature of school contexts.

This involves three phases of socialization. First, aspiring leaders require professional socialization, preparing to become a principal. Second, they need to change their identity from teacher to principal, a process of personal socialization. Third, they need a period of organizational socialization, learning to lead in a specific school. Crow and Moller (2017: 755) link identity formation to leadership development: 'Understanding ... how cultural and historical factors influence the fluid and developmental nature of identities should motivate us to take such factors into account in our leadership preparation and professional development programs.'

Grant, in her chapter on Namibia, adds the notion of anticipatory socialization (Crow, 2006), which relates to the opportunity for teachers to develop as leaders in their classrooms and beyond. She adds that this form of socialization may also be construed as a potential form of leadership development.

Leadership preparation

The discussion in earlier sections suggests that specific leadership training is required if principals are to operate effectively in challenging African environments, but, in practice, there are few formal leadership preparation or development opportunities. There is an important distinction to be made between leadership *preparation*, which is learning that occurs before appointment, and leadership *development*, which is training that takes place after accession to headship (Bush, 2008). Moorosi and Bush (2011: 71) note that 'many Commonwealth countries focus more on leadership development than on preparation'.

Bush and Oduro (2006) comment that principals are usually appointed without any qualifications or training in most of Africa. In Ghana, for example, longevity of service, or implied 'rank', is a pre-requisite for appointment, although basic teacher training, certification and experience are also required before promotion to headship. Arikewuyo and Olalekan (2009: 73) stress the need for training before potential leaders in Nigerian schools take up service, because 'teaching experience is not the only yardstick'. In a review of literature in Nigeria, they comment on the risks inherent in moving teachers from the classroom to managerial positions. 'The danger here is in promoting an individual from a position of competence to a position of incompetence'. Ibara (2014: 684) makes a similar point, noting that Nigeria's National Policy on Education 'is silent on the training of school principals'.

This view is reinforced by Ibukon et al.'s (2011) study in Nigeria's Ekiti state. They conclude that appropriate training for principals is required to fill the competence gap between experienced and inexperienced principals. Similarly, in relation to Ghana, Donkor's (2013) research with teachers and school leaders led to the view that the country lacks efficient and effective leadership:

> The study confirmed the inadequate attention that policy-makers … give to basic school leadership. The bottom line is that basic school leaders in Ghana need to be equipped with knowledge and skills in management and leadership to enable schools to improve in performance. (2013: 1)

Even where training opportunities are available, they may be unfit for purpose. The training also usually occurs after appointment, leaving new principals unprepared for their responsibilities. Oduro (2003: 309) reports that all 30 participants in his Ghanaian study 'complained that the training was not organized at the right time and should have preceded their appointment as headteachers'.

Zame, Hope and Repress (2008: 117) also comment on the lack of training for heads and aspiring heads in Ghana:

> Currently there is no comprehensive reform initiative that addresses the need to develop head teachers' leadership proficiencies. As it stands, individuals are promoted to the head teacher position without extensive leadership training …

Without effective basic school leadership, the chances of systemic educational reform, leading to a quality education system, will more likely than not remain elusive.

Arikewuyo and Olalekan (2009: 73) surveyed 235 recently appointed heads in junior high schools in the south and south-west regions of Nigeria to ascertain their development needs. The overwhelming stated need was for training in the functional areas of personnel, finance and school community relationships, suggesting that the need for instructional leadership was underestimated, even though the respondents were all appointed on the strength of their teaching service.

Ofoegbu et al. (2013: 75) argue that 'the contemporary complexity of the internal and external school environment in Nigeria has increased the need for principals to receive effective preparation for their demanding roles ... Leadership preparation is therefore an important agenda item necessary for charting the path to improved Nigerian schools'.

Bush and Oduro (2006: 373) conclude that 'specific preparation is required if teachers, learners and communities are to have the schools they need and deserve'. The various chapters in this book show that leadership preparation and development, where it occurs, takes several different forms.

Formal leadership and management programmes

Pansiri and Mwajabe show that the University of Botswana offers a B.Ed. Educational Management programme, reconstituted as a Bachelor of Educational Leadership and Management programme in 2017 following an external evaluation (Bush, 2015). This programme also includes four weeks of experiential learning.

Moorosi and Komiti explain that some Lesotho teachers registered for specialist leadership and management qualifications as part of a clear intention to become a principal. In Kenya, provision includes formal university courses and short Ministry of Education needs-based courses, but Okoko reports uneven access to such programmes, with teachers in poorer communities less likely to be able to participate.

Mestry notes that, in South Africa, the Department of Basic Education (DBE) piloted the Advanced Certificate in Education: School Leadership (ACESL) as a threshold qualification for aspiring and practising principals and members of school management teams. Bush and Glover (2012) show that this programme led to enhanced student outcomes.

The main provider of educational leadership programmes in Tanzania is the Agency for the Development of Educational Management (ADEM), which offers training at various levels, mainly targeting educators who already hold leadership positions. Abdalla and his colleagues comment that Tanzanian programmes reflect generic educational leadership content rather than addressing content specific to the widespread leadership challenges in Africa, such as curricula inherited from developed countries, dramatic increases in demand for schooling and widespread poverty.

In Ghana, two well-established universities offer programmes in educational administration, leading Amaki and Ampah-Mensah to argue that the absence of the requirement for aspiring school heads to take prescribed courses in educational administration cannot be ascribed to the non-availability of opportunities.

The patchy and limited provision of formal programmes in Africa contrasts with the position in many developed countries. Bush and Jackson (2002) report on the outcomes of study visits by teams appointed by the former English National College for School Leadership (NCSL). These teams of academics and practitioners visited 15 leadership centres in seven countries and jurisdictions to gather 'intelligence' about how these leading centres operate. Four of these territories (Canada, Hong Kong, Singapore and the United States) have mandatory programmes for new principals, while the other three (Australia, New Zealand and Sweden) all have optional formal programmes.

Teacher training programmes

Moorosi and Komiti note that some Lesotho teachers were introduced to some basic leadership and management modules and concepts during their teacher preparation programme. It appeared that these modules were a deliberate attempt to introduce teacher trainees to management concepts, as it was common for newly qualified teachers to be asked to take over headship of the school within a few months of taking up their first teaching post. This contrasts with most Western countries, where the inclusion of leadership modules in teacher training programmes is unusual.

Experiential preparation

Moorosi and Komiti discuss three forms of experiential preparation in Lesotho. Perhaps the most significant example is what they describe as the 'promotion route', whereby teachers gain 'hands on' experience as head of department or deputy principal. They note that this provided opportunities to 'learn through practice'.

Similarly, Abdallah et al. comment on 'informal' leadership preparation in Tanzania. This mode allows for the immediate transfer of what is learnt to leadership practice, but the disadvantage is that the leader is restricted to what the role model knows and does.

Ebot-Ashu reports that there is a mix of on-the-job training experienced by school leaders in Cameroon, including one-to-one meetings and peer support, together with broader school meetings. He argues that on-the-job training provides an opportunity for successful managers and leaders to make the most of their leadership knowledge and expertise.

Amaki and Ampah-Mensah comment that many school heads in Ghana rely on 'craft knowledge' for their development, including learning from other heads. They add that such peer assessment has become a useful device for supporting the socialization into school leadership of novice heads and the continuing development of practising heads because of its focus on dialogue and shared interpretations of events.

Most Western countries prefer to offer structured programmes rather than to rely on experiential learning, but England is unusual in relegating its flagship programme, the National Professional Qualification for Headship (NPQH), from mandatory to optional status in 2013. Subsequently, it also closed the NCSL, which had been regarded as a world leader in leadership development. The ostensible reason for these changes was to give schools more choice, but the effect was to de-professionalize school leadership, a backwards step (Bush, 2018). Meanwhile, Malaysia, for example, has made its National Professional Qualification for Educational Leaders (NPQEL) mandatory for aspiring principals (Ministry of Education, 2013, Ng, 2016).

Recruitment and selection

The recruitment and selection processes are key aspects in determining the effectiveness of schooling. A requirement for aspiring principals to be qualified leaders limits the pool of candidates but serves to ensure that only those with at least threshold competence can be appointed (Bush, 2018). It also limits the possibility of people being appointed for reasons unrelated to professional competence, including personal or political affiliations. For example, Moriba and Edwards (2009: 106) claim that leadership appointments in Sierra Leone are subject to corruption, with nepotism, based on tribal considerations, being more significant than quality or competence in selecting principals. Similarly, Ofoegbu et al. (2013: 67) criticize the factors used to select school principals in Nigeria. 'There are no formal requirements for people to be appointed into leadership positions. It is not uncommon for school heads to be appointed on the basis of god-fatherism, political affiliation, ethnicity or some indices of culture or religion.'

African researchers report on the appointment processes in their countries. Ibukon, Oyewole and Abe (2011) say that principal appointments in Nigeria are more effective when experienced teachers are chosen. Ibara (2014: 684) adds that the appointment of Nigerian principals, who have only teaching qualifications, means that school leadership and management are 'in the hands of technically unqualified personnel'. According to Donkor (2013), Ghana does not have uniform or well-defined criteria for appointing basic school leaders, leading to animosity among teachers. In their review of school leadership in West Africa, Bush and Glover (2016) conclude that there is only limited evidence about the appointment process for principals in West Africa, leaving open the prospect of personal factors and affiliations being more important than leadership capability when such appointments are made. They conclude that only the most capable professionals should be appointed as principals.

The various chapters in this volume outline the recruitment and selection processes in several African countries. For example, Moorosi and Komiti comment that the Education Act (2010) spells out the role of school principals as managers of schools in Lesotho, in collaboration with school governing boards. The only requirement for the appointment of school principals is qualified teaching status, with no provision for any specific form of preparatory training.

Similarly, Okoko notes that, although Kenyan school leaders are required to have at least a bachelor's degree, they are not expected to have any formal leadership preparation before they are appointed. Most of them progress through seniority, where they move from classroom teacher to senior teacher or head of department, to deputy head teacher or deputy principal and then to head teacher or principal. This model assumes that the knowledge, skills and dispositions they acquire at the various levels are transferable to leadership. She adds that promotion from classroom teacher to head teacher takes an average of 19 years.

Abdalla et al. report that, in Tanzania, official policy requires that head teachers have a leadership qualification but, in practice, vacant positions are filled by promoting teachers based on their teaching experience, often without prior experience in junior leadership positions.

Ebot-Ashu comments that heads in Cameroon are frequently appointed on the foundation of a successful record as teachers, on the assumption that this offers a sufficient starting point for school leadership. The selection and recruitment of head teachers is, therefore, mostly based on a teacher's seniority in rank and teaching experience.

The Ghana Education Service (GES) has no requirement for a prospective school head to complete preparatory programmes in educational administration or related areas. Amaki and Ampah-Mensah explain that the requirements relate to qualifications (the candidate is a professional graduate teacher with satisfactory work history and conduct), experience (the candidate has served as an assistant headmaster/mistress, or in an equivalent position, for at least three cumulative years) and age (the candidate must not be over the age of fifty-five years).

These chapters confirm that the appointment of principals is largely unrelated to their leadership knowledge or skills. At best, appointments are based on successful classroom experience, a necessary but insufficient criterion for successful headship. It seems likely that the success of China, Hong Kong and Singapore, for example, in the Programme for International Student Assessment (PISA) is partly attributable to their insistence that only qualified leaders are appointed as school principals.

Induction

Given that new principals often experience anxiety, uncertainty and isolation, an effective induction process seems to be essential. However, in practice, induction is usually limited and, where it occurs, it is often a one-off event, typically offered by a local administrator, unconnected to previous or subsequent development and often provided just before, or just after, the principal takes up the post. This type of induction is usually confined to procedures and reporting processes and is rarely customized to the specific needs of the principal or the school. Bush and Oduro's (2006: 364) review of beginning leadership in Africa indicates that induction is very limited, often staffed by people of limited experience, using repetitive and inappropriate teaching styles and failing to link the training with nationally legislated norms. Similarly, the chapters in this volume offer a mixed, but largely negative, picture of induction in Africa.

Moorosi and Komiti report that in Lesotho, provision of induction programmes was inconsistent. Those who were not offered induction felt that they were just 'dumped' in the principal's office and left to their own devices. Similarly, Grant comments that the world of the newly appointed Namibian principal is one of chaos and accompanying hardship, despite the provision of regional induction workshops. In Cameroon, Ebot-Ashu states that induction is ill-suited to the development of effective school principals.

Mestry notes Msila's (2015) South African research, which shows that many principals felt helpless in the absence of any formal induction. They were filled with anxiety, frustration and professional isolation because they did not understand their leadership responsibilities. Mestry adds that the principals confirmed that the ACESL course had effectively promoted their professional growth and given them a better understanding of their role in the school. He concludes that this course could serve as induction as well as being a leadership preparation programme.

Designing an effective induction programme requires consideration of the nature of the process. As noted above, if induction is provided by a local administrator – often the principal's superordinate within a hierarchy – it is likely to be confined to administrative procedures and reporting processes. Given the increasing emphasis on instructional leadership, such a limited approach is inadequate.

Bush (2018) identifies two alternative approaches to induction. The first is underpinned by the view that principals are part of a wider system and need to operate primarily as administrative leaders. The second arises from understanding that the principal is a professional leader and that his or her growth is an indispensable element for school improvement. Table 11.1 illustrates the components of these two models.

Column two of Table 11.1 shows a narrow approach to induction focused on administration and formal accountability. In contrast, column three illustrates

Table 11.1 Alternative Induction Models

Component	Administrative leadership	Professional leadership
Nature of provision	Group	Individual
Leadership model	Administrative	Instructional
Main focus	Adherence to procedures	Professional learning
Purpose	System conformity	School improvement
Accountability	Through the formal hierarchy	To professional and lay stakeholders

Source: Bush 2018.

a personalized approach designed to promote on-going professional learning and an instructional approach. The administrative emphasis is found in many centralized systems, including Africa. While policy-makers increasingly recognize that instructional leadership is more likely to promote student and teacher learning than traditional administrative approaches, this is rarely reflected in induction procedures in Africa or in other centralized systems.

Mentoring

The international literature (e.g. Bush, 2008; Hobson and Sharp 2005) shows that mentoring is a highly effective approach to leadership development. Hobson and Sharp (2005) comment that all major studies of formal mentoring programmes reported that such programmes have been effective. It is a successful element of Singapore's principal preparation programmes (Chong, Stott and Low, 2003).

Mentoring may be seen as a distinctive aspect of professional socialization, especially where the mentors are highly experienced and successful leaders. However, Crow (2004) cautions that this may lead to a conservative approach, one based on current and previous practice rather than designed to meet the future needs of schools and leaders. Similarly, Bush et al.'s (2011) evaluation of the South African principals' programme found significant benefits from mentoring but also noted a tendency for the process to lead to 'cloning', with uncritical acceptance of mentor advice or 'prescriptions'. Crow's (2004) advice is for leadership development to include theory and research as well as mentoring.

There is only limited discussion of mentoring in the various chapters in this volume, suggesting that it rarely occurs. In Namibia, however, Grant reports that there was substantial evidence of coaching and mentoring in schools by senior staff, most notably, the principal. This was regarded as a positive influence on leaders' development. As a consequence, it strengthened organizational socialization and enhanced succession planning.

In-house coaching and mentoring was considered effective when school principals invoked the leadership of their colleagues and involved them in the daily routines of leadership and management. Succession planning was taken a step further in some schools, with teachers being mentored into leadership roles. However, a few participants in the Namibian study did not receive strong mentorship and, instead, were left to fend for themselves.

In South Africa, according to Bush et al. (2011), as noted here, mentoring was a distinctive and central feature of the ACESL programme, designed to facilitate the transfer of learning to principals. However, Bush et al. (2011) and Bush and Glover (2012) also made some critical comments. Mentors were responsible for large number of principals (between 9 and 38) and the facilitation sessions took place in groups or 'cohorts' which did not match the generally accepted definition of mentoring, namely, a one-to-one relationship (Bush, 2008). Mentees were reluctant to open up and discuss their inadequacies because they learnt that the district office would soon know of their shortcomings (Msila, 2015).

Carefully planned and implemented mentoring would be major assets for any leadership development programmes and could contribute in a powerful way to developing school leaders and their schools. However, there are two major constraints: the cost of providing one-to-one mentoring, and the limited availability of well-trained and motivated mentors. These problems suggest that in-house mentoring, as in Namibia, might be the best way forward, although this would be fragmented rather than systemic.

Networking

Networking between and among principals is regarded as an effective mode of leadership learning (Bush, Glover and Harris, 2007). It is a form of peer support and has the potential to build the confidence and capability of new heads. A meta-analysis of more than 40 programme evaluations for the English NCSL showed that participant perceptions of networking were almost always positive, especially when it involved leaders from similar contexts, for example, small primary schools (Bush et al., 2007).

There is evidence of successful networking in some of the African countries featured in this volume. Moorosi and Komiti comment on networking clusters in Lesotho, reported in research by Komiti (2017) and Moorosi (2017). In Komiti's (2017) study, female principals appreciated the support they received from the association of high-school principals. In Moorosi's (2017) study, network clusters were found to be a regular form of professional development for the principals that was district co-ordinated and involved principals of both primary and secondary schools. It is through these networks that most principals attested to feeling empowered and learning more from their peers.

In Namibia, there was a Principals' Association that met once a term to share information and best practices, discuss common problems and take common decisions before taking up issues with the regional office. However, the meeting seldom had a 100 per cent attendance. Despite this, the association offered a platform to support committed principals in their development as leaders.

Research conducted by Bush et al. (2011), and Mestry and Singh (2007) in South Africa revealed that the ACESL programme attended by principals promoted collaborative networks among peers in neighbouring schools. Schools benefitted from sharing resources, finding solutions to challenges and resolving conflicts through discussion networks and professional learning communities. The survey findings were positive, with 76 per cent stating that developing networks were of great help (Bush et al., 2011). However, Bush and Glover (2012) indicated that networking was not fully established, was inclined to focus mainly on assignment preparation and did not provide a sustainable basis for collaborative working across schools.

There was also evidence of networking in Cameroon, which took the form of an informal network of school leaders sharing best practice. Ebot-Ashu reports that the evidence supports the central agency's encouragement of an informal network of school leaders to share best practice since there are small formal and informal networks already in Cameroon. The central agencies can help the different systems and schools to share ideas, issues and best practice of learning initiatives at all levels of the system, and in school communities.

These African examples confirm the international evidence that networking can be a helpful mode of leadership development. The main difference is that, in Western contexts, it usually forms part of a wider development programme, while in Africa, it tends to act as a substitute for formal preparation. This does not obviate its value and, given the challenges of leadership in such contexts, it may be even more valuable for African leaders.

Conclusion

It is widely accepted that leadership is central to school improvement and student learning. There is also growing evidence (notably Robinson et al., 2009) that instructional, rather than administrative, leadership is required to produce the best outcomes. However, in many countries, including most of Africa, leadership preparation is neglected, and teachers may become principals without any specialized training. The career path of many professionals, from classroom practitioner to middle leader, senior leader and principal means that they gradually reduce what they are trained for – teaching – while increasing what they may not be prepared for – leadership (Bush, 2018). Funding is always a constraint in developing countries, and this may be the main reason for the lack of formal programmes almost everywhere in Africa.

Induction arrangements are also usually inadequate in Africa, leaving potential principals to draw on an ad hoc apprenticeship model, whereby they learn the job from their own principals while holding more junior leadership posts. However, this is a narrow approach that is likely to lead to replication of previous practice, while the complex needs of African schools in the twenty-first century require a broader range of knowledge and skills. Lack of systematic preparation and induction at best delays principals' effectiveness and, at worst, wholly inhibits it.

Patterns of leadership preparation and development are highly variable across national contexts, ranging from prescriptive mandatory programmes, as in Malaysia and Singapore, to ad hoc 'on-the-job' learning in most of Africa. Given the limited resources available for education in most of the continent, effective leadership preparation opportunities are likely to depend on donor funding, although the evidence is that such initiatives are rarely sustained when the funding stream is withdrawn. Developing sustainable leadership programmes is a major challenge, but Africa's children deserve the best teaching and leadership.

References

Arikewuyo, M. and F. Olalekan (2009), 'Professional Training of Secondary School Principals in Nigeria: A Neglected Area in the Educational System', *Journal of Educational Administration & Policy*, 2 (2): 73–84.

Bush, T. (2008), *Leadership and Management Development in Education*, London: Sage.

Bush, T. (2015), *External Review of the B.Ed (Educational Management)*, Gaborone: University of Botswana.

Bush, T. (2018), 'Preparation and Induction for School Principals: Global Perspectives', *Management in Education* 32 (2): 66–71.

Bush, T. and D. Glover (2012), 'Leadership Development and Learner Outcomes: Evidence from South Africa', *Journal of Educational Leadership, Policy and Practice*, 27 (2): 3–15.

Bush, T. and D. Glover (2016), 'School Leadership in West Africa: Findings from a Systematic Literature Review', *Africa Education Review*, DOI:10.1080/18146627.201 6.1229572.

Bush, T., D. Glover, and A. Harris (2007), *Review of School Leadership Development*, Nottingham: NCSL.

Bush, T. and D. Jackson (2002), 'Preparation for School Leaders: International Perspectives', *Educational Management and Administration*, 30 (4): 417–29.

Bush, T., E. Kiggundu, and P. Moorosi (2011), 'Preparing New Principals in South Africa: The ACE: School Leadership Programme', *South African Journal of Education*, 31 (1): 31–43.

Bush, T. and G. Oduro (2006), 'New Principals in Africa: Preparation, Induction and Practice', *Journal of Educational Administration*, 44 (4): 359–75.

Bush, T. and J. Heystek (2006), 'School Leadership and Management in South Africa: Principals' Perceptions', *International Studies in Educational Administration*, 34 (3): 63–76.

Chong, K. C., K. Stott, and G. T. Low (2003), 'Developing Singapore Leaders for a Learning Nation', in P. Hallinger (ed), *Reshaping the Landscape of School Leadership Development: A Global Perspective*, 163–74, Lisse: Swets and Zeitlinger.

Crow, G. (2004), 'The National College for School Leadership: A North American Perspective on Opportunities and Challenges', *Educational Management, Administration and Leadership*, 32 (3): 289–307.

Crow, G. (2006), 'Complexity and the Beginning Principal in the United States: Perspectives on Socialisation', *Journal of Educational Administration*, 44 (4): 310–25.

Crow, G., J. Lumby, and P. Pashiardis (2008), 'Introduction: Why an International Handbook on the Preparation and Development of School Leaders?' in J. Lumby, G. Crow and P. Pashiardis (eds), *International Handbook on the Preparation and Development of School Leaders*, New York: Routledge.

Crow, G. and J. Moller (2017), 'Professional Identities of School Leaders across International Contexts: An Introduction and Rationale', *Educational Management, Administration and Leadership*, 45 (5): 749–58.

Daresh, J. and T. Male (2000), 'Crossing the Boundary into Leadership: Experiences of Newly Appointed British Headteachers and American Principals', *Educational Management and Administration*, 28 (1): 89–101.

Donkor, A. (2013), 'Basic School Leaders in Ghana: How Equipped Are They?' *International Journal of Leadership in Education: Theory and Practice*, 4: 1–11.

Heck, R. (2003), 'Examining the Impact of Professional Preparation on Beginning School Administrators', in P. Hallinger (ed), *Reshaping the Landscape of School Leadership Development: A Global Perspective*, Lisse: Swets and Zeitlinger.

Hobson, A. and C. Sharp (2005), 'Head to Head: A Systematic Review of the Research Evidence on Mentoring New Head Teachers', *School Leadership and Management*, 25 (1): 25–42.

Ibara, E. (2014), 'Professional Development of Principals: A Path to Effective Secondary School Administration in Nigeria', *Africa Education Review*, 11 (4): 674–89.

Ibukon, W., B. Oyewole, and T. Abe (2011), 'Personality Characteristics and Principal Leadership Effectiveness in Ekiti State, Nigeria', *International Journal of Leadership Studies*, 6 (2): 247–59.

Kitavi, M. and P. van der Westhuizen (1997), 'Problems Facing Beginning Principals in Developing Countries: A Study of Beginning Principals in Kenya', *International Journal of Educational Development*, 17 (3): 251–63.

Komiti, M. (2017), 'Exploring the Career Paths of Female Principals in Lesotho High Schools', Unpublished MA Thesis, North-West University, South Africa.

Leithwood, K., C. Day, P. Sammons, A. Harris, and D. Hopkins (2006), *Seven Strong Claims about Successful School Leadership*, London: Department for Education and Skills.

Mestry, R. and P. Singh (2007), 'Continuing Professional Development for Principals: A South African Perspective', *South African Journal of Education*, 27 (3): 477–90.

Ministry of Education (2013), *Malaysia Education Blueprint*, Malaysia: Ministry of Education.

Montecinos, C., T. Bush, and F. Aravena (2018), 'Problems Encountered by Novice and Experienced Principals during a Succession Process in Chile', *International Journal of Educational Development*, 62: 201–8.

Moorosi, P. (2017), 'School leadership development in Lesotho', in L. Mapheleba (ed), *Education in Lesotho: Prospects and Challenges*, New York: Nova Science Publishers.

Moorosi, P. and T. Bush (2011), 'School Leadership Development in Commonwealth Countries: Learning Across Boundaries', *International Studies in Educational Administration*, 39 (3): 59–75.

Msila, V. (2015), 'The Struggle to Improve Schools: Voices of South African Teacher Mentors', *Educational Management Administration & Leadership*, 44 (6): 936–50.

Ng, A. M. Y. (2016), 'School Leadership Preparation in Malaysia: Aims, Content and Impact', *Educational Management Administration & Leadership*, 45 (6): 1002–19.

Oduro, G. (2003), 'Perspectives of Ghanaian Headteachers on Their Role and Professional Development: The Case of KEEA District Primary School', unpublished Ph.D. thesis, University of Cambridge.

Ofoegbu, F., A. O. Clark, and R. O. Osagie (2013), 'Leadership Theories and Practice: Charting a Path for Improved Nigerian Schools', *International Studies in Educational Administration*, 41 (2): 67–76.

Robinson, V., M. Hohepa, and C. Lloyd (2009), *School Leadership and Student Outcomes: Identifying What Works and Why, Best Evidence Synthesis Iteration*, Auckland: Ministry of Education.

Sackney, L. and K. Walker (2006), 'Canadian Perspectives on Beginning Principals: Their Role in Building Capacity for Learning Communities', *Journal of Educational Administration*, 44 (4): 341–58.

Walker, A. and H. Qian (2006), 'Beginning Principals: Balancing at the Top of the Greasy Pole', *Journal of Educational Administration*, 44 (4): 297–309.

Zame, M. Y., W. C. Hope, and T. Repress (2008), 'Educational Reform in Ghana: The Leadership Challenge', *Journal of Educational Management*, 22 (2): 115–28.

Index

CPSIA information can be obtained
at www.ICGtesting.com
Printed in the USA
LVHW080149270821
696254LV00006B/198

9 781350 205956